Power, Choice and Vulnerability

Power, Choice and Vulnerability

A CASE STUDY IN
DISASTER MISMANAGEMENT
IN SOUTH INDIA
1977–1988

Peter Winchester

earthscan
from Routledge

First published 1992 by James & James (Science Publishers) Ltd

This edition published 2013 by Earthscan

For a full list of publications please contact:
Earthscan
2 Park Square, Milton Park, Abingdon, Oxfordshire OX14 4RN
Simultaneously published in the USA and Canada by Earthscan
711 Third Avenue, New York, NY 10017

First issued in paperback 2016

Earthscan is an imprint of the Taylor & Francis Group, an informa business

ISBN 13: 978-1-138-99518-5 (pbk)
ISBN 13: 978-1-873936-05-4 (hbk)

British Library cataloguing-in-publication data

Winchester, Peter
    Power, choice and vulnerability – a case study in
    disaster mismanagement in South India, 1977–88.
    I. Title
    363.309172

Typeset by Columns Design and Production Services Ltd, Reading

Contents

CONTENTS

Acknowledgements

In the course of my voyage through the troubled waters of disasters, I have been helped by many people in England and India. There are some special people, of course, without whose support I could never have written this book and if they read the book they will know that I am grateful to them for all their help. Instead of acknowledging them individually I would like to dedicate this book and the following passage from *The Spirit of Man* to them and to the many others about whom I have heard, but whom I have never met:

> If this life be not a real fight, in which something is eternally gained for the universe by success, it is no better than a game of private theatricals from which one may withdraw at will. But it *feels* like a real fight, as if there were something really wild in the universe which we, with all our idealities and faithlessnesses, are needed to redeem . . . .
>
> . . . Be not afraid of life . . . . The "scientific" proof that you are right may not be clear before the day of judgement (or some stage of being which that expression may serve to symbolize) is reached. But the faithful fighters of this hour, or the beings that then and there will represent them, may turn to the fainthearted, who here decline to go on, with words like those with which Henry IV greeted the tardy Crillon after a great battle had been gained: "Hang yourself, brave Crillon! We fought at Arques, and you were not there!"

Preface

An understanding of vulnerability governs the art of disaster mitigation. The aim of this book is to explain how a view of vulnerability that is different from the one currently being used can improve some aspects of disaster management and can go some way to making disaster mitigation and post-disaster development more effective. The view centres on the concept of **differential vulnerability** which is applicable to all types of disaster but has here emerged from a study of cyclone mitigation policies and post-cyclone disaster development.

Cyclone mitigation programmes equate vulnerability with exposure to physical risk, but I will argue that cyclone vulnerability is a function of exposure to a much wider range of risks, which cyclones only accentuate. These risks stem from the power and economic relations within the societies themselves which create precarious everyday conditions for the majority of people whose daily lives are on the brink of economic disaster in any event. The power to control the allocation and distribution of resources by a minority of people in many societies limits the choices of the majority leading to their vulnerability to a wide range of events. This occurs in cyclone-prone areas as much as it does elsewhere and the restricted choices for the majority living in cyclone-prone areas severely limits their risk-reduction strategies to cope with the exigencies of cyclones as well as debilitating them to cope with the many other pressures within their communities.

The national and state governments of India are perfectly aware of the precarious existence of many people in cyclone-prone areas and because they see the main threat coming from cyclones, their cyclone policies are geared accordingly. Other programmes are also implemented in cyclone-prone areas which focus on development, the so-called anti-poverty programmes. These are designed to work together so that while the anti-poverty programmes focus on building up people and assets, the cyclone mitigation programmes focus on protecting both people and assets.

However, the key to cyclone vulnerability is to understand the phenomenon of differential vulnerability, whereby the differences between households are such that some people are more at risk than others to exactly the same threat in the same place. The cyclone mitigation programmes do not take the differences between households fully into account, partly because the measurement of differential vulnerability imposes additional administrative burdens and partly because the debate on vulnerability and risk has been so confused and the ensuing programmes have become counter-productive. An extension to the argument is that development in disaster-prone areas can also be counter-productive and increase vulnerability unless the concept of differential vulnerability is recognised. This concept is crucial for disaster mitigation in so far as disaster mitigation relates to *pre- and post-disaster development policies*.

The book is neither an attack on cyclone mitigation programmes nor on development programmes in cyclone areas. It is an attempt to untangle the complexities of vulnerability, which takes into account the differences within a society so that a more relevant concept can be incorporated into policies within current political realities. The book offers a concept of vulnerability which has been tested against empirical data collected over 10 years in one cyclone-prone area of south India – a concept which, in the author's view, will improve attempts to reduce poverty and hardship in these and, hopefully, in other areas.

Cyclone Mitigation Policy

1.1 INTRODUCTION

Cyclone disasters make dramatic reading. Every few years headlines like these appear in Indian newspapers: "Cyclone toll 500; 1 million homeless" . . . . "Storm havoc, heavy loss of life feared . . . whole villages washed away" . . . . "Cyclone strikes coast; heavy damage to crops; 1 million hectares submerged" . . . . "Cyclone leaves 900 dead; total harvest destroyed" . . . . "A.P. toll exceeds 8,000; 2 million hectares affected" . . . . "A.P. toll may touch 13,000; 2 million homeless" . . . . and so on.

Every year the numbers increase: if not the number of casualties – and these have reduced dramatically in the last five years – then the number of losses, and, every time the same questions are asked with varying degrees of fury or righteous indignation. Why are cyclones so lethal? Why do they cause so much damage? Can the damage be reduced? Why do people live in such exposed places? Can't anything be done to protect them? These questions, rightly, focus on how to alleviate the effects of cyclones in the short and long term, and the power of the Press has had a considerable influence on shaping government policy over the years, as we shall see. However, once the disaster is over and the area is restored "to normality" both it and the people are forgotten by the Press until the next cyclone strikes and then the same questions are raised once more.

The answers to these questions are the subject of this book and we hope, in the following chapters, to convince the reader that there are ways of reducing damage and protecting people in cyclone areas that will be effective in the long term, but which are not being implemented at the present. But, before we can look at policies and solutions we must first introduce the cyclone phenomenon within the context of the east coast of India and the Krishna delta.

1.1.1 The characteristics of cyclones

Formation

Tropical cyclones are formed from a progressive intensification of westerly moving disturbances of patterns of cloud and rain up to 1,000 km long and 500 km wide which turn into depressions and then into cold-cored tropical storms. These can only form where the ocean surface temperature exceeds 26.5°C (Palmen 1948) and where there is no temperature inversion (Gray 1968).

An anti-cyclone in the upper troposphere is essential to the formation of cyclones. This allows high-level outflow which permits development of very low pressure and high wind speeds at the sea surface. A distinctive and essential feature of the cyclone is its warm vortex. The warm core develops through the action of cumulo-nimbus towers releasing latent heat in the form of condensation. The warm core is vital for growth because it intensifies the upper anti-cyclone thus stimulating the low-level influx of heat and moisture which intensifies convective activity (Barry and Chorley 1976: 290–295). The outstanding feature of a fully-formed cyclone is that it resembles a narrow funnel. Although its periphery may grow to 1,000 km, the most powerful area of a cyclone is within the 100 km radius and the highest wind speeds are around the 'eye', which is created by the temperature difference between the core and its surroundings, and which is on average 60 km in diameter. Nearly all the inflowing air escapes upward in the funnel which may be 5–20 km high. A tropical cyclone with a maximum sustained wind speed of 65 kmph may last for four or five days whereas a severe cyclonic storm of hurricane intensity with wind speeds greater than 120 kmph usually lasts from two to three days.

Movement

Tropical cyclones follow a basic parabolic path and are steered by the great anti-cyclones overlying the tropical oceans (Koteswaram 1958; Desai *et al.* 1979). When they reach the edge of the tropics where the east winds change to west winds they recurve. They can also recurve quite suddenly if the vortex, determined by the upper tropospheric flow, is taken over a cool sea surface or over land, and they reach their greatest intensity shortly before or just at the recurvature point (Riehl and Simpson 1981: 168–175). Tropical cyclones move at between 16–24 kmph over the ocean (Barry and Chorley 1976) but landfalls are difficult to predict, the implications of which are discussed later. Over land the behaviour of cyclones is less erratic (Riehl and Simpson 1981: 248–253); rough ground and vegetation will decelerate them rapidly but coastal areas with large shallow water bodies will counteract this tendency and winds of cyclonic speeds may still be found 24–36 hours after the landfall of a slow moving storm.

Sea and coastal waves

A tropical cyclone imparts enormous energy to the sea by wind stresses which can create huge and precipitous waves out to sea. In shallow water the stresses result in the formation of short low waves each transporting huge amounts of water causing an upslope of the sea at the coast and generating powerful long-shore currents which can extend for 300 km (Dube *et al.* 1981).

Storm surges

These occur when the level of the sea is raised by direct wind-driven water combined with an uplift of the sea surface induced by the low pressure at the cyclone centre (Hoover 1957). The height of a storm surge will also depend on tides, water run-off from the land, on-shore winds (Bhaskara Rao and Mazumder 1966), other waves and the configuration of the coast (Das *et al.* 1974). A storm surge can be up to 50 km wide and 7 m high (Bhaskara Rao and Mazumder 1966: 34). High water will last up to six hours or several days in areas of poor drainage (Subbaramayya *et al.* 1979).

Wind

A tropical cyclone is principally defined by the measurement of its wind speed and barometric pressure. The Government of India, Meteorological Department, measures cyclones according to the wind speed. It defines **depressions** as weather systems where the greatest sustained wind speeds are less than 65 kmph sustained for more than 12 hours, **cyclonic storms** (CS) where wind speeds are maintained at between 65 and 95 kmph; **severe cyclonic storms** (SCS) where sustained winds are more than 95 kmph and **severe cyclonic storms of hurricane intensity** where sustained wind speeds exceed 120 kmph. These measurements are used throughout in all references to cyclonic storms (I.M.D. 1960).

Rain

Rain is usually associated with cyclones and although 250 cm has been recorded during a cyclone, sometimes only a trace will fall (Beckinsale 1969; Barry and Chorley 1976). Rainfall of 50 cm during a two-day cyclone is quite common (I.M.D. 1960). Heavy rainfall is also associated with monsoon activity (Lockwood 1965) and with what is known as cyclonic weather where a system of cloud and rain about 300 km wide with a broad eye of 150 km brings heavy rain for up to 30 days without ever developing a wind system (Barry and Chorley 1976).

1.1.2 Tropical cyclones in the north Indian Ocean

Almost all the initial disturbances from which tropical storms and tropical cyclones develop are found within 10° latitude of the location of the Equatorial Trough (Riehl and Simpson 1981). In the Bay of Bengal (Map 1.1) there are two maxima of cyclone development associated with the onset and retreat of the monsoon and these occur during May–June and October–November. During the period 1877–1977, 20 per cent of all cyclones emanating from the Bay of Bengal crossed the east India coast in November and 18 per cent in May (Subbaramayya *et al.* 1979). During this period 337 cyclonic storms (CS) and severe cyclonic storms (SCS) crossed the east coast of India and Bangladesh between the latitudes 8°N and 22°N, and of these 101 were severe cyclonic storms. Nearly a third of the cyclones during the 100-year period made a landfall on the north Orissa and Bengal coast between latitudes 20–21°N, and the next highest have been in the latitude of the Krishna delta 15–16°N (Subbaramayya *et al.* 1979; and Map 1.2).

1.1.3 A brief history of cyclones along the coast of Andhra Pradesh

Cyclone disasters along the coastline of Andhra Pradesh have been well documented. In 1679 the British East India Company recorded that 20,000 people had been drowned by a storm surge which swamped Masulipatnam in the Krishna delta. Since then, more than 100 cyclones have struck the stretch of coast 150 km either side of Masulipatnam, which is the second-highest cyclone-prone stretch of the east Indian coast, killing more than 250,000 people. The most famous cyclones since 1697 have been at Coringa in 1764 (30,000 drowned), at Masulipatnam in 1864 (30,000 drowned and the town destroyed), at Nellore in 1927 (5,000 dead), and in Masulipatnam again in 1949 (1 million acres flooded and 4,000 dead) and again in May and November 1969 (1 million acres damaged and 4,000 dead). The most famous recent cyclone and the starting point for this book was the one with a storm surge that struck the Krishna delta just south of Masulipatnam in November 1977 which devastated an area of 2 million acres and left 10,000 dead. In May 1979 a severe cyclone hit Nellore in the south of the state (1,000 dead and 2 m acres

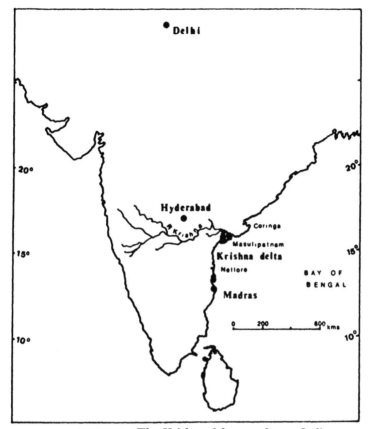

MAP 1.1: *The Krishna delta, south-east India*

damaged). (A.P. Government 1981a and 1981c). In October 1983 a cyclone devastated large areas of the Godavari delta damaging 2 million acres of crops and leaving 800 dead (*Times of India* 5.10.83). More recently, in May 1990, a cyclone struck Masulipatnam again, leaving 900 dead and 2 million acres damaged (*Hindu* 18.5.90).

Damage from cyclones

The extent of damage sustained as a result of cyclones is basically a function of the size and intensity of the storm, the structure of the population, and the character of the area affected. The effect of the sea, either in a storm surge or in tidal flooding, is by far the most destructive element of a severe cyclonic storm causing the most casualties and damage (see Table 1.1) although the excessive rain that sometimes accompanies a cyclone can cause devastating

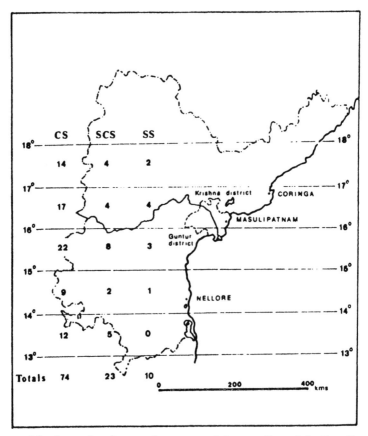

MAP 1.2: *Numbers of cyclones to have crossed the coastline of Andhra Pradesh, by latitude, 1877–1977*

Sources: A.P. Government 1980b; Subbaramayya *et al.* 1979; Subbaramayya and Subba Rao 1981.

flooding. High winds create much damage to crops by flattening them; high winds can also blow down electrical and telegraph lines, uproot trees and kill and injure people by causing structural failures in buildings.

When storm surges occur, they are *the* most destructive features of cyclones, killing on average seven times more people and creating three times more damage to crops than severe cyclonic storms unaccompanied by storm surges. In severe cyclonic storms with storm surges more than 90 per cent of the deaths are from drowning, whereas in severe cyclonic storms without storm surges the deaths are more or less evenly spread between drowning and collapse of buildings. The collapse of buildings features very often in policy documents as a major cause of cyclone deaths and yet compared to deaths by drowning, it is fairly insignificant.

TABLE 1.1: *Twelve severe cyclonic and two cyclonic storms to have crossed the coastline of Andhra Pradesh, classified by their principal meteorological characteristics correlated with the mean number of deaths and extent of damage to crops: 1949–83*

	Severe cyclonic storms		Cyclonic storms	
	High wind[a] + High rain[b] + Storm surge	High wind + High rain	Low wind + High rain	Low wind + Low rain
Number of cyclones	5	4	3	2
Mean number of people killed	5591	833	59	17
Mean extent of damage to crop in lakh acres[c]	24.25	8.7	4.3	2.8

Sources: A.P. Government 1980b: 9–11; *Times of India* and *Hindu*, October 1949 – October 1983.
[a] High wind is a wind speed greater than 95 kmh.
[b] High rain is rainfall of more than 30 cm in 24 hours.
[c] 1 lakh = 100,000.

Table 1.2 shows the extent of damage and casualties following the two key cyclones (SCSs) from which current cyclone policy has developed; these are the 1977 cyclone which struck the Krishna delta, and the 1979 cyclone which struck an area 200 km further south. The variation in damage is due to different land uses and cropping patterns and the relative wealth within and between the same cyclone-affected areas.

The relative differences in wealth *within* the same cyclone-affected areas can be seen in the first two columns. The 1977 cyclone (columns 1 and 2) occurred in November at the time of the *paddy* (rice) harvest. The storm surge-affected area (column 1) in Krishna district was a densely populated predominantly rice-growing area in which extensive damage and heavy casualties were caused by the storm surge; in the larger and also densely populated area of Guntur (column 2), unaffected by the storm surge, the value of the damage was much greater, since this was predominantly an area devoted to varied and lucrative cash crops such as cotton, sugarcane and betel trees.

The relative differences in wealth *between* areas can be seen by comparing columns 2 and 3. The 1979 cyclone (columns 3 and 4) which occurred in May (the second crop and the harvest for dry-land crops) affected an area in Nellore district two and a half times greater than the equivalent cyclone in Guntur district in 1977; however, the damage to crops and loss in Guntur were somewhat less than twice that of Nellore, although casualties were higher in Guntur – illustrating differential population densities. The differences in damage *between* intensities of cyclones can be seen by comparing columns 3

7

TABLE 1.2: *Comparison of losses and damage following two cyclones of varying intensities, 1977 and 1979*

	Severe cyclone 1977		Severe cyclone 1979	
	Storm surge area of Divi Seema[a]	Cyclone area of Guntur[b]	Severe cyclone area of Nellore[c]	Cyclone area of Guntur[d]
Size of affected area (sq km)	80	350	850	80
Human lives	7,300	1,759	706	65
Livestock				
Cattle	20,000	46,970	77,000	1,536
Others	n.a.	14,865	n.a.	5,708
Property[1]				
Crops		5.6	10.57	21.61.24
Buildings[2]	17.2	23.00	69.1	7.39
Houses[3]	25,000[4]	120,000	250,000	10,000

Sources: [a] and [b] A.P. Government 1977; [c] A.P. Government 1981c; [d] A.P. Government 1981a.

[1] Value in Rs crores (1 crore = 10,000,000).

[2] Private and public buildings damaged and destroyed (but not houses).

[3] Number of houses destroyed.

[4] Estimated total of houses destroyed in Krishna district 125,000.

and 4. The 1979 cyclone was deemed to be a severe cyclonic storm (SCS) in Nellore district but by the time it arrived in Guntur district it was deemed to be a cyclonic storm (CS). The differences in damage is approximately ten fold. We shall be returning to both cyclones in some detail in later chapters.

1.2 THE EVOLUTION OF CYCLONE POLICY

1.2.1 Governments' perception of cyclone disasters

Historically, governments' explanation for the extent of cyclone devastation has been "the savagery of Nature", (*Hindu* 21.11.69; 22.11.77; 10.5.79; *Times of India* 4.11.71; 19.11.77). This is used to explain economic hardship in the coastal areas (A.P. Government 1979a: 14) and is further reinforced by the focus on the awesome physical characteristics of cyclones in *all* their policy documents. Governments regard cyclone vulnerability as a function of exposure to the physical fury of cyclones and they regard their duties as (i) saving life and protecting property; (ii) relieving suffering; and (iii) rehabilitating stricken populations as quickly as possible by means we will discuss later.

Despite the historical perception that the "savagery of Nature" causes cyclone vulnerability, criticisms have emerged over the years which suggest that the fault may not be all Nature's but partly Man's. However, the focus of both government policy and criticism in the national Press has consistently been on Nature as the chief culprit and the unusual and unexpected aspects of cyclones that cause the problems (*Hindu* 18/19.5.69; *Times of India* 3.11.71). Man's inability to cope in the face of these exigencies is deemed as obvious. The Andhra Pradesh State Government's (referred to hereafter as the government) perception of natural disasters is that NATURE is wild and uncontrollable and that disasters are always "out there" beyond human control just waiting to pounce on hapless MAN, a view typified by the Editorial in the *Hindu* newspaper on the 22nd November 1977, two days after the 1977 Andhra cyclone:

> . . . a catastrophe of this kind has many lessons to offer. It brings out the deficiencies in preparing for a disaster and providing relief, more, it poignantly shows the extreme vulnerability of the poor in particular, and lends urgency to the task of insulating them from *the savagery of Nature*. (*Gruesome visitation*, Editorial: *Hindu* 21.11.77.)

Running through government policy statements is the theme that disasters are situations just short of war – i.e., "situations resulting from man-made or natural catastrophes, other than war . . . which demand the total integration and management of rescue and life support systems" (Government of Maharashtra 1981: 3); and in many cases the headlines in the Press and statements by ministers reflect these sentiments and we see and hear the constant use of such phrases as "war footing" and "war against nature". This perception is heightened by official pronouncements and statements in the Press that use words that detach the problems associated with extreme natural events from the rest of day-to-day relations and social life, stressing the problem as unexpected, unprecedented and uncertain; unawareness and unreadiness are used to describe the state of the victims but even they are not always to blame:

> What happened on the 19th at Divi Seema happens once a century and no human power could have visualised such a calamity, much less prevented it . . . . The destruction caused by the fury of Nature could not have been prevented even by the presence of the Army. (A.P. Government 1977a: 8.)

In the government's view there is a direct link between cyclones and poverty because of the cumulative effect of cyclones, summarised neatly by the Chief Minister of Andhra Pradesh when making the case for extending more credit to farmers after one severe cyclone in 1979:

> Cyclones have been an annually repeating phenomenon. Farmers have been losing their repaying capacity and are falling into arrears year after year and cumulatively the burden is becoming unrealistic. (A.P. Government 1979a: 14.)

But is the cumulative effect of cyclones the cause of poverty in the coastal areas? After all, the coastal areas include two very rich delta areas (the Krishna and Godavari deltas) which between them produce half the rice in the state (A.P. Government 1982a).

1.2.2 Development of cyclone policy

In cyclone-prone areas there are two complementary sets of programmes operating simultaneously. They are: (i) the **Cyclone Mitigation Programmes**; and (ii) the **Integrated Rural Development Programmes (IRDP)** which are sometimes called anti-poverty programmes. Both sets of programmes should be seen together. Since this book is about the recovery of a rural population from a cyclone disaster we will look at the cyclone mitigation programmes in some detail first and then briefly at the anti-poverty programmes at the end of this chapter.

Cyclone mitigation policies evolved out of famine relief policies which themselves developed from concepts of social security (see later discussion on anti-poverty programmes) from earlier times enshrined in the Hindu codes of *Sukraniti* and also under Islamic law (Guhan 1986). In India one of the historic duties of the ruler, or the state, was to relieve suffering caused by natural calamities; it was not their duty to try and avert the inevitable effects of such natural calamities. When the British ruled India, the burden of relief was taken over by the Presidencies and in 1878 the Famine Inquiry Commission recognised that the paramount duty of the state was "to offer protection . . . from the effects of the uncertainty of seasons" and identified areas that were prone to drought and subsequent famines. The Famine Commission laid down principles of famine relief administration which included "the provision of employment opportunities . . . through relief works" and "arranging gratuitous relief to destitutes through the village community". One of the Commission's major recommendations was the creation of a separate department for the administration of famine relief and the appointment of a full-time Famine Commissioner to co-ordinate relief activities in times of scarcity (Government of India 1981: 4, 5). It was the Famine Commission's duty to relieve suffering but not to prevent it. That would have been considered interfering and the British were well aware of the inherent dangers of such a course which ran counter to their "laissez-faire" doctrines at the time.

The conceptual framework of famine relief was extended into cyclone mitigation when elements of the current system of disaster preparedness were laid down in the 1930s and public works programmes (take from the Famine Codes) were started in cyclone-devastated areas "as a prophylactic measure to prevent deterioration of the rural economy" (Government of India 1981: 4). As well as these programmes, the notion, again taken from the Famine Codes, of giving "gratuitous relief" to cyclone victims was woven into cyclone

10

mitigation policy. From the 1930s until the late 1960s the standard response by governments to cyclone disasters was to relieve suffering and restore the economy of stricken areas. The procedure was aptly encapsulated in the report of the Collectors' Conference held in Vijayawada after the May cyclone of 1969:

> Top priority was given to disposal of carcasses and the provision of drinking water . . . establishing communications, repairing roads, restoring irrigation channels, repairing breached bunds and giving (short term) financial assistance to farmers who had lost their crop. (*Hindu* 27.5.69.)

After the two cyclones in Andhra Pradesh in 1969 (A.P. Government 1980a) and the colossal devastation of the cyclone and storm surge in the neighbouring state of Orissa in 1971 (10,000 dead) it became clear that individual states could not cope adequately with such extreme events and more reliance was placed on the Army to take the necessary remedial actions. The Press was increasingly critical of the government's inabilities to cope with such colossal devastations and outside aid was increasingly sought. In 1969 the Chief Minister of Andhra Pradesh had appealed to the Red Cross for help (*Hindu* 5.11.69) and in 1971 the Red Cross appealed to the world for help (*Hindu* 5.11.71). The emphasis on relief increased and the fact that there was not enough relief anyway was highlighted in a stinging editorial in the *Times of India* (4.11.71) after the Orissa cyclone:

> In other countries a similar disaster would have stirred the entire nation and relief organisations would have swung into action. But here the apathy created by long exposure to suffering seems to be growing into a hard crust.

Up until that time cyclone mitigation had the character of crisis management, with governments and the Army "rushing in supplies to stricken populations" and administrations "put on war footing" and so on. The two cyclones in 1969 initiated the first phase of activity in cyclone mitigation policy for years, and in their aftermath the government of Andhra Pradesh set up a Cyclone Distress Mitigation Committee (CDMC), consisting of meteorologists, engineers and administrators. The Committee produced a set of recommendations (A.P. Government 1971) which, sadly, were not incorporated into state policy until the late 1970s and have not yet been incorporated into legislation. These recommendations were focused almost entirely on preparedness and mitigation measures and are presented in some detail below because in principle all of them became the basis of subsequent cyclone policy (A.P. Government 1977a; 1979a; UNDRO 1981).

Phase One: the Cyclone Distress Mitigation Committee

The two cyclones of 1969 had painfully revealed the inadequacies of the government to cope with the after-effects of cyclones and instead of suggesting

11

ways of diverting resources to accelerate relief and rehabilitation programmes, the committee focused its attention on ways to improve preparedness and prevent loss of life and assets. We should note that only one recommendation out of 25 referred to post-disaster measures. The recommendations were set out under six broad headings culminating in a Model Cyclone Plan which it was hoped would be the blueprint for future policy and were as follows:

1.   The physical protection of low-lying areas

Under this heading the committee recommended that the government should build cyclone shelters in the main villages along the coast; plant wind breaks up to 20 miles inland; take up extensive afforestation along the coastal belt as a substitute for the natural vegetation that had been stripped away by population encroachment over the years; build flood-storage reservoirs and improve and maintain the drainage facilities in the low-lying areas. Also under this heading the committee recommended that dryers should be provided for stored crops (cyclones often occur in November while the harvested crop is still lying in bundles in the field drying out, and encouraging farmers to build raised platforms in their fields to save the harvested crops from subsequent flooding (Recommendations 24–29).

2.   Dissemination of warnings

Under this heading the committee recommended that the government improve communications between the storm-warning centres in Vizaghapatnam and Madras (in Tamil Nadu) and the flood-forecasting centre in Hyderabad; upgrade the Air India radio stations; co-ordinate the transmission of warning by the state and inter-state police forces; provide telephones at *taluka* (the smallest administrative unit of government and equivalent to a district council in Britain) headquarters; provide VHF links in the Post & Telegraph Department and set up control rooms at district level (the equivalent of a county in Britain) under the control of the District Collectors. Certain officials at these headquarters would have been previously designated for special duties to disseminate warnings, and, finally, Cyclone Relief committees should be formed at state level – i.e., in Hyderabad with close links with the Chief Minister and Secretary to government (Recommendations 30–37).

3.   Arrangements for evacuation of populations from affected areas

Under this heading the committee recommended that road improvements should be carried out between the major villages in the cyclone-prone areas, and that in the areas which were not accessible by road the "people be educated to heed warnings" (Recommendations 38–40).

4.   Safety of government property and undertakings

Under this heading the committee recommended that bus depots and transport organisations should be suitably notified about the nature of cyclone warnings and that Indian Railways should have comprehensive instructions for their passengers and staff about what to do in the event of a cyclone in order to ensure the safety of the trains, passengers and other property (Recommendations 41–46).

5. Post-disaster measures

Under this heading the Committee recommended that the government should prepare Hazard Location Maps of the coastal areas to make search and rescue operations easier; establish priorities for the restoration of communications and power supply after a cyclone strike; ensure the availability of amphibious vehicles for rescue purposes; co-ordinate all sea searches, and "encourage fishermen to wear easily distinguishable items of clothing" (Recommendation 47).

6. Community-preparedness programmes

Under this heading the Committee recommended that the government should organise mass education programmes in the cyclone-prone areas and have special preparedness meetings in the coastal areas in April and September using films, posters and pamphlets to communicate their message.

Finally, these six groups of recommendations were brought together in Recommendation 48, *the Model Cyclone Plan for a Coastal Area in Andhra Pradesh*, and the formation of Standing Committees who would be responsible for (i) educating the public on cyclone hazards and protective measures that can be taken; (ii) making arrangements for emergency action; (iii) effecting evacuation from coastal villages when authorised; and (iv) effecting rescue work. The last two responsibilities were quite impractical because only the armed forces and the police had the resources to carry out evacuation and relief operations on the scale envisaged, as previous events had shown, and future events were to prove.

The scope of the CDMC recommendations was far wider than the government's resources could cater for, with the result that only a few of the recommendations were taken up. However, the government took them as a cue to change policy and although it was impossible to provide sufficient protection for the populations in the coastal areas on the scale recommended, government concluded it would be possible to prevent large-scale loss of life and assets if resources were shifted from post-disaster measures to preventive action. The principal result therefore of CDMC recommendations was that from 1972 onwards the government concentrated on improving the forecasting, warning and evacuation procedures. This in turn, however, required improving the infrastructure and physical communications in the coastal areas, many of which were remote and almost inaccessible.

Phase Two: the cyclone of 1977

The cyclone of November 1977 became the catalyst for the second burst of activity in cyclone policy. Meteorologically the cyclone was unusual (Subbaramayya and Fujiwhara 1981) due to the influence of the "Fujiwhara" effect (two cyclones interacting with each other); it was also unusual from the political point of view and the way it attracted world-wide attention and an unprecedented influx of national and foreign Non-Government Organisations (NGOs). Coinciding with forthcoming state elections, it soon turned into a "political cyclone" and its political nature largely influenced the character of the responses.

The government's diagnosis of the colossal devastation and loss of life was that they were due to a combination of "the ferocity of the storm" (A.P. Government 1977a: 2); "the lack of adequate protection due to the disappearance of mangrove forests in the coastal areas" (A.P. Committee of Inquiry "to look into the physical factors that contributed" – A.P. Government 1977a); faulty infrastructure – i.e., blocked drainage channels *ibid*.); faulty warning (*ibid*.: 4–6); inadequate forecasting (*ibid*.: 5, 8, 9); and the failure of the people to take notice of the (belated) warnings (*ibid*.: 9); and, the people, of course:

> A facile assumption is made that the Army could have been used to evacuate the people. Apart from the nature of the calamity, anyone who is reasonably acquainted with people of such areas, constantly exposed to cyclones etc., would know that nothing would induce them to move out of their homes . . . . Besides, physically it would have been impossible to move out thousands of people over the long coastline to 14–20 kilometres inland. (A.P. Government 1977a: 7.)

In fact, it was everyone else's fault except theirs. The Press diagnosed the colossal devastation and loss of life as being principally due to the government's failure to implement any of the previous Cyclone Distress Mitigation Committee's recommendations, rendering warnings futile and evacuation difficult; but they also blamed "the stubbornness of the people" for refusing to take any notice of the warnings (*Hindu* 28.11.77; *Times of India* 26.11.77). But the *Hindu* foresaw a problem; "moving people out of a densely populated 80 km stretch would have been difficult . . . especially since communications were disrupted" (29.11.77), but "crying wolf too often has reduced the credibility of warnings so the task of the weathermen is to win greater credibility by improving the accuracy of their forecasts" (Editorial, *Hindu* 30.11.77).

Most of the criticism levelled at the state government (Congress I) was directed at its failure to have carried out any of the major CDMC recommendations (*Hindu* 22.11.77); but the criticisms had political overtones "A.P. Government blamed for laxity" (*Hindu* 26.11.77) and "Central Government (Janata Party) ready to step in if the situation becomes unsatisfactory" (*Times of India* 26.11.77). The criticisms of the government

14

response could be summed up in the Editorial from the *Times of India* of 8.12.77:

Nothing has been done, either by the Centre or the States concerned to implement any of the . . . recommendations of C.D.M.C. . . . that steps be taken to provide for more accurate forecasts, early warning systems, construction of reinforced concrete shelters and . . . standby relief operations.

Since this is the cyclone from which we have initiated this study into vulnerability, we will return to it in more detail in later chapters. For the time being it is sufficient to say that this cyclone left the affected area and the administration in chaos. Heroic efforts were made by many but it was generally felt that sins of omission rather than sins of commission were to blame for the extent of the tragedy. The cyclone two years later was less embarrassing politically because by then the 1977 opposition party was in government and it had swiftly ordered the mass evacuation of the coastal areas where the landfall of the cyclone had been predicted and fewer people were killed than otherwise.

Following these two cyclones, policy changed in two further respects. First, the concept of rehabilitation within the restoration programmes changed from one of simply restoring an area to its previous levels of development to a concept linked with the longer-term development of a stricken area; secondly, the concept of protection was enlarged from *community* protection to include *individual* protection in the form of "durable" housing, some aspects of which we will discuss shortly.

In 1981 the Cyclone Contingency Plan of Action (CPA) was approved as the official policy document governing cyclone mitigation (A.P. Government 1981d). The CPA set out clearly and unequivocally, for the first time, what the duties and responsibilities were for all levels of administration (from state to district) in the event of a cyclone threat. The plan is divided into sections that set out (1) the designation and status of cyclone warnings from the two state cyclone forecasting stations; (2) the preparedness measures necessary before a cyclone and the evacuation procedures in the event; (3) the convening of committees to oversee rescue operations, removal of the dead, restoration of traffic and the distribution of relief after the cyclone; (4) the need for mass publicity for community preparedness; and (5) specific measures to be taken by state government irrigation, animal husbandry, forestry, medical, public health, roads and building and railway departments in the event of a cyclone. A full-time Commissioner for Cyclone Relief and Rehabilitation (similar to the Commissioner for Famine Relief), supported by permanent officers and funded by the Revenue Department, was designated by CPA to be "in overall charge of rescue, relief and rehabilitation operations in the State" (A.P. Government 1981d). In 1981 the National Assembly at Hyderabad had placed before it the Andhra Pradesh Legislative Assembly Bill No. 38 of 1981 of the Natural Calamities Act (1981b) which amongst other things gave the government powers to exclude anyone from a designated disaster area.

In October 1983 another severe cyclone meandered up the coast from Madras and then remained stationary for about a week 100 miles off the coast of the Godavari delta in the north of the state. Heavy and continuous rains preceded the actual strike which made it difficult for the government to carry out the mass evacuation of the coastal areas that it had prepared. Nevertheless, 200,000 people were evacuated and when the cyclone struck, then only in a relatively mild form, less than 100 people were killed but the crops were ruined and a huge relief programme had to be carried out (*Times of India* 3.10.83). Once again the Press had plenty of criticisms and some solutions to offer:

> . . . no preventive or protective measures can cope with such a visitation . . . except marginally. Current estimates indicate heavy crop loss (in the Godavari delta) besides the destruction of private assets of those who can least afford it . . . . There is a need for a permanent fund, for offering disaster relief *instead of on an "ad hoc" basis* [my emphasis]. (*Times of India* 11.10.83.)

A further mix of programmes was proposed still emphasising the physical nature of the problem but linking it for the first time with a crucial requirement – crop insurance:

> The feasibility of risk mapping as suggested by UNDRO [United Nations Disaster Relief Organisation] should be explored. The Centre has Rs 1,700 crores to organise control measures against flooding [for the whole of India] . . . but no headway has been made because the States will not co-operate . . . . Another part of the Control programme is the slow pace of the extension of the benefits of Crop Insurance. (*Times of India* 11.10.83.)

1.3 SOME ASPECTS OF CYCLONE POLICY

1.3.1 Difficulties facing governments

Governments in cyclone-prone states in India face many difficulties in dealing with cyclones, most of which centre on competition for scarce resources and the differential political impacts these resources make. How the political system perceives and responds to impending disasters, both in the short and long term depends on their potential for politicisation, which depends on two things; the first is the time span and duration of the event which presents more or less time to mobilise resources, and the second is the perceived differential effects on victims. Because of their "quick onset" nature, cyclones have a far more dramatic appeal and potential for political capital than "slow onset" disasters such as droughts, desertification and so on. The potential for politicisation is underpinned by the fact that cyclone disasters are more

16

successful in attracting funds than droughts, and the opportunities to spread the benefits over a wide electorate are far greater. For instance, droughts most affect the poorest, and measures are targeted directly at the poorest groups; whereas cyclone disasters are perceived by government as affecting everybody equally and governments tend to spread disaster relief homogeneously, so that not just the poorest benefit.

Responses to cyclones and other disasters are principally governed by rivalries and conflicts of interest at all political and administrative levels; these occur between various ministries within central government, between the central government and the state government, between state and state, and between various levels within the administrative machinery of state governments. The politicians at the central and state level bargain amongst themselves since they have not only local but national power groups and vested interests to protect. A natural disaster in one area is commonly perceived as being a disaster in another, because scarce funds will be diverted from one part of the state to the disaster-affected area. The Godavari and Krishna deltas are among the richest areas of the state, but both are cyclone-prone. The people in the inland drought-prone areas (Telenganna in the north and Rayalaseema in the south) resent greatly the fact that aid should be going to these rich areas when their own everyday conditions are wretched. Politicians and administrators are aware of these feelings and act accordingly.

A key determinant in shaping the nature of disaster policies is the source and extent of funds to cope with the disaster. Until 1972 central funding was determined by an *ad hoc* assessment of the situation by a central time of officials and money was advanced as part grant and part loan to the affected states. The Sixth Finance Commission altered this because it was thought that the states were "not making proper use of the grants" (Government of India 1978: 53) and the Seventh Finance Commission suggested that beyond a margin previously set, the central government could contribute 75 per cent of the required expenditure in excess of the margins, but subject to the recommendations of its own assessors.

In the negotiating process that takes place after a disaster there is always a disparity between the estimates of damage made by state governments and central government. In 1977 the state government, by way of the Press, estimated that the damage caused by the cyclone was of the order of Rs 250 crores (1 crores = 10 million) but the central government only paid Rs 56.52 crores in disaster funding (A.P. Government 1977a: 19). In 1979 the various estimates of the damage in the Press ranged from Rs 290–570 crores and the State government claimed Rs 180 crores but was paid only Rs 37 crores (A.P. Government 1979: 13).

1.3.2 Rehabilitation programmes

Before the 1970s, governments had concentrated on public-works programmes, hand-outs and gratuitous relief (doles) as the mainstay of their rehabilitation programmes. The influx of national and foreign Non-Government Organisations (NGOs) after the 1977 cyclone, bringing with them $US 10 million of aid (Raghavulu and Cohen 1979) showed up the relative poverty of the government cyclone relief and rehabilitation programmes, with the result that the government subsequently enlarged its rehabilitation budget and broadened its concepts of disaster relief. For instance in 1969 the rehabilitation costs after the two cyclones of 1969 was the equivalent of 1 per cent of the state's annual expenditure on irrigation; in 1977 it had grown to 3 per cent and by 1979 it was 5 per cent (Winchester 1986: 27–28, 59–61).

The content of rehabilitation programmes also changed from one of handing out gratuitous relief and restoring public and some private assets on a one-to-one basis, to programmes which included giving loans, subsidies and grants to some sections of the community who had previously been excluded – i.e., the marginal farmers, fishermen and artisans – as part of the longer-term development of the area. Replacement of private assets traditionally only covered animals and household goods but under the new policies assets such as animals, equipment and crops were replaced through subsidies and grants (funded partly through IRDP and partly through Cyclone Relief) to enable their owners to recover to their previous levels of ownership (A.P. Government 1977a: 15–17, 19; 1979a: 7, 8, 12).

In 1977 an estimated Rs 15.0 crores was spent on relief and Rs 19.0 crores on rehabilitation after the cyclone (A.P. Government 1977a: 19–21). In 1979 the government spent Rs 12.5 crores on relief and Rs 30 crores after the 1979 cyclone (A.P. Government 1979a: 8, 12). In both cases the rehabilitation costs were in the form of short-term credit and/or subsidies to farmers, artisans and fishermen. This in turn spurred the banks into pushing more credit into the rural areas which had to some extent been a neglected activity, even though it had been a major plank in central government policy after the banks had been nationalised in the mid 1960s. However, the evidence from the fieldwork suggested that a high proportion of the extra credit that the banks channelled into the affected area after the 1977 cyclone did not reach the intended beneficiaries but was diverted to the powerful and influential members of the society.

1.3.3 Long-term protection programmes

The high death toll of the 1977 cyclone was a major political embarrassment and a contributory factor in the downfall of the government six months later.

The notion of physically protecting people from cyclones *before* the event, instead of mitigating their losses after the event, became the key issue in government cyclone policy for the first time and the concept of protection expanded from community protection to individual protection. Due to the nature of the resources they had at their command, the government concentrated on community and individual protection while the NGOs concentrated on individual protection. Community protection was implemented in the form of the cyclone shelter programme and physical coastal protection, and individual protection was encapsulated in the *pucca* housing programmes – later to become known as durable housing – which were initiated by the NGOs who came into the town.

The great majority of the hundred or so NGOs who rushed into the cyclone- and storm-surge-affected areas in 1977 unilaterally decided that "durable housing" was the top priority and consequently set about adopting villages and promising *pucca* (concrete-roofed) houses. The government were not keen on this but decided to capitalise on the enthusiasms of the NGOs and together they worked out a cyclone housing programme whereby the NGOs would share the cost of the houses on a 50/50 basis and the government would pay for the infrastructure (A.P. Government 1980c). There were grave doubts expressed at the time about the value of these houses, mainly on cost grounds, but the argument that India and the people needed status symbols won through and thousands of "pucca" houses were built. We will be discussing this issue later. The housing programmes were complemented by plans to build 1,500 cyclone shelters (A.P. Government 1980a), again with help from the NGOs.

After the 1979 cyclone which destroyed 2 million houses (A.P. Government 1981a), the government were able to legitimise the cyclone housing programme on the plausible cost-benefit grounds that:

> It has been the sad experience that the worst hit in cyclones . . . are those who live in huts and temporary structures. Several lakhs of such temporary structures were blown away during the recent cyclone. The government have been spending crores of rupees as immediate relief for restoring/rebuilding temporary structures again to be exposed to the next cyclone. The government have therefore decided that as a permanent *rehabilitation measure* [my emphasis], construction of pucca cyclone proof houses have to be taken up on a priority basis in the 20 km belt from the coast . . . . (A.P. Government 1979a: 10, 11.)

Thus the housing programme was accelerated and cyclone housing was taken under the wing of the Andhra Pradesh Housing Corporation drawing funds from central as well as state sources.

The durable housing programme has subsequently become the mainstay of disaster mitigation policy in the coastal areas, with its emphasis on reducing the physical effects of cyclones. Durable housing affords some protection and expands a villager's range of choices – i.e., whether to stay in his house or not during a cyclone – but in our view it does not widen his economic options to any significant extent. It could be argued that durable housing is only there to protect him but we think that the focus on durable housing is misplaced for reasons we will present shortly. While durable housing, of course, is better than nothing, the emphasis on it detracts from the main cause of vulnerability, the analysis of which is the main purpose of this book.

1.4 CRITIQUE OF CYCLONE POLICY

1.4.1 Questions

Do government cyclone policies reduce vulnerability or increase it? It could be argued that cyclone policies, with their stress on forecasting, warnings and evacuation systems and on increasingly physical protection, increase risks by making people think it is safer to live in cyclone areas than it really is. However, as examples show from the east coast of the United States and elsewhere in the world, it is virtually impossible to make cyclone-prone areas safe places to live in (White 1974). All that programmes can do is to limit the damage and not put lives at risk unnecessarily. Unless there is a safety net beyond the cyclone programmes (and we will discuss some of these in the next section) then increased risk means increased vulnerability. Others would argue the opposite; by saving people's lives with timely warnings and evacuations and even partially protecting them and their assets, the people survive to work another day – even though the risks are still high. Basically the main queries about cyclone mitigation programmes which focus on protection are (i) is protection necessary? and (ii) does protection work? – i.e., are cyclone areas safer than they were before?

In the cyclone-prone areas there is now a much higher expectation of relief and rehabilitation than there were 10 years ago. Many people inside and outside government think that the government over-reacted to the 1977, 1979 and 1983 cyclones and is now trapped in a cycle of increasing aid to cyclone areas, increasing expectations and perhaps limiting choice. Choices of actions by individuals and communities are affected by their expectations, sometimes with disastrous results, so that those with the least choices face the greatest risks. (For example, one village hamlet in the study area "collectively" refused to accept the concrete houses offered by the government, preferring the more spacious alternatives built by the voluntary agencies, which were not forthcoming. Despite the collective decision in 1977, the richer people had rebuilt their own traditional houses by 1983 and the poorest remained in the same huts they were given in 1977, and were still at risk.)

Some would argue (Hewitt 1983: 10) that the increasing tendency for governments to respond to disasters with technology leads to rural (and urban) communities becoming increasingly dependent on expertise and technology that is not available in their communities, which leads to some sections of the communities become more dependent on others than they were say 50 years ago when there was only limited outside expertise and technology and when the need for intra-village links and a system of mutual dependence was essential (Srinivas 1960; 1962; 1976; Beteille 1965). The assertion that technology produces dependence may be true, depending on the "technology" used; but, in the case of improving monitoring, forecasting and warning technology, the benefits are theoreticlly available to all (transistors are cheap in India and standards of forecasting and warning are as good as they are anywhere in the West) and many lives have been saved as a result of this improved technology. The crucial point is that the over-reliance on technology may exclude other aspects of cyclone vulnerability from being taken into consideration – a point which is developed later.

In the previous section we said that there were two major aspects of change in cyclone policies over the last 20 years; these were changes in the approaches to rehabilitation and protection. Now we will present a brief critique of only one of them – protection – because protection encapsulates nearly all the aspects of pre- and post-disaster development that dominate government thinking. We will start with forecasting, warning and evacuation because the main thrust of policy over the last 10 years or so has been on this aspect of disaster mitigation; and then go on to a short critique of physical protection itself, both for communities and for individuals.

1.4.2 Over-emphasis on warning and evacuation

Warnings

The effectiveness of warning systems depends as much on technological and administrative factors as on whether the warnings are taken seriously and acted upon. Governments tend to over-warn to reduce emergency rescue, relief and political costs, and people who are exposed to hazards tend to play them down and also the warnings. A prevailing, though ethnocentric, view of the early 1960s about how people perceived natural hazards (and in particular floods) was that they "were prisoners of their past experience . . . seeing the future as the mirror of the past" (Kates 1962: 12) and the evidence of fieldwork tends to bear this out for widely varying reasons (Winchester 1990: 95–109).

The main difficulty in getting people to take warnings seriously and leave their homes, lies in the difference between villagers' and governments' perceptions of probabilities of cyclone strikes. Villagers will "rationalise" the probability of a cyclone hitting their villages as very low by recalling how many times within their own memory cyclones have missed them and they will calculate the costs of taking action by equating them with the costs of moving. On the other hand the government, with a potential strike area of at least 100 km in length and knowing that they face relief and rehabilitation costs, will rationalise their actions by calculating the political and economic penalties of not taking action by equating them with the costs of *not* moving.

Apart from the difficulties in persuading people to move, there are problems associated directly with the nature of cyclones. We saw earlier that the movements of cyclones are notoriously difficult to predict. Forecasting errors increase with the duration of the forecast and distance of the cyclone from the coast and the average error for a 24-hour prediction is about 240 km while the average landfall error for a 24-hour prediction is about 180 km. A predictive error of 10° in direction of motion would shift the scene of greatest danger by 100–150 km (Simpson 1971).

Evacuation

The high death tolls after cyclone strikes in the past could reasonably be attributed to failures in warning systems *and* to an absence of evacuation measures, but there is evidence from the fieldwork to suggest that people do not willingly leave their homes and possessions even when they can see a cyclone approaching. In 1977 the government belatedly instructed District Collectors to evacuate people along a coastline of approximately 900 km but the warnings were not heeded and evacuation measures were minimal and at least 10,000 people were killed. Forecasting techniques and warning systems have been greatly improved since 1977 and were applied successfully in the cyclones of 1979, 1983 and 1990. In 1979 the landfall of the cyclone was more accurately predicted and the government ordered the evacuation of low-lying areas along 300 km of the coast between Nellore and Prakasam, in the south of the state, and 300,000 people were successfully taken to safety (*Times of India* 14.5.79) and in 1983 the evacuation of 50,000 people was successfully carried out in the Godavari delta due mainly to more accurate forecasting (*Times of India* 5.10.83).

Greater penalties for politicians combined with the refusal or failure by populations in coastal areas to take warnings seriously in the past have led to evacuation measures being automatically implemented after the first warning as standard procedure and the evacuation of populations in lorries and buses to a few kilometres inland is now the duty of the revenue department assisted by the police. The wholesale movement of thousands of people inland causes other problems, not least of which are the high costs of maintaining temporary relief camps for hundreds of thousands of people who require feeding and adequate sanitation facilities.

For the people, the costs of moving are linked with their preoccupation with either reducing debts or not increasing them and they tend to see their courses of action more in terms of penalties rather than of opportunities. In all but the most severe cases it would seem that most people would sit tight and hope the cyclone passes, pinning their hopes on their past experiences of having survived. Response, however, is governed according to social and economic viewpoint. The fieldwork interviews revealed that most people would not move unless forced or unless there were devices that could insure or compensate them for losses, either from the event or from theft as a result of moving. Their unwillingness to move voluntarily was mainly governed by the high costs of moving – i.e., the difficulties of getting transport and travelling on crowded or flooded roads – and the empirical evidence of their own experience that any possessions they might have to leave behind would be stolen.

If costs of evacuation (and the relief costs) could be reduced, then a policy of evacuating long stretches of the coastal areas might be justified on cost grounds. The government, in fear of the political backlash, tends to pin its hopes on better forecasting and warning systems but in our view they are still on "a hiding to nothing". An over-reliance on warning and evacuation procedures is compounded by (i) the inaccuracy of predictions of the landfalls of cyclones; and (ii) the high probability that most of their costs are likely to be abortive if the forecasts prove inaccurate.

Evacuation costs are cheap compared to other cyclone mitigation costs and other programmes (see below); in 1983 they were budgeted at Rs 0.1 crores for the whole state – i.e., 10 per cent of total cyclone relief (A.P. Government 1983a, 1983b) – but can vary from almost nothing in 1977 to Rs 1.0 crores (1982: personal communication with a senior official in the Revenue Department, Government of Andhra Pradesh). Evacuation programmes since 1979 have been successful, but, from the fieldwork interviews in 1988 we found that there were still some people who were willing to risk their lives and not leave their homes, unless they were forced to *or otherwise induced*.

We have concentrated on warning and evacuation in this section although emergency relief and rehabilitation also come into this category of short-term programmes. These programmes with their emphasis on warning, evacuation and relief programmes, perfectly justifiable on humanitarian grounds, seem utterly reasonable on cost grounds too, especially when the costs of evacuation and relief are compared with other programmes, as presented in the budget estimates for 1983–84 (A.P. Government 1983b; 1983c):

Relief (including evacuation– Rs 1.2 crores;
Animal husbandry   – Rs 16.5 crores;
Food for work programmes– Rs 2.5 crores;
Minor irrigation   – Rs 11.5 crores;
Fisheries   – Rs 5.0 crores.

1.4.3 Reliance on long-term protection

Turning now to protection; we saw before that policy had evolved from almost zero *community protection* in the late 1960s, except for a few tidal bunds in some of the coastal areas, to extensive community protection by the mid 1980s in the form of sea walls, afforestation and dune control programmes (A.P. Government 1979b); and, again, from almost zero *individual protection* before 1977 to extensive individual protection by the mid 1980s in the form of the concrete housing and cyclone shelter programmes (A.P. Government 1981a; 1981e; 1982b; 1982c; 1982d; 1983a). We will start first with community protection.

The case for physical protection in cyclone-prone areas seems obvious enough although the degrees of protection depends largely on the resources available. Mangrove swamps used to provide "natural protection" along stretches of the coast but these have nearly all disappeared as a result of development and population expansion. The physical protection of coastal areas from sea- and river-flooding, by way of tidal and river bunds has always been part of government policy, stretching back go the mid 1850s when the deltas were first irrigated, but maintenance has always been a major problem. It is easier to protect people from the ravages of high winds than it is from flooding by devising small-scale cost-effective technology that provides wind protection, but wind protection measures have fewer economic and political pay-offs than flood protection. Flood control is largely governed by geomorphological constraints and resources, but the economic and political rewards of carrying out large-scale flood-control projects which are protecting the people as well as the crops are potentially far greater. Flood-control works along the River Krishna have proved successful in reducing loss of life from riverine flooding in the past but those along the coast have proved far less successful. We will briefly examine the economic argument and some of the implications of large-scale coastal flood-control projects that the government have undertaken.

The argument that links the need for physical protection and the reduction of poverty rests on the premise that reducing the physical and therefore economic risks associated with cyclones leads to increased investment in an area which in turn provides work for the poorest sections. The flaw in this argument is that physical protection induces people to bring previously unprofitable land into cultivation (the risks and costs were too high before) which indeed increases the costs of cultivation which are then in turn offset by reducing labour costs (by tractorisation amongst other methods) which does result in less work for the poorest and a greater reliance on temporary migration. We will substantiate this claim in Chapters Five and Six.

Historically, the wealthier cultivators with the widest range of choices in the coastal areas have tended to reduce their risks not necessarily by investing

24

more *per se* but by diversifying from subsistence crops into more profitable but higher-risk cash crops such as fruits, fish farming, cotton, sugarcane and so on. These crops have tended to require more irrigation and more expensive agricultural inputs than subsistence crops and the costs have been offset by reducing labour requirements, resulting in less work for those who depend on agricultural labouring as a living – i.e., the landless labourers who are among the poorest in any agricultural society.

Both the processes of bringing more land under cultivation and the tendency to offset risk with high profits could lead either to permanent migration from coastal areas, which some think is desirable (Khan 1982), or, to the increased marginalisation of the poorest in the coastal areas as they are driven out to the least fertile land, inevitably the most exposed and therefore the least protected, increasing their risks, and, potentially the government's relief and rehabilitation costs. In Chapter Two we will bring evidence to show that this is exactly what happened in the study area over a period of years.

The construction of large-scale community protection programmes tends to give people a sense of security that may not be completely false but nevertheless may not be an altogether accurate one. Flood-control programmes undoubtedly encourage people to continue to live in high-risk areas which they otherwise might leave if they had a choice (however, the vast majority simply do not have such a choice). The increasingly high density of population could lead to heavier loss of life if flooding was unexpected and overtopped the tidal bunds.

The government would argue that the warning and evacuation programmes are the "fail safe" to the flood-control programmes, should the floods overtop the bunds or should the works themselves erode and become useless. The argument to evacuate low-lying areas was proved to be valid even though they were (normally) protected by flood-control works, because in the May cyclone of 1990 (as severe as the one in 1977) when the government evacuated 400,000 people from densely populated areas over a 800-km stretch of the coast, the tidal bunds in the study area collapsed and 50 sq km (population 100,000) were up to 6 m under water (*Hindu* 9.5.90). The loss of life in this instance was reduced of course by the evacuation but also because the storm-surge waters rose very slowly. One might venture to suggest that these figures show an over-reaction to a situation that cannot be justified on economic grounds and one argument against wholesale evacuations at this scale is that the costs of evacuating the other 300,000 people might be more profitably spent in other ways, which we will discuss in subsequent chapters.

As long as the problem of cyclone vulnerability is seen in terms only of cyclone damage and loss of life then a problem with policy which concentrates on community protection through flood-control projects is that the pay-offs of a minimum investment for a maximum protection might encourage the government to do less to improve the position of the weakest sections than it might otherwise be pressured to do. Another issue that emerges from this discussion is the extent of government responsibility *after* it has protected the environment; and another is whether long-term protection measures can be combined successfully with other programmes, for instance education, training programmes, a health service, a social security system. The discussion also raises questions about who benefits from these improvements and who loses; the assumption underlying the thinking behind these programmes, and throughout disaster mitigation generally, is that everyone benefits equally, but more about this later.

1.4.4 Cyclone shelters and permanent housing

Community cyclone shelters

The first aspect of protection programmes that we should comment on is the cyclone-shelter programme (A.P. Government 1980a) briefly described before. Critics argued that only 12 per cent of the coastal population could be accommodated in the number of cyclone shelters being proposed and that the shelters would not be used as community buildings as envisaged due to bureaucratic difficulties (subsequently verified in the fieldwork). Other critics foresaw caste frictions in multi-caste villages creating situations where some castes would not be permitted to use the shelters under any circumstances (Cuny in UNDRO 1982) and this was also verified in the fieldwork programme. Another criticism was that in freak conditions a storm surge higher than 10 m (Gosh 1977; Islam 1971) might engulf the shelters and turn them into death traps which many churches, temples and schools turned out to be in 1977.

However, the cyclone shelters have proved to be possibly the most successful part of the cyclone mitigation policies. In some respects they have taken over the role of the large and extremely well-built four-truss traditional houses in so far as most people in the villages will now go to them (depending on size) if they can. Most of the cyclone shelters in Divi Seema (the study area) were completed by 1979 and they have been used in numerous occasions since. The cyclone shelters have now become a primary insurance device against theft for the people who do not want to leave the village and who can still keep an eye on their possessions. Instead of refusing to leave their houses for fear of having their possessions stolen, the poorer villagers now go to the shelters, which are, however, too small to accommodate their animals and possessions. The better-off villagers will leave the villages anyway.

However, there are dangers. In a survey of 24 shelters in Divi Taluk carried out in August 1983 only two shelters showed any signs of structural failure due to subsidence and poor construction that might raise doubts about their durability to withstand hurricane winds and flooding. The cyclone shelters, unlike the concrete houses, look as if they will last and be life-savers, or death traps?

Permanent housing schemes (concrete housing)

The next aspect of protection programmes that we should comment on is the permanent housing programme that the government has been pursuing vigorously since 1978. Since the 1977 cyclone the government's aims in rebuilding the traditional villages in coastal areas as housing colonies with concrete-roofed houses were (i) to protect the inhabitants from future cyclones and afford some protection of their assets; (ii) to improve the environmental conditions in the villages by increasing space standards; and (iii) to reduce the recurrent repair and replacement costs of traditional houses. This position was summed up in a paper presented by the Director of Weaker Sections Housing at a conference in Hyderabad in 1980:

> The most striking manifestation of poverty is the poor quality of housing preponderance of deficient structures, over-crowding, squalid surroundings, and limited access to essential services like water and sanitation. The fundamental dilemma is that the community and Government cannot afford the resources to meet the housing needs, but the great population is too poor to build adequate houses without public assistance. (Ayyar 1981: 56.)

The underlying policy was that all villages in the coastal areas where the death tolls had been so high should be rebuilt as housing colonies with special cyclone-proof houses. These were to be constructed on the same sites as the previous villages and in some areas adjacent to the coastal strip for particular caste groups (Harijans and Muslims). The housing colonies were connected to the main roads by all-weather approach roads and were provided with electricity at the government's expense. The colonies were laid out orthogonally according to space standards laid down by the Roads and Bridges Department of the Housing Directorate and in accordance with standards set out for all low-cost housing in the state (A.P. Government 1982f), the layouts being governed by engineering concepts of access and fire hazard. The design of the houses was left to the agencies but they had to meet specific technical criteria governing construction, materials and waterproofing, based on standards for urban housing.

Due to the high costs of materials and construction, the plinth areas (that is the raised platform on which the house is built) were uncomfortably smaller (18 sq m) than the most prevalent two-pole traditional house (26 sq m). All village households who had lost their houses, irrespective of status, were deemed to be eligible for concrete houses, providing they were willing to give up their claims to their previous house sites so that everyone could have equal-sized house sites. But, inevitably many house sites were increased or decreased in size during construction and in some villages the more influential households with the power to divert resources received two houses.

The intention was to build the houses as durable cores from which extensions would be built in traditional materials when the owners could afford them; the idea being that even if a cyclone destroyed the flimsier extensions the core would still be left. The cores would be used much in the same way as the central portions of the traditional houses, namely, for the storage of precious belongings, additional storage of food grains, sleeping in the cooler months and some protection during cyclones. It was estimated that the durable concrete core would cost Rs 5,500, shared equally by the government and voluntary agency, and that this provision would save anyone who would otherwise have to build a house, an equivalent of Rs 1,000 at 1981 values. A financial penalty associated with the concrete houses was that they were classified as "permanent housing" after a year and as such attracted an annual tax of Rs 25–50 depending on the plinth area. The traditional non-brick *katcha* houses were not classified as permanent and therefore did not attract site tax.

The engineering space standards that were adopted led to excessive amounts of space being taken up by roads, resulting in small house sites with no space for housing expansion (see Tables A.1.1 and A.1.1.2, Appendix 1). As a consequence some households had to live on the peripheries of the colonies which were only accessible through another caste's "territory", which at one stage threatened to become a serious social issue in the study area. (In the traditional villages the castes are separated physically; the overlapping of caste territories does not occur and is an important feature of the culture.) In the housing colonies in the study area it would have been possible to have increased the average house site by about 50 per cent, without re-creating the restricted and squalid (in winter) environments of the more cramped areas of the traditional villages. The extra 40 sq m would have been large enough for "income-generating activities" such as providing shelter for animals or fowls, growing produce to sell from a kitchen garden, using the space as a workshop, or leasing it out. One of the overriding realities of life was that where was no guarantee that the extra land would have been used for other income-generating activities *unless* the owner could have got formal credit and help from a government programme. The most likely scenario would have been that other family members would have moved in and the larger house site would have been used to extend the existing house or in some cases to build another house. Having more family members close at hand is the pattern of living in this area and is one of several risk-diffusion and risk-reduction strategies that people use. However, households with few assets, living in flimsy houses in cyclone-prone areas face a cruel dilemma; by increasing the numbers of family members living together and the household's earning capacity, they also put more people at risk to cyclones.

In terms of durability the houses did not live up to their name and many were perceived by their owners to be unsafe (Tables A.1.2.1 and A.1.2.2,

Appendix 1). Many households had to build traditional one- or two-pole houses up against the concrete boxes, using them for temporary storage, because the concrete houses were inadequate. In the rainy season (July–October) the concrete cores became virtually useless as dry storage; most leaked badly and in most of them a fine spray would descend from the ceiling during rain storms. The widely-known heat-retention properties of concrete created uncomfortable conditions for sleeping made worse by the custom, or necessity, of closing windows at night against evil spirits and robbers. The smooth plastered walls were less attractive to mosquitoes than the unplastered mud walls of the poorer traditional houses and there were many fewer reports of snakes and rodents entering the concrete houses. Although health conditions inside the concrete houses were probably an improvement on the traditional houses, the large areas of unclaimed public land in the colonies became voracious breeding grounds for mosquitoes in the rainy season and these public areas were invariably closer to the houses in the colonies than they were in the traditional villages.

One of the precepts underlying policy was that the construction of housing colonies might provide extra local employment, but in fact the programme produced very little local employment in Divi Seema, the study area. The houses were built by contractors from the towns on the mainland and Avanigadda, who brought with them their own carpenters, steel-fixers, bricklayers, plasterers, and their mates. Only unskilled labour for general coolie work such as building the internal roads and levelling sites was provided by the local contractors from the nearby villages (Appendix 1, section 1.3).

Another precept underlying policy was that the free provision of concrete houses would save many people the costs of building a new house themselves. If the houses had been more durable some savings could have been made and there would have been some justification in providing such expensive houses. Savings could possibly have gone into providing dowries (the majority of families in Divi were unable to meet the cost of any dowry), medical expenses – which as we will see are relatively exhorbitant – or paying off previous debts, or as the priorities of the households demanded. It was extremely difficult to extricate the facts about savings, but our findings showed that people living in free houses were no better off than their opposite numbers in traditional houses (Table A.1.3.1, Appendix 1).

The second important aspect of this housing programmes was that of status. Status may appear to be an erroneous issue to an outsider, but it is an issue that is deeply felt by the villagers. Despite the criticisms about the concrete houses in terms of their comparatively high cost and total climatic unsuitability, there was a dilemma facing those wanting to build durable houses for the poor. The dilemma centred in the late 1970s (and still does) on the issue of status. Concrete houses were regarded as status symbols by almost everybody and mud and thatch huts were associated in the minds of everybody (except the foreigners) with poverty. The dilemma was expressed in the following passage by Raghavalu and Cohen writing after the 1977 cyclone:

> It is hard not to agree . . . that the cost of providing pucca houses to everyone will be prohibitive, and that the programme will not deteriorate into favouritism and corruption . . . . But, is the demand for pucca housing and shelters so irrational . . . ? What the critics tend to ignore (or label as "politics") is the genuine need in India to demonstrate governmental involvement with the welfare of the survivors. Symbolic gestures and statements in the form of pucca houses and concrete structures, are absolutely essential for politicians, however costly and irrelevant they may be in terms of rational strategy of rehabilitation. (Raghavalu and Cohen 1979: 60.)

This argument has been used countless times by governments all over the world and it surely raises the question whether the best way for governments to show their concern for their people is through such overtly visible projects such as housing (with immediate results) or whether there are other less visible ways? Where would the balance be struck? We return to these questions later.

1.5   A SUMMARY OF CYCLONE POLICY:
THE CONVENTIONAL VIEW

In summarising the development of cyclone mitigation policy over the last 20 years we can see that the government went through a learning process that has produced an effective cyclone mitigation policy, in parts. The learning process was accelerated by the growing awareness of the wider economic and political effects of cyclone devastation, better communications and the power of the Press. We have seen that the focus of policy changed from measures designed to reduce the impact of events *after* they had happened, to measures designed to reduce the impact of events *before* they happened. In doing so the government widened their area of concern and their policies changed from dealing with the effects of devastation in one area on an *ad hoc* basis to dealing with the potential devastation of many areas on an *integrated* basis. It is hard to say to what extent policy is still shaped by the process of *post facto* fund management (a euphemism for haggling) because the threat of cyclone disasters is so politically omnipresent.

The government's cyclone mitigation programmes of individual protection (pucca cyclone-proof houses) and collective protection (cyclone shelters and a sea wall) were greatly influenced by comments in the Press and to some extent by what the NGOs were doing. From the evidence of the losses and devastation (Table 1.2) the government's perceptions were correct in so far as the key factors in accounting for the extent of damage were exposure, topography and the ferocity of the storm. We can encapsulate these perceptions in what we will call the **Conventional View**, taking the details from their policy documents, some of which we have quoted in this chapter, and their subsequent actions, and relating them specifically to the study area. The structure for this version of the Conventional View was first used in an analysis of land degradation in Kenya by Randall Baker (1981) but it has been found to be applicable to other situations too. In the Conventional View we link cause and effect, taking one factor as the independent variable and the others as dependent variables. In this case all the evidence points to the *physical* vulnerability of cyclone-prone areas as being the most suitable independent variable, and the argument is shown in Figure 1.1.

On the face of it the Conventional View seems plausible enough. However, we should note that it omits any reference to the historical development of Divi Seema or to the underlying political economy. In the light of present-day knowledge, these omissions would appear to be quite serious.

FIGURE 1.1: *The Conventional View* (after Baker and Winchester in Winchester 1986: 30)

THE PROBLEM DEFINED:
   The physical vulnerability of cyclone-prone areas.

THE SYMPTOMS AS PERCEIVED:
   High death tolls attributable to the severity of cyclones.
   Widespread damage to crops and property requiring extensive and recurrent relief and rehabilitation.
   Widespread hardship and poverty in rich irrigated coastal areas.

THE CAUSES:
   The large scale and uncontrollable characteristics of cyclones.
   The low-lying nature of coastal areas with their poor drainage and proneness to flooding.
   The exposed nature of coastal areas and inadequate physical protection.
   The failure of forecasting and warning (technology) and evacuation (administration) systems.
   The ignorance and bad habits of coastal populations.

THE SOLUTIONS:
   Improve forecasting, warning and evacuation systems.
   Formulate disaster plans, develop disaster management techniques; enact legislation, carry out hazard analysis and risk mapping of physically vulnerable areas.
   Improve the physical protection of coastal areas: by building control works, barriers, levees, and earth stabilisation; planting afforestation belts; improving draining systems.
   Increase the protection of the populations of coastal areas: by building cyclone shelters; improving the techniques and the technology of traditional and modern building practices; improving design of buildings to resist high winds and flooding; raising the ground levels of villages or house sites in flood-prone areas.
   Eradicate ignorance and "bad habits", by introducing cyclone-preparedness training programmes; control supply of liquor in coastal areas.

1.5.1 Philosophy underlying the Conventional View

The underlying philosophy of the Conventional View needs to be explained. While we are discussing it, we should also contrast it with the underlying philosophy of a range of views we will be presenting in the next chapter (the Alternative View). The philosophy underlying the Conventional View – that the environment is physically vulnerable and that people need protecting from risks such as cyclones – is one of "*maximising* safety". The philosophy on which the Alternative View is based (which will be explained and justified in Chapter Two and tested in Chapters Five and Six) is one of "*minimising* avoidable suffering" and derives from Karl Popper's "agenda for public action" (Popper 1966, vol. 2: 237) and deals with threats that are *internal* as well as external to societies.

The more affluent and powerful members of society subscribe to the philosophy of "maximising safety" because they think they should be protected from risks of high severity but low probability, such as cyclones. The least affluent – i.e., the weak, the old, the sick and the poor – want to be protected from day-to-day risks of low relative severity but high probability, as well as cyclones, and would subscribe more to the philosophy underlying the Alternative View, because everyday risks are far more damaging to them than the occasional cyclone. However, the statistics of probabilities are unknown to the vast majority of people, as the astrological columns of newspapers and the industry testify, so that official perceptions and responses to risks such as cyclones are determined more by their political consequences than by probabilistic estimations, as we have seen. The extent of visible damage is a powerful determinant of subsequent policy and policies of maximising safety have the great political advantage of being more or less instantly visible.

The loss of life triggers emotions more quickly than other losses so that anything that can reduce threats to people's lives has a high priority in policy formulation. However, the terms in which human life is measured usually lie in political realities, and in such situations the most pertinent question is the cost of saying "no" to protective measures. The costs of saying "no" to protection, raises questions that lead to the Alternative View. Supporters of the Alternative View argue that resources should be directed less to saving lives on the catastrophic scale of events that are unpredictable and random, and, more to saving lives on the everyday scale of events, and would make the case that preventing people from dying from starvation and disease is a more practical basis for a philosophy than saving them from catastrophes, although, of course, saving them from catastrophes is also important. Programmes based on the Alternative View would aim to improve living conditions and reduce social injustices, the causes of which are internally generated in societies where suffering is found, and are predicatable and occur continually.

Both views overlap to some extent and draw attention to problems which are basically ones of disadvantage, but their emphases are different. The philosophy of "maximising safety" of the Conventional View also minimises avoidable suffering to some extent by protecting the environment, as well as improving the conditions of the occupants of the flimsiest houses and of the most dangerous sites. The Alternative View not only focuses on the occupants of the flimsiest houses and on the most dangerous sites, it actively seeks out the reasons why the people were in those houses and on those dangerous sites in the first place. Both views are concerned with preventing situations from getting worse but the main difference between them is that the Conventional View is less concerned with the process of change, whereas the Alternative View is concerned *specifically with change*. The Alternative View has another important difference from the Conventional View by concentrating on problems associated with resources allocation and dispersement for the disadvantaged sections of the community, the Alternative View would have the effect of extending their range of choice. Logically this extension of choice should lead to removing the causes of disadvantage in the first place, which, the Alternative View would argue, derives more from policies and institutions, and powerful sections working within them, and less from physical phenomena. We shall be discussing these implications in later chapters. For the time being we will rest the government's cases on the Conventional View and return to the omissions in the next chapter after we have completed an overview of the other relevant programmes in cyclone-prone areas.

1.6 OTHER GOVERNMENT PROGRAMMES IN CYCLONE-PRONE AREAS

We now return briefly to the anti-poverty programmes which are regarded by government as being complementary to the cyclone mitigation programmes. The anti-poverty programmes are aimed specifically at reducing poverty in rural (and urban) areas and have developed over the years as part of rural development policy, set within the Integrated Rural Development Programmes (IRDP) which targeted groups of disadvantaged people within larger populations. To give the reader an idea of the scope and range of the programmes within IRDP we now present a short resumé of how these programmes evolved within the changing concepts of rural development since Independence in 1947.

At Independence, the leaders of India were quite aware of the backwardness of agriculture and the lack of an industrial base for the Indian economy. In the first 10 years after Independence great emphasis was placed on the development of the rural areas in order to complement the drive for industrialisation. It was recognised by the Government of India that rural poverty was rooted in the system in which the poor were deprived of assets and their lack of access to employment in the organised sector. Their aim was to redress this imbalance by mixing employment programmes with asset-accumulation programmes, the mix depending on location, and these were the basis of their rural development programmes.

Rural development programmes were targeted at "communities as a whole" and based on concepts such as "Community Organisation" (First Five-Year Plan) and "Participation" (Second Five-Year Plan) backed up with land reform and workers co-operatives. The development projects were aimed at improving agricultural performance by improving rural infrastructure programmes, health and education facilities and providing credit to the small farmers and landless groups through special agencies. Intermediate technology was fashionable at the end of the 1960s which coincided with the aspirations of many politicians, who shared Mahatma Gandhi's vision of India – a collection of self-sufficient villages.

By the mid 1960s the rural development programmes had collapsed. Partly because the large farmers had syphoned off the bulk of the credit programmes and had successfully excluded the poor, but mainly because the introduction of the bio-technology of the "Green Revolution" inexorably shifted the impetus of agricultural production from people to technology. The extent of mass poverty was increasing, in fact, although this was not acknowledged officially. A change in direction was required. The new Conventional Wisdom led in two directions (Fourth Five-Year Plan); the first to anti-poverty programmes which promoted *employment* through National Rural Employment Programmes (NREP) and public works programmes rather than provide unemployment relief, the ultimate purpose being to give purchasing power to the poor, which could be done most efficiently via direct payments in cash or foodgrains, rather than through *works*, which involved overheads and leakages (Guhan 1980); and the second to massive investment in rural development programmes which were targeted at the "most vulnerable sections" of populations, instead of whole communities.

Governments were aware of poverty, and, using incomes as a measure they developed the anti-poverty programmes to try to prevent populations at risk from falling below certain income levels. They were also aware that people who suffered from ill health, lack of assets, lack of work or had no education or limited skills were particularly vulnerable to poverty. Where the facilities were thin on the ground they tried to improve the quality of their lives through their IRDP programmes as best as they could within the arena of competition for resources.

These anti-poverty programmes included setting up agencies known as Small Farmers' Agencies (SFDA) and Marginal Farmers' and Agricultural Labourers' Development Agencies (MFALDA) aimed at helping specific target groups of farmers, artisans and the landless to accumulate assets which would increase their incomes. SFDA and MFALDA prepared the schemes, identified the small and marginal farmers and agricultural labourers, presented the schemes and recommended the farmers to the local financing agencies. The agencies provided subsidies of 25 per cent for the small farmers and 33 per cent to the others at the same time as covering some of the financing risks of the funding agencies. The programmes provided the targeted groups with the means to acquire the following assets: for *Agriculture* the provision of pairs of bullocks, bullocks and carts, pumpsets and dairy animals; for *Other animal husbandry* the provision of sheep, pigs, goats and buffaloes; for *Village industries* the equipment and means to carry out wool-weaving, pottery-making, leather-working and brick-making; for *Service trades* the equipment to carry out trades for cobblers, washermen, carpenters, blacksmiths, barbers and so on; for *Trading* activities the means to set up and run petty shops, cloth businesses, fish-vending and sea and canal fishing.

Many of the larger programmes depended to some degree on technology, supplied by the state and the multinationals. Past failures had shown that management was a key factor in achieving economic prosperity and there was a growing realisation that to conquer poverty and economic hardship it was necessary to bring together experts in many different fields in a "multi-disciplinary integrated approach" and this led to the Integrated Rural Development Programme (Fifth Five-Year Plan) which gathered together the strands of the SFDA and MFALDA programmes. One of the main problems with the SFDA and MFALDA programmes and the IRDP programmes was that they relied overmuch on government administration and were taken over by bureaucracies, as a result of which many of the intended beneficiaries lost control of the development process.

By the late 1970s many social scientists had concluded that technology had failed to resolve the continuous and endemic problem of poverty (Kothari 1981) and that the much-vaunted "targeting vulnerable groups" programmes had failed abysmally too and that a return to "community organisation" was required, but this time through a third party, the voluntary organisations. A view developed inside and outside government that voluntary agencies or Non-Government Organisations (NGOs) were the best catalysts through which the people could control the development process. These agencies (many of them operational for 20 years) had the experience of the micro-level problems of people's everyday lives, whereas government were incapable of this degree of involvement with people since they had neither the trained manpower to operate at this level, nor, in many cases, the motivation.

The desire inside and outside government to see NGOs resuscitate the moribund concepts of "community organisation" and "participation" was the prevailing mood in 1977 when the cyclone struck, and, partly accounts for the inundation of the area by NGOs, with the active encouragement of the state government, at the time. Since then, NGOs have come in for a great deal of criticism and the whole idea of development from the outside has been questioned (Nandy 1987; Sheth 1983; 1987). Many NGOs in India are turning

FIGURE 1.2: *Government perception of vulnerability and poverty in cyclone-prone areas.*

POVERTY		CYCLONE VULNERABILITY
Widespread distribution	PROBLEM:	Recurrent impact of cyclones
Low level of assets and resources in poor households	SYMPTOMS:	Overall devastation; loss of life; loss of assets
Geography; lack of resources	CAUSES:	Characteristics of cyclones and topography
Build up assets in targeted low-income households	SOLUTIONS:	Physical protection of people and assets; evacuation
IRDP anti-poverty programmes	FORM:	Cyclone mitigation programmes

to "social activism" as an alternative to project implementation and we will discuss some of these aspects later in Chapter Four.

Bringing the anti-poverty and cyclone mitigation programmes together we can summarise governments' perception of the causes of both poverty and vulnerability in cyclone-prone areas (Figure 1.2) as being a combination of lack of assets and loss of assets, their claims that anti-poverty and cyclone mitigation programmes are complementary are justified to some extent since anti-poverty programmes mitigate the effects of poverty by *building up assets* and cyclone policies mitigate the effects of cyclones by *protecting people and their assets.*

However, in relation to concepts of vulnerability, the IRDP programmes are regarded as faulty by some:

> . . . IRDP programmes seek to raise incomes but at the same time entail a loan and indebtedness. But poor people are reluctant to take debts and increase their vulnerability. One implication for policy is that government programmes, which, whatever their benefits, make poor people indebted or in other ways more vulnerable, should be treated with caution. Such vulnerability can be reduced through group loans and through insurance which covers debt is the asset is lost. Reducing vulnerability can be an important as reducing poverty. (Chambers 1989: 2.)

Others are also critical of the IRDP programmes (Kurian 1987; Guhan 1980; 1986). Nevertheless, without anti-poverty programmes in the cyclone-prone areas the populations are at greater risk than they are with them and they provide a minimum level of economic protection from the ravages of cyclones. The questions to which we now turn are "Is that protection sufficient?" and "Is it protection from cyclones that people want?"

A Conceptual Model of Vulnerability

INTRODUCTION

In Chapter One we showed that Nature was the prime culprit of devastation in cyclone-prone areas, according to the government's perception, and that vulnerability was a function of exposure measureable by losses. In this chapter we expand this perception and widen our understanding of vulnerability by suggesting that Man is the major culprit in creating cyclone devastation compounding the destructive capabilities of cyclones by his own actions. We start by offering other ways of looking at the problem of cyclone vulnerability, starting with a brief resumé of the progress in disasters research since Gilbert White's work in the 1950s and 1960s and how this work has resulted in the view that is widely held today – that so-called natural disasters are *primarily* the products of political economies and not the natural hazards themselves.

2.1 A RESUMÉ OF DISASTERS RESEARCH

From the late 1960s there was growing evidence that the devastation caused by natural disasters was only partly attributable to the severity of the events themselves and was more a function of the social and economic characteristics of the populations in which they occurred. The principal contribution to this perception was made by Gilbert White and his colleagues who were the first social scientists to acknowledge that the devastating effects of natural phenomena were partly the result of Man's actions as well as the phenomena themselves (G. F. White 1961; 1964; Kates 1962: Burton *et al.* 1968; Hewitt and Burton 1971). In their concept, the important distinction was between extreme natural-hazard *events*, which were not necessarily hazardous to people, and the *character* of the hazardous events. In White's concept a hazard was the risk encountered in occupying a place subject to extremes of natural phenomena (Burton *et al.* 1968: 19) so that the characteristics of risks in hazard areas and the perception of them became the focus of study (Burton and Kates 1964; Mitchell 1974) and not the characteristics of the hazard event itself. This introduced the need for a wider understanding of measuring risk and vulnerability. Underpinning White's concept were two methodological requirements; (i) the need to define and measure hazard events so that their description was of value to non-physical scientists; and (ii) the need to describe and analyse perceptions of hazards and the choices people made to cope with them (Burton *et al.* 1968). This distinction between the nature of a hazard and its effect was a crucial one because until then hazards had been measured only in geophysical terms unrelated to human activities (A. White 1974).

White and his colleagues found that people transformed their environments into resources by using natural features for economic, social and aesthetic purposes and by so doing created hazardous circumstances which sometimes created disasters (Burton *et al.* 1968: 20; Islam 1981) and that people sharing the same overt threat would appraise the same risk differentially (Kates 1962) depending on a variety of factors including economic penalties. The great contribution to an understanding of natural disasters made by White and his colleagues was that *differential perceptions of risk* were as important a factor in risk management as the characteristics of the the hazards themselves.

However, their approach to solutions remained mainly anchored in the geophysical aspects of hazards and technically based adjustments, exemplified by Ann White's "Adjustments to the hazard of tropical cyclones" (in White 1974: 260) summarised as follows:

Modification of the event itself:
Before the storm: Seeding cyclone clouds to lessen the intensity of the storm (too expensive – see Riehl and Simpson 1981).

Modification of damage potential:
Before the storm: Making use of protective shore-works, afforestation, warning systems, evacuation, construction of raised areas; use of zoning codes, building codes, design of wind resistant buildings, construction modification, flood- and wind-proofing.
During the storm: Evacuation, seeking shelter or praying.

Distribution of losses:
Before the storm: Buying insurance, stockpiling of emergency supplies of water, food and building materials.
After the storm: Claims on insurances (non-existent in the coastal areas of India); emergency relief and reconstruction or "bearing the loss".

This was similar to the approach taken by the Andhra Pradesh Government – i.e., the recommendations of the Cyclone Distress Mitigation Committee (see Chapter One, 1.2.2). The ethnocentricity of Ann White's model and the approach that it exemplifies, and its very partial relevance to developing countries, has since been severely criticised by Torry (1979), who claimed that the "vast anthropological and sociological hazard/disaster literature is virtually ignored" (1979: 369), and also by geographers for its failure to recognise the differential socio-political aspects of disasters (Watts 1983).

Despite its ethnocentricity, (or perhaps because of it) the model was taken up by governments all over the world, including the state governments along the eastern seaboard of India, with their predilection for technology and administration. However, they seem to have ignored the reasons why people appraise the same risks differently and this is a crucial omission.

By the end of the 1960s more evidence was coming to light to suggest that people's *unregulated* activities were a contributory factor in the creation of natural disasters (Chen 1973) and by the mid 1970s the view that a disaster was

". . . a severe, relatively sudden and frequently unexpected disruption of normal structural arrangements *within a social system*, or subsystem, resulting from a force . . . over which [the social system] has no control" (Barkun 1974: 51)

was becoming more widely understood by many social scientists. This may have partly echoed governments' views that disasters were uncontrollable and outside the social system, but suggesting that the causes of disasters were perhaps rooted within the social system itself was not recognised officially.

However, until the end of the 1970s the dominant definition of disaster vulnerability in disasters research and practice was that vulnerability was the direct relationship between Risk and Hazard (UNDRO 1979b), the assumption being that the hazard was the event and the risk was the exposure to the hazard, not the same way that Gilbert White had proposed years before, and that the risk therefore was the same for everyone exposed to it. The underlying assumption in this definition was that populations exposed to natural hazards were homogeneous, except for degrees of exposure. The definition made it much more convenient for disaster managers to deal with disasters than having to cope with the obvious differentiations within societies.

Sociologists had long maintained that disasters were "social crisis periods" (Dynes *et al.* 1967; Dynes *et al.* 1972; Dynes and Quarentelli 1977; Dynes *et al.* 1987; Britton 1987), but crises occur at all scales of human activity from the individual to the nation and the difficulty with definitions of disaster has always been to perceive different levels of crisis, as *relative disasters*, without becoming suffocated by minutiae or overwhelmed with generalities. Neil Britton (*ibid.*) has made an important contribution to this debate by focusing on three types of a social-crisis period – accidents, emergencies and disasters – which help to disentangle the different scales of disaster and bring them into the sphere of everyday conditions, which has been hinted since Gilbert White and many others, but never made explicit. Britton clarifies three types of crisis that can all be relatively disastrous depending on who they affect, and this relativity of effect is a point we shall return to later in this chapter (2.4).

During the 1970s the view developed that economic processes could increase the vulnerability of populations to natural disasters and should be considered as causes of disasters in the same way as were the more obvious physical or environmental phenomena (Baird *et al.* 1975; O'Keefe *et al.* 1976). One of these was the process of spatial and economic marginalisation which was considered to be an extreme form of vulnerability occurring at the margins of society:

> ... in such a way, socio-political and economic marginality produced eco-demographic marginality, i.e. marginal people are, through the process of social allocation ... quite literally pushed into marginal places. (Wisner 1976: 2.)

Baird *et al.* (1975) referred explicitly to the dependency theories of Gunder Frank (1966; 1973) and Samir Amin (1974) *inter alia* and used these theories in understanding the process of marginalisation. They also pointed to a relationship between relief and underdevelopment and argued that relief merely reinforced the *status quo*, produced greater marginalisation and greater disaster susceptibility and furthermore that relief hindered adjustments to future natural hazards and increased dependence. These claims will be substantiated by our own findings which we discuss later (Chapters Five and Six.

It was suggested that populations were able to adapt to a certain range of hazards but that external factors such as government policies affecting the environment could change the population–environment relationship, reducing or restricting the population's capacity to deal with hazard and thereby increasing its vulnerability to natural disaster. Westgate and O'Keefe (1976: 64) proposed a working definition of a disaster event as:

> ... an interaction between extreme physical or natural phenomena and a vulnerable human group ... [which] results in general disruption and destruction, loss of life, and livelihood and injury".

The importance of this definition lay in its emphasis on disasters as the interaction between the physical phenomena and vulnerable human groups and the suggestion that a contributory cause was the state of the human society as much as physical phenomena. In the same paper (p. 65) the authors define vulnerability

> ... as the degree to which a community is at risk from the occurrence of extreme physical or natural phenomena, where risk refers to the probability of occurrence and the degree to which socio-economic and socio-political factors affect the community's capacity to absorb and recover from extreme phenomena.

Westgate and O'Keefe also pointed out that the distinction between vulnerability from a hazard environment and vulnerability from socio-economic status, was a false one and they proposed that vulnerability should be a term which embraced not merely risk from extreme phenomena but *the endemic conditions* inherent in a particular society that may exacerbate that risk.

A clear implication was emerging that disasters were an extreme situation within a series of normal events and should be analysed in that context and not as unique happenings: "disaster is the extreme situation which is implicit in the everyday condition of the population" (Baird *et al.* 1975: 2). Also, there was more than a hint that government intervention caused vulnerability in rural areas leading to the conclusion that natural disasters were principally man-made.

> . . . an additional explanation [of vulnerability] to be the changing relationships between agriculturalists and the land leading to a change in their concern for the preservation of the environment. The changes were observed as induced by Government policies spread of the market economy. (Hewitt 1976: 34.)

Hewitt argued that the major ingredients of a natural disaster were the causal processes of the social relations of production. This theme was powerfully developed by Watts (1983: 242): ". . . the forces and social relations of production constitute the unique starting point for human adaptation". Watts suggested that the focus of any examination into the effects of natural disasters should be radically changed and he summoned support:

> From the latter perspective the production focus dovetails directly with problems of access to and/or control over the means of production in a given society; and most importantly how the total product of that society is allocated among various groups within its populations. (Cook 1975: 45, cited by Watts 1983)

In his own case-study on drought and famine, Watts (1983: 256) makes the point that

> . . . hazards had been redefined by the transformation in the social relations of production. Indeed the rural poor were vulnerable to any sort of perturbation . . . . Poor farmers shackled by their poverty are largely powerless to effect the sorts of changes that might mitigate the debilitating consequences of environmental hazards. Hazard response is thus contingent upon their situation in the productive process.

Another study on the famine in northern Nigeria between 1968–74 (Apeldoorn 1981) put forward the hypothesis that the cause of the famine, which followed a long drought, was that the mechanisms evolved over time by the communities to cope with hazard and climatic phenomena had been diminished or destroyed by changes in the social relations of production. These changes were the direct result of government policies. The problem is diagnosed as one of marginalisation and inequalities in access to resources. The author was critical of the government's focus on relief because it indicated its crucial failure to recognise the true nature of the problem – relief was regarded as the only means of coping as efficiently as possible with what the government termed "an Act of God" – and the solution put forward was for the government to produce disaster-preparedness and self-reliance programmes.

The issue that was avoided by Apeldoorn was the analysis of the socio-political elements of power, which was attempted in analyses of desertification (Baker 1981) and soil erosion (Blaikie 1981). Baker and Blaikie's analyses were similarly based and focused on the political economy and the analysis of the social relations of production; their basic hypotheses being that the social relations of production were the result of the *interaction* between the political economy, "the system within which problems are defined and decisions taken" (Baker 1981: 1), and the physical environment.

In Blaikie's analysis the critical elements of the process did not necessarily occur at the place where the relations were evident, and different social formations had different effects in similar physical environments. He argued that it was crucial to distinguish between the various processes that created those differences:

> The implications of a political economic approach . . . are problematic. The first is that the focus is not necessarily place based, but on the human relations that do not necessarily locate themselves where soil erosion occurs and sometimes have no spatial expression at all. So if aspects of the causal explanation . . . lie outside the area, so do the remedies and these embrace the strong political, economic, social factors . . . . The direction of analysis also leads . . . to a critique of existing policies and other attempts on the part of the State to control or protect the environment. Thus the approach is characterised by (a) a combination of 'place based' concern with the area itself (affected by soil erosion) with (b) an analysis of often invisible not necessarily place-based political-economic relations. (Blaikie 1981: 4).

The central theme of Blaikie's and Baker's analyses was that environmental degradation from which marginalisation and risk intensification developed

> . . . directly results from cumulative land use decisions through time and that the decisions must be considered as part of the wider political economic analysis (Blaikie 1981: 14).

The political-economy context is basically the product of the inter-relationship between: climate and physiography, the social relations of production and historic development policies (see Figure 2.1), and people are more or less vulnerable according to their relationship with these interrelationships and processes. These relationships will be fully discussed later but for the time being we should acknowledge that the relationship between a community (and a household) and the political economy is a crucial one, as illustrated in Figure 2.1.

FIGURE 2.1: *A conceptual model of vulnerability showing the external factors affecting vulnerability* (after Blaikie and Winchester: Winchester 1986)

CLIMATE

| **PHYSIOGRAPHY** | **SOCIAL RELATIONS OF PRODUCTION** | **DEVELOPMENT POLICIES** |

COMMUNITY/HOUSEHOLD

2.2 THE ALTERNATIVE VIEW

We saw in Chapter One how official statements and press reports used words that detached the problems associated with extreme natural events from the rest of Man/Environment relations and social life "stressing the events as unexpected, unprecedented and uncertain . . . and the victims as unaware and unready" (Hewitt 1983: 10). By stressing the unusual aspect of disasters, the governments put the natural calamities outside the assured order of knowledge and of reasonable expectation and tended to place disaster outside the everyday responsibility of society and individuals; they made monitoring and scientific understanding of geophysical processes the top priority of disaster management (Chapter One, section 1.2.2).

The whole basis of the concept underpinning the Conventional View was that people were

> . . . committed to removing known manageable risks from everyone's life, failing to do so only where the risk is highly uncertain. There is a lot of evidence that human groups and institutions are rather less fervent about equity and social justice than that. (Hewitt 1983: 14).

The Conventional View assumed that everyday life and disasters were opposites, that everyday life in relation to disasters was normal, secure and productive, and that disasters resulted in life being insecure, and unproductive – i.e., the occasion of losses. Another assumption was that the sources of stability and instability in human affairs occured at times and places where damaging extremes destroy ordinary life.

> Natural hazards, like disease, poverty, even death, become simply the unfinished business of our endeavours. We can then focus daunting technical equipment and expertise upon . . . forecasting physical conditions, more complete containment of natural processes (physical protective works): educating government and the public; devising . . . centrally controlled systems to protect those at risk to some high [risk] hazard areas; redesign installations and if all else fails, organising relief on a grand scale. (Hewitt 1983: 19).

In contrast to this we now propose an *Alternative View* (see Figure 2.2) which derives from the political-economy model, based on the work of many social scientists in the field of development and other studies (Bernstein 1973; 1979; Cuny 1984; Oxall *et al.* 1975; Lehmann 1979; Mitra 1977; Sen 1975; Seers 1979; Wijkman and Timberlake 1984, *inter alia*) who had found that government policies had resulted in drastically altering the social relations of production in many societies, resulting often in the spatial and economic marginalisation of many of their members.

Central to the main idea in the Alternative View is the relationship between crisis and everyday conditions. We will bring evidence later that substantiates our claim that conditions of crisis exist every day for most people in cyclone

FIGURE 2.2: *The Alternative View* (after Baker, Blaikie and Winchester in Winchester 1986: 73–74)

THE PROBLEM DEFINED:

The physical vulnerability of cyclone-prone areas is a symptom of their economic vulnerability so that the everyday conditions of some groups of people make them extremely vulnerable to the impact of cyclones, in which case cyclones only accentuate existing conditions of vulnerability.

THE SYMPTOMS AS PERCEIVED:

High death tolls partly attributable to the severity of cyclones and subsequent flooding.

Extensive poor-quality housing. Extensive damage and losses to crops, animals and buildings during cyclones.

The recurring need for large amounts of aid and extensive rehabilitation after severe cyclones.

THE CAUSES:

Land-use, land-distribution and resource-allocation policies by successive British and Indian governments which have led to the spatial and economic marginalisation of large sections of populations in coastal areas.

Land-use policies that have encouraged rapid population growth leading to environmental deterioration, the deforestation of coastal areas and the increased use of inadequately protected land, increasing the numbers at risk of suffering losses and damage through cyclones.

Resource-allocation policies that have failed to provide sufficient or adequate alternative protection to most of the exposed population within 20 km of the coast, and reduce the numbers of losses, or other forms of insurance to reduce the impact of the losses.

Insufficient alternative employment opportunities in a monoculture area, resulting in over-dependence of the majority of the population on one source of income.

Deterioration of social insurance within the society as a result of commercialisation and increasing Government intervention.

THE SOLUTIONS:

Change the bias of cyclone mitigation programmes from physical protection and over-reliance on technology and administration, to building up the resources of the most vulnerable sections of the society through long-term credit, health and educational improvement programmes, based on a wider definition of the term vulnerability, so that it applies to a much wider field than an exclusive relationship to the probability of a natural phenomenon occurring.

---

areas, and we will argue that the relationship between crisis and cyclones is not the crucial one. Cyclones are the most extreme risk that people face but their effects only heighten the existing symptoms of the real disaster of development policy. We will argue that disasters are not out there in nature, savage and intensive, waiting to pounce, but exist in society in our social organisation of knowledge and production. The underlying argument in the Alternative View is that the phenomenon of *differential vulnerability* exists, whereby different people suffer differentially in response to the SAME physical phenomenon in the SAME area, and we should be concentrating on these aspects, as well of course as the physical ones, in cyclone prone areas. To do this we need a clear understanding of the nature of vulnerability and its components.

2.3 THE NATURE OF VULNERABILITY

2.3.1 Vulnerability: a definition

Westgate and O'Keefe (1976: 65) defined vulnerability as "the degree to which a community was at risk from the occurrence of extreme physical or natural phenomena, where risk refers to the probability of occurrence *and the degree to which 'socio-economic and socio-political factors affect the community's capacity to absorb and recover from extreme phenomena"*. This definition, derived from the dictionary definition – "the state or capacity for being liable to injury or damage, likewise it reflects the capacity to withstand injury or damage" – was more or less accepted by social scientists within the field of disasters research at the time, although it was largely ignored by governments and technocrats. More recently, the susceptibility for damage and the capacity to resist has been sensitively transferred to the personal level in the work of Robert Chambers (1982; 1983) who defines vulnerability thus:

> Vulnerability . . . is not the same as poverty. It means not lack of want, but defencelessness and an inability to cope with risk, shocks and stress. (Chambers 1989: 1.)

The definition could apply to a community but we would have to be careful in doing this because communities are not homogeneous and are composed of individuals each with different capacities to resist or recover, as we shall see later from the analysis of the empirical data. Chambers (*ibid.*) goes on to make a distinction between poverty and vulnerability, which is crucial to the debate:

> Failure to distinguish vulnerability from poverty has bad effects. It blurs distinctions and sustains stereotypes of the amorphous and undifferentiated mass of the poor. Poverty is often defined by professionals for convenience of counting, in terms of flows of incomes or consumption. Anti-poverty programmes are then designed to raise incomes or consumptions and progress is assessed by measures of these flows. Indicators of poverty are then easily taken as indicators of other dimensions of deprivation, including vulnerability. But vulnerability, more than poverty, is linked with net assets. Poverty in the sense of low income, can be reduced by borrowing or investing: but such debt makes households more vulnerable. Poor people with a horror of debt appear more aware than professionals of the tradeoffs between poverty and vulnerability – to make more secure – are not for one, the same as programmes and policies to reduce poverty – to raise incomes.

Poverty and vulnerability are inextricably linked and the empirical evidence we discuss in later chapters will substantiate the above thoughts as well as throw more light on the condition of vulnerability.

From our own everyday experiences we know that our *personal* ability to take a risk or endure a shock, stress or loss depends largely on how "strong" or "weak" (healthy/ill; rich/poor; employed/unemployed) we are at the time, and that our strength or weakness (ability to cope with these events) is determined by how well we have faced and dealt with similar previous events, as well as on the nature of such events. Both our capacity to be wounded and our capacity to resist depend also on the personal resources we can raise *outside ourselves* (the family, the group, the community) to deal with the event at the time and these outside assets and resources, together with our own, will largely determine our susceptibility to future risks, shocks, stresses or losses. We also know that the same risk or loss will have different effects on other people because their strengths and weaknesses are different from ours. Thus from our own personal experiences, we are aware of the phenomenon of *differential vulnerability*.

This extends to the household level where the *SAME* shock, say a fire or a flood, will have quite *different effects* on different households in the same area depending entirely on who or what is lost and the *relative* value of those losses. The people or things (assets or resources – later referred to as investments) that are lost will determine how the household recovers and survives the future.

When we come to examine assets in more detail we should keep in mind some of the characteristics that govern their role. First there is *susceptibility* of assets to damage or loss, which centres on the types of assets; for instance how much more likely is a cow to be lost or injured in a flood than jewellery? Secondly, there is *dependence* placed on assets, for instance what is the difference in the dependence of a household on the health of a minor wage-earner or the health of a milch animal? Thirdly, the *transferability* of an asset will determine the vulnerability of a household to a large extent, for instance can the household move away their assets from the hazard? These are the sort of questions that are constantly asked by officials in disaster areas and are difficult to answer in the absence of a clearer understanding of vulnerability.

2.3.2 Instability

The essence of vulnerability is that it is a condition that evolves over time. It either increases or decreases and either way will affect the stability of a household or community (or an individual) and their ability or inability to cope with outside events. One of the ways of measuring vulnerability is to look for the point, where, say, the economy of a household or the health of an individual) moves from being in more or less a state of equilibrium to becoming unstable, usually, the result of some sort of shock event (internal or external to it). Another way is to chart the point in time at which an individual, household or community, loses its ability to regain the position it was in before it became unstable. In economic analysis the position at which a household becomes unstable and the position at which it is unable to regain its former position of stability is most acutely reflected in its income. If a household is economically unstable then it follows that any larger scale instability will increase its own instability, but, it does not follow that because a household is economically stable under one set of conditions that it will necessarily remain so when those conditions change.

General Equilibrium Theory (Arrow and Hahn 1971) is useful here in so far as it provides a framework in which we can examine some of the components of vulnerability, and according to stability analysis in General Equilibrium Theory the tendency towards equilibrium (see Figure 2.3) depends on three broad factors; (i) *the nature and size of a shock*; (ii) *the initial conditions* (that is the conditions prevailing before the shock); and (iii) *the paths of adjustment to recovery*.

FIGURE 2.3: *General Equilibrium Theory: external shocks, household characteristics and paths of adjustment to recovery*

SHOCKS

| **CLIMATIC** | | **NON-CLIMATIC** |
| (Normal & Extreme) | | (Loss, Illness, Death) |

**HOUSEHOLDS
CHARACTERISTICS**
(Assets & Resources)

LOSSES

**PATHS OF ADJUSTMENT
TO RECOVERY**

Catastrophe Theory (Woodcock and Davis 1978; Zeeman 1978) is another useful tool in looking for these critical points in so far as it deals with sudden and discontinuous change, whereas traditional stability analysis relies on gradual and continuous changes. Catastrophe Theory is additionally useful because one can use qualitative features, rather than quantitative ones – i.e., household characteristics – to explain how a household moves towards collapse by coming to a point of instability, **suddenly**, beyond which it becomes unstable, usually as the result of a loss, but not always so (for instance, the death of the major wage-earner in a household can upset the household economy for a considerable time, depending on, say, the ages and sex of the other wage-earners). Catastrophe Theory is also useful because it illustrates that in vulnerable households there is a point beyond which anything can tip the balance between stability and instability and the effect of this event may be out of all proportion to its size. Tawney writing about China in 1931 describes this condition:

> . . . There are districts in which the position of the rural population is that of a man standing permanently up to the neck in water, so that even a ripple is sufficient to drown him. (Scott 1976: 1; quoting Tawney 1966.)

Taking the ideas behind these theories of the overall processes that create vulnerability we can now go deeper into its characteristics by looking at (i) shocks; (ii) losses; and (iii) adjustments.

The impact of any event or shock that tips the balance between stability and instability depends on the nature and characteristics of the event and the nature and characteristics of the household or individual receiving that shock. Our next step into the labyrinth of vulnerability analysis should start with an examination of the nature of shocks and how their effects can vary according to their characteristics. The term shock is used in its widest sense and is taken as meaning any event that upsets equilibrium which is outside the normal course of day-to-day events. For instance, an argument with a traffic warden could hardly be called a shock to an urban motorist, although it might be temporarily unpleasant, whereas to find the tyres of your car slashed might well be a shock, both psychologically and economically.

2.4 SHOCKS, LOSSES AND PATHS OF ADJUSTMENT TO RECOVERY

The external factors or shocks that can precipitate a crisis and cause instability in households can be examined in a number of ways. Chambers (1983: 104–134) groups them as follows: (i) Social conventions; weddings, funerals and dowry payments; (ii) Natural disasters; floods, cyclones, drought; (iii) Physical incapacity; illness, accident, child-bearing; (iv) Unproductive expenditure; and (v) Exploitation. Political changes, civil disturbances, changes in wages and prices and markets and taxes can also be included as crisis precipitators. Another way of classifying shocks is to examine their characteristics – such as their size, incidence, frequency, predictability and linking effects. We will start with the latter classifications used by some geographers (Burton *et al.* 1978) and then include some of Chambers's groupings in the analysis that follows in later chapters. Taking the geographers' classifications as our cue, we will now briefly unravel some of the characteristics of shocks in the first stage of our attempt to explain vulnerability and differential vulnerability.

2.4.1 The nature of shocks

Size

One aspect of shocks is their size. Shocks can be large or small and differ in severity and their impact should be evaluated *relative to* a household's susceptibility to loss or damage at the time of the event; otherwise, the rich, who have more to lose, could then be defined as more susceptible to shocks and could be deemed to be more vulnerable. The impact of the shock is of greater concern if it takes the household below some measurable absolute boundary such as starvation or death, which would be unacceptable on humanitarian grounds, but we shall see later that a small-size shock such as the loss of an application form for some coveted favour (land, house site, job and so on) could have devastating effects on one household that another household might hardly notice.

Timing

As well as their size, another crucial aspect of shocks and the effects they can have is their timing. This may be crucial in determining whether a household survives (physically and/or economically) or becomes destitute, and on who is affected. Although any climatic risks may be spread over a small or wide area, the timing of a drought or a flood may affect one household more critically than another in the same area, say one whose working head fell ill or was injured at the critical time of harvesting. The timing of shocks at a larger scale can also have differential effects, for instance, excessive rain at harvest time will damage the livelihoods of more farmers than fishermen but a cyclone will damage the livelihoods of fishermen more than farmers. (The reasons for this will be explained later). Timing becomes less important when land use and cropping patterns are taken into account where different areas with different land use and cropping patterns are exposed to the same cyclone and this strategy is widely used by the more prosperous farmers in the study area.

Frequency

The frequency of a shock event will have a critical bearing not only on the effect of the shock but also on the *persistence* of its effect. Random events – such as excessive rain at harvest and cyclones – that nevertheless occur in cycles, can have cumulatively dehabilitating effects on agriculture; seasonality is the best example of this where a recurrent event has both random and systematic components. Much has been written about seasonality (Chambers 1982; 1983; 1989; and Chambers *et al.* 1981, *inter alia*) which is now generally considered not to be the cause of poverty but a major factor in bringing regular crisis points to the lives of the poor. Seasonality and intra-seasonal variability can have what has come to be known as a ratchet effect (Chambers 1983: 113).

An economic ratchet occurs when a household needs to raise money to deal with a crisis of some sort, say an accident or a bribe that has to be paid immediately. Shortly afterwards another crisis happens and more money is required so an asset is sold. Shortly after that, before the household has had time to recoup its losses another crisis happens, say this time, a death which requires more financial outlay for an appropriate funeral. Perhaps all this happens during a poor harvest and the household members are unable to find work. Gradually the household borrows more money which will perhaps take years to repay and as it become increasingly indebted so its choices shrink and it finds itself in a syndrome of poverty and despair. An example of a physical ratchet with economic implications is increasing soil erosion and land degradation in some drought prone countries as *one* consequence of recurrent droughts (Baker 1981; Blaikie 1985), where the increasing degradation steadily decreases the range of choices available to the community at large and the poorest in particular; another is the diminution of the viability of risk-reduction strategies (i.e, range of choices) practised by traditional societies, through the over-use of common property resources such as forests, pastures and river beds as these become taken over (Jodha 1983). Similarly, the recurrence of cyclones creates a ratchet effect in cyclone-prone areas by the gradual destruction of the cultivable lands that are recurrently inundated with salt water or exposed to high winds. In our case, the government is correct in arguing that the recurrent incidence of cyclones is one factor – they argue that it is the major factor (A.P. Government 1979: 6) – in increasing the vulnerability of the people who depend on such land in cyclone prone areas.

The most devastating ratchet effects are more likely to be provoked by large external shocks, such as a severe failure of seasons due to cyclones or rainfall variations, which may affect a whole region, although as we shall see the effects of such devastating events are widely varied even within the same area.

Predictability

Another feature of shocks that we should take into consideration is their predictability and it would be useful if we could predict them. Predictions are based on theories of probability and some events have a very low probability and cannot be predicted with accuracy – e.g., some categories of accidents. Other events are more or less predictable and have a higher probability – such as epidemics, wars and elections. Others are even more predictable, such as cyclones in the Bay of Bengal in November and May rather than in September or June (Subbaramayya and Subba Rao 1981), but that does not rule out random and freak cyclones occurring in the latter months. Even if events could be predicted with a high degree of accuracy, people will react to them in different ways. The Theory of Bounded Rationality (Slovic *et al.* 1974; Burton *et al.* 1978: 187–204) attempts to explain why people make apparently suicidal and irrational responses even to predictable events.

Linkage effects

The most destructive feature of shocks is when several of them cluster or happen together in a sequence, each event decreasing the household's or community's resources and lowering their ability to recover, combining to produce a multiplier effect. In the case of a sequence, the first event intensifies the impact of previous events, and if the household has not recovered from those then the sequence that follows will have more disastrous effects than perhaps otherwise. Even if the household can withstand the first shock, a sequence of them may gradually increase its incapacity to cope; for example, an illness, deteriorating health or an accident can result in loss of income through an inability to work. This loss of income might force the household to borrow money at rates that they would not normally consider and the exhorbitant repayment terms could easily result in having less money to buy treatment. Lack of appropriate treatment at the appropriate time could lead to a more prolonged illness or a permanent disability leading inexorably to either a reduction or the termination of work thereby decreasing still further the productivity of the household and its ability to survive.

2.4.2 Losses

In an agricultural society in a cyclone-prone area all types of losses tend to be serious because they affect the way that households earn their living, which is precarious enough for the majority under any circumstances. The loss of assets and resources in cyclones is widespread and can present serious consequences for households, depending on the relative value of the assets or resources that are lost. The two types of losses that we are concerned with derive from *climatic* and *non climatic* causes. We will look at losses in the study area in detail in later chapters but since we investigating vulnerability we will briefly outline the types of losses that can be sustained under these two conditions.

Losses from extreme climatic conditions

Loss of land
In an agricultural society, land is the most important asset. Damage to land can be classified as the most serious loss, although it may only be a temporary one. Following a cyclone accompanied by a storm surge, the productivity of the land can be severely curtailed by sand-casting and salinisation from sea inundation, but land can be restored to productivity quickly or slowly depending on the resources available. After such an event, it is the government's priority to clear the land and restore the economy as soon as

possible and they direct their resources accordingly. Losses after a severe or normal cyclone are not so great for reasons we will explain later when we discuss risk strategies.

Crop losses

Where standing crops are damaged or destroyed they represent a property loss to the farmers who own them and a loss of income for the people who would have been employed harvesting them. The coincidence of the cyclone season with the harvest creates a major risk but crop varieties have been adapted to reduce these risks (see discussion later).

Animal losses

Animals losses are lost income as well as lost assets. They are profoundly felt in an agricultural society because so many people depend on them for an income one way or another. The wealthier farmers depend on their draught animals for ploughing, taking produce to markets and to some extent for fuel; the poorest households depend on milch animals for income, sustenance and fuel; others depend on herding animals for income, milk and meat. Many households keep ducks or fowls as sources of food and income, and particular caste trades make a living from using animal skins. A fairly obvious example of the difficulty in measuring vulnerability by losses is if a rich farmer who loses his four milch animals in a cyclone is deemed to be more vulnerable than a poor farmer who loses his only animal.

House and domestic losses

The loss of a house can be a major setback, depending on the house-type. In this climate the houses are used less for living in but more for keeping things in. Food stores, jewellery and household utensils (cooking pots, water vessels) are kept inside even the humblest mud and thatch house. The loss of a house is less of a financial setback in terms of time and replacement costs than the loss of stores, partly because of the prevailing system of "swapping" labour time, and partly because the traditional mud houses are cheap and easy to replace and are gradually improved (see discussion later). Finances for housing replacement after a cyclone are limited and reserved for more pressing needs.

The loss of a traditional "*pucca*" house (two- and four- truss roof with clay tiles and stout walls) is a severe blow. Not only because these large houses tend to be the homes for up to three families but also because sometimes part can be rented out as offices or stores. If this type of house is destroyed then the animal shelters will have been destroyed as well. The replacement costs for traditional houses are very high (25 per cent of the average income of a typical "pucca" house-owning family) and require specialist skills that cannot be arranged on a reciprocal basis.

Losses from non-climatic conditions

Deaths

The most serious loss to a household, usually, is the death of one of its members by natural causes, illness, drowning or fatal injury, but it depends on who dies. If it is a major wage-earner then the effect may be serious, if it is an old member who can't work then the effect, although perhaps sad, may be slight. The effect of any death will of course vary according to the characteristics of the household. In some households the loss may increase the "ratchet effect", in others it may be a timely relief.

Disability and illness

We classify a variety of illnesses as losses because they affect the earning capacity of households and become a drain on their resources. Illnesses can be classified into those with short-term and those with long-term effects. Short term illnesses such as "village fever" are not sufficiently debilitating to affect permanently the economic well-being of the household, but longer-term epidemic water-borne type diseases, such as gastro-enteritis, which are endemic in the coastal areas, have long-term debilitating effects that gradually sap the economic resources of households and produce another turn of the ratchet. Chambers (1989: 2) summarises the work of Jane Corbett (1989: 58–62) in her study of poverty and sickness by emphasising the

> . . . vulnerability to sickness and the high economic costs to households of ill health, including how sickness makes poor people poorer through delayed treatment, the costs of treatment and loss of earnings.

The distinction between permanent and temporary disability is important and which member of the household is affected, as this has a significant effect on the labour power of the household. Many cases of mental and physical disabilities result from accidents or illnesses that have not been treated early enough in their development, usually through lack of money. Permanent-type illnesses tend to affect the older members of the society but not exclusively. In many rural areas there are a high proportion of deformed people from rickets and malnutrition and cripples from intermarriage. These losses to potential labour power have a significant effect on the capacity of households with such people to survive a range of shocks and increase their vulnerability to other types of shocks. This acute threat to survival has been vividly summarised by Robert Chambers:

... The main asset of the poor people is their bodies .... At the same time, the bodies of the poorer people are more vulnerable than the bodies of the less poor; they are most exposed to sickness from insanitary, polluted and disease ridden environments, both at work and at home, and to accidents at their work; they are weaker with malnutrition and previous sickness tending to reduce resistance to disease and slow recovery; and the poorer have less access to prophylaxis or to timely or effective medical treatment .... Medical costs can impoverish. Where treatment is sought it often entails heavy expenditure until the household exhausts its tangible assets it can sell or mortgage. Where the treatment fails but the sick person survives this leaves the household assetless and chronically poor, the costs of any treatment may be spread in only small amounts, which are then greatly exceeded by the earnings foregone from work lost through disability. (Chambers 1989: 4.)

The impact of losses

The impact of losses on different households varies to a great extent on the patterns generated by the socio-economic system they live in. One factor affecting vulnerability and which is a direct reflection of the social relations of production is *Class*, which together with prevailing *Caste* patterns forms a particularly virulent form of differentiation in India. Class is one way in which access to resources and assets is socially differentiated. Caste is another (see later discussion). Class usually determines "Who owns What" (i.e., the social relations of production) which then largely determines where people live, what work they do, how they are paid, the daily and yearly pattern of work, their social activities and the role they play in cultural activities. Those who suffer the most in a cyclone disaster, which is not necessarily the same as those who lose the most, are unlikely to be able to do much about the processes that have generated their vulnerability, but some groups are definitely more vulnerable than others. These classes of people can be distinguished by their gender (female) and ethnicity (Scheduled castes and Tribes).

Before we leave the subject of losses we should briefly mention the concepts and realities of insurance. We shall see later in the discussion on risk-reduction strategies that there are a number of insurance devices operating in traditional societies, but, in reality they tend to operate in respect to sustaining life rather than supplementing losses. In terms of the realities of insurance, only a small minority of people living in cyclone-prone areas are insured with companies for crop and animal losses, although a larger minority have insurance against losses in forms that can be encashed quickly – gold and/or jewellery. But, uninsured people with no reserves of cash lose out twice in a disaster. They lose vital assets that are essential to life, and they have to divert other scarce resources to replacing them, usually in the form of distress sales or further crippling debt burdens. Opportunity costs are very low (in Divi Seema) so that time taken in earning the money to replace the lost assets is unlikely to be spent doing anything else (for instance, agricultural activities take precedence

54

over house replacement). The major impact of losses on people who are not "insured" against them is that it proscribes their range of choices – already severely limited – about what to do with any surplus assets they might have built up, say since the last cyclone.

In general those who control the means of production or have control over assets that are not destroyed in a cyclone are economically less vulnerable, not only because they will be less physically vulnerable (their more substantial houses and animal shelters and storage sheds are less likely to collapse) but because they will be able to sustain their losses by one means or another. The opposite is true for those with neither control over their means of production nor secure livings or assets that will survive a cyclone.

2.4.3 Household characteristics

We shall be going into some detail later about household characteristics since they are an essential part of the model of vulnerability. For the time being we should introduce the reader to some of the more obvious household characteristics as we gradually build up the picture of differential vulnerability.

Family type

In coming to grips with vulnerability, an important household characteristic to understand is that of family type, since it largely determines how people live and what assets they share; it also gives some idea about the nature of the support networks in which people live. In India there are three fundamental family (household) types; these are (1) those that comprise a *residential family unit* which includes those tied by genealogical relationships; (2) those whose *members who are coparcenary* – i.e., sharing entitlements to land or other assets whereby basic property rights are not divided and although ownership of assets is separated some assets are still shared; (family types 1 and 2 are what are known as extended family types); and, (3) those *hearth groups who share common domestic arrangements* – i.e., families living together under the same roof and sharing the same kitchen (called a joint Hindu family), and those living under the same roof but cooking and eating separately (called a joint household).

Household size

Another important household characteristic is household size since this largely determines the labour power and hence productivity of a household in terms of its income. Household size depends to some degree on living arrangements and if the families are of the extended, joint, single-parent or individual types, the latter being very rare in rural India. Fertility patterns and associated stages of the family life cycle will have a significant effect on household size and consequently on the economic standing of the household, and migration will also alter the size of the household. We shall be taking all these factors into consideration in later chapters.

Age

An important characteristic of a household that bears on differential vulnerability is the age of its members. Age in a rural society such as Divi Seema is only significant economically when it is associated with ill health. Old people are generally looked after by the younger members of their families although in some cases they live separately. Old people will work in the fields as labourers in the agricultural seasons or minding animals at home. Children start working in the fields at about the age of 10; the boys who are too young to work in the fields will look after herds of water buffalo; the young girls who do not work in the fields will look after the youngest children, collect dung and firewood, work at home and so on.

Sex composition of the household

In a segmented labour market, where the greatest income opportunities are with men, the composition of the household by sex will significantly determine its access to resources, markets and income-earning opportunities. Other factors influencing a household's opportunities with a high female : male ratio are the legal position of women and property acquired during marriage, access to credit and absolute discrimination in the wage rates. Many jobs are sex-typed; in Divi, jobs involving weeding, transplanting and cutting the paddy are carried out by women. However, the sex specificity of some jobs will make the situation worse for women with modernisation and technological change. The life cycle of women's work is quite different from men's; the differential impact of natural reproductive cycles together with seasonality of employment results in quite different employment and wage opportunities for women.

Skills: education and caste

Rural areas are characterised by individuals or families with a high degree of task specialisation. Sex differences act as a major constraint in the acquisition of skills and there are also strong caste distinctions acting against changes in households' opportunities of increasing their incomes by the acquisition of new skills. Both of these depend to some extent on opportunities of education but these too are variable and can be overtaken by household priorities. The caste characteristics of the household may strongly determine its opportunities in the market, even more so when linked with associated skills. The distinction to be drawn here is the one between belonging to the untouchable or scheduled castes and to other lower castes in the hierarchy. Although there appears to be now a positive discrimination in job reservations and higher education in favour of the scheduled castes and tribes it does not seem to have altered their position in the rural labour market in this part of India.

2.4.4 Paths of adjustment to recovery

Risk strategies

In continuing to build up a conceptual model of vulnerability we will sketch in the last link between a household's (or community's) vulnerability and the external world; the link being risk strategies which are part of the adjustments and sometimes referred to as coping mechanisms. Basically there are two types of adjustment against risks; risk-reduction strategies implemented *before* events, which can range from technical and social arrangements at a collective level, to diversifying assets at a household level, and in an extreme form to migration; and, risk-diffusion strategies implemented *after* crisis, referred to sometimes as loss management. These strategies include techniques to minimise potential losses by diversifying income-earning opportunities (Beck 1989), and by using skills and techniques to manage the consequences of the inevitable losses after crisis, mainly by means of short term borrowing or lowering short-run consumption requirements (Binswanger and Sillers 1983).

Social arrangements in traditional rural societies were organised around the problem of obtaining a minimum income for their members and minimising their exposure to risk, on account of the limited techniques and technology available and the unpredictability of the climate. Social arrangements would include patterns of reciprocity, work sharing and the use of communal lands as in the "moral economy" (Scott 1976). In periods of duress and economic crises, the traditional range of networks and institutions outside the immediate family which would act as shock absorbers, included caste fellows, villagers, patrons and landlords.

Societies as a whole evolved to cope with the problems of income variation and exposure to risk, but, within that structure, each household still had to have a minimum level of resources to meet its necessary social obligations as well as to feed itself and continue to work. One example of a labour system in a social structure which depends for its cohesion on subsistence guarantees is the *jajmani* relationship between the landed and landless castes, in an agrarian system that was generally fraught with risks (Bremen 1974). The *jajmani* system prevailed in the study area as a residue of the *zamindari* land-holding system (discussed in Chapter Three) until the mid 1950s (A.P. Government 1977b: 53–54) and it meant that for workers hired on an annual basis there was a social insurance system whereby when a yearly worker fell ill or could not work, the landlord would provide for some of his basic needs such as food and a part of his wages. Chambers discusses some of the innate risk-insurance processes within traditional societies but points too to their possible erosion.

> In parts of [some countries] . . . trends can be discerned which make poor people more vulnerable. Where their incomes rise they have the means to make investments, to build up stores and to establish claims which make them less insecure. Where services improve, isolation and vulnerability diminish . . . . Where tenure of land, water, trees is clearly vested in the poorer, they become more secure . . . [However] there are two trends against this: first, the decline in patron-client relations . . . and second, declining support of the extended family. (Chambers 1989: 3.)

Household adjustments

Adjustments by households to shocks are determined primarily by their pre-shock asset position and then by the nature of claims they can make on (i) their own members; (ii) friends and relations and caste fellows; (iii) the village society; (iv) the state; and (v) the market. Adjustments can be made before, during and/or after a crisis and are reflected in differential rates of recovery over time. Every household pursues different strategies for the accumulation of assets, just as it pursues different risk-reduction and risk-diffusion strategies to minimise the effect of potential losses which may affect the social and economic status of the family, but basically strategies are governed by choice.

The crucial issue in pursuing either a risk-reduction or a risk-diffusion strategy, or both – if one has a choice, and we will come to the contraints on choice later (in Chapter Three) – is the effectiveness of the strategy in terms of the cost and the extent of recovery possible. Adjustments are ineffective if they lead to a sustained decline in necessary consumption or a permanent loss in productive assets so often seen in the high incidence of distress sales after some natural calamity. They are also ineffective it they lead to a sustained decline in family labour or in large-scale out-migration.

A decline in necessary consumption of food and other basic needs will have longer-lasting negative effects (Jodha 1976; 1978; 1983), than a decline in social consumption such as expenditure on weddings, which can be postponed (if one has a choice!). The cycle of building up assets and then depleting them for whatever reasons – cyclones, distress sales, dowries and so on – will mean that households are sometimes in surplus and sometimes in deficit. This surplus/deficit cycle is not necessarily undesirable but its effects are dependent on the time-lag between depletion and recovery. If assets that were sold to meet one crisis are not replenished before the next crisis then the household moves into a progressively more vulnerable position over time.

The recovery of a household from a shock such as a cyclone, and the effect of its impact, will largely depend on the household's characteristics at the time of the shock and what it loses. Its characteristics at the time of a shock are largely determined by the range of previous shocks it has endured, by the interrelationships between the social relations of production, development policies, physiography and climate, and its own biological characteristics, all of which have also largely determined how the household has recovered from previous shocks. Recovery is directly linked with vulnerability (i.e., the initial conditions of the household at the time of the shock) which we can call its Siamese twin. This close relationship is fully explained and justified in Chapters Five and Six, but here it is important to notify the reader that recovery and vulnerability are part of the same condition although we are distinguishing between the two here. The choice of the paths of adjustment to recovery will also reflect the vulnerability of households and we can get a good idea of the vulnerability of a household simply by asking what strategies it uses.

Temporary or permanent migration is the risk-reduction strategy most used in rural socities in India, depending on whether there are areas to migrate to. Migration strategies are a response to collective risks. Many families' principal source of income is from remittances sent from a family member who has migrated permanently (Connell *et al.* 1976). Migration has wide-ranging implications on the composition of households and the choice of whether to migrate or not is often determined by the structure of the household, for instance, it is easier for adults to look for jobs elsewhere in a household with several adults, some of whom can stay and look after dependents. The reasons for migration can sometimes be complex but migration is a channel of opportunities through which the economic vulnerability of a household can be altered. Fundamentally, migration is a strategy of risk-minimisation through diversification of opportunities for additional incomes (*ibid.*). However, by migrating to cyclone areas this strategy of risk aversion is threatened by the additional risk of being killed in a cyclone.

2.5 A RECENT MODEL OF VULNERABILITY

Introduction

A recent model of vulnerability has emerged from the work of Jeremy Swift (1989: 11) who suggests that one way of measuring vulnerability is through asset accumulation or depletion over time. He proposes a model which identifies three types of "assets" – investments, stores and claims – the data for which are relatively easy to collect. Before we discuss Swift's model, which derives from his analysis of famines, it might be useful to describe briefly how the model has developed since it might provide others with useful insights for the development of disaster management and be applicable to disasters other than famines.

Famines were thought to be caused by production failures, but Amartya Sen in *Poverty and Famines* (1981) showed that famines could take place where there was no production failure and he identified failures in the exchange market mechanisms (wage labour, agricultural and pastoral commodity markets – Figure 2.4). Today, after a decade of withering famines in Africa and elsewhere we know that people starve because they cannot afford to buy food even when food is available in the famine areas because the assets they have to sell (i.e., animals or labour) lose their value relative to the price of food.

FIGURE 2.4: *The relationship between production, exchange and consumption* (Swift 1989: 10, after Sen)

PRODUCTION		CONSUMPTION
	EXCHANGE Wage labour; Agricultural and pastoral commodity markets.	

Sen's analysis identified some important sources of vulnerability by focusing on the "exchange" or "terms of trade relationship" which made some people and some communities more vulnerable than others. In Sen's view vulnerability to famine was a direct function of relative poverty, and relative poverty is a direct function of a household's ownership of tangible "endowments" (assets) of land, labour and animals and the *rate at which it can exchange these for food*. But, according to Swift, the analysis did not explain a number of problems associated with differential vulnerability within some communities, and on a smaller scale, between households or individuals in the same households. (In Swift's view, Sen's work also did not explain the behaviour of many households who go to considerable lengths to *preserve their assets* at almost any cost, and nor did it explain why people hoarded relief food in order to acquire further assets in an attempt to aid recovery and reduce future vulnerability).

60

2.5.1 Components of the model

Swift expands on Sen's model. He analyses in more detail the "entitlements" classified by Sen and expands the concept of assets to include "stores" of value and "claims" for assistance that can be called on in times of crisis. The model consists of three types of asset: investments; claims and stores and is set out in Figure 2.5, to which we have made some minor modifications (for instance we have changed Swift's "stores" to "stocks" and have taken out the particularly African references "big men, chiefs") but have otherwise not altered its essence.

Assets

The way that asset levels fluctuate depends as much on the forces acting externally on a household – i.e., cyclones and flooding – as on the internal forces that act on the household – i.e., its life-cycles: births, deaths, marriages (Figure 2.5). The decisions to get rid of assets reflect the choices open to the household from a position "where other things are equal" to those made under extreme duress, i.e., distress sales. When a household has enough assets to meet its immediate needs (i.e., a surplus) it may choose to pay off a debt, invest in educating a son or concentrate on health provision; it may put some of the surplus into building up its physical assets such as house expansion, house strengthening, buying or leasing farm equipment, building animal shelters, increasing food stores and so on. Another household may invest in maintaining or furthering its social position in the community by enhancing future claims through dowries and ceremonies; another may maintain or further its claims with the government or influential people with gifts, bribes, donations and so on.

In all these activities the range of choice open to the household will depend entirely on the extent of its surplus and its priorities, and we shall see later how varied these can be (Chapter Three, section 3.2.7, and Table 3.6). Priorities will be governed to a large extent not by opportunities but by penalties; for instance a poor household will regard paying back a private loan as a higher priority than a richer household, simply because of the stigma attached to private loans and the penalty for a poor household defaulting on a bank loan is that it will not obtain another one (unlike the better-off households).

The main reason for assets to fluctuate is crises and when a household faces a crisis then assets are cashed in and productive assets (animals, land, equipment) are sold, bank accounts emptied, loaned animals recalled, debts called in and so on. But the poorest people have the fewest assets and the least

FIGURE 2.5: *Assets and a model of vulnerability* (after Swift 1989: 11)

INVESTMENTS

Human investments
Household members available for work; Investments in health and education.

Individual productive assets
Land; Trees: Wells; Houses; Farming equipment; Animals; Specialised equipment; Domestic utensils.

Collective assets
Access to common property resources; Soil conservation schemes; Water-harvesting; Irrigation systems.

CLAIMS

Claims on other households in community:
Production resources, food, labour, animals.

Claims on patrons, chiefs, landlords
Claims on other communities
Claims on Government, NGOs
Claims on the international community

STOCKS

Food stores
Granaries, fodder

Stores of value
Jewellery, gold

Money or bank accounts

---

choices so in general they reach the threshold of "collapse" faster than others (collapse here meaning the economic level at which they cease to have either any support or claims for support).

Claims

By expanding the notion of assets to include claims ("tangibles and intangibles"), Swift makes a significant contribution to the debate on vulnerability. In his view, claims are:

> a variety of redistributive processes within smaller and larger communities, ranging from households and extended families, through shallow kinship groupings to major lineages, up to traditional and modern political formations. (Swift 1989. 11.)

Swift points to the wider social forces that govern vulnerability and which were *not* included in previous models of vulnerability, to which Westgate and O'Keefe, and others, referred. The inclusion of claims as an asset is particularly interesting in so far as many people in disaster-prone areas are now supremely adept at "claiming" upon the politicians and voluntary agencies who work in such areas, and this type of claim forms an important part of their risk-reduction strategies.

2.6 SUMMARY:
A CONCEPTUAL MODEL OF VULNERABILITY

From the preceding discussion we can assemble a model of vulnerability for a household or a community that takes into account those relationships and processes that are external *and* internal to it and which affect its vulnerability. We identified the external relationships and processes as being climate, physiography, the social relations of production and development policies (Figure 2.1), to which we added the relationship between production, exchange and consumption (Figure 2.3). Both these groupings directly affect the asset levels of households (or communities) and these in turn directly affect the risk-reduction and risk-diffusion strategies a household may be able to use.

FIGURE 2.6: *A conceptual model of vulnerability*

	CLIMATE	
PHYSIOGRAPHY	**SOCIAL RELATIONS OF PRODUCTION**	**DEVELOPMENT POLICIES**
PRODUCTION		**CONSUMPTION**
	EXCHANGE Wage labour; Agricultural and pastoral commodity markets	
	HOUSEHOLD CHARACTERISTICS Investments	
Assets	Claims	Stocks
RISK-REDUCTION STRATEGIES		**RISK-DIFFUSION STRATEGIES**
	HOUSEHOLD VULNERABILITY	

We have slightly altered Swift's nomenclature, using the word investments to mean the range of assets and resources available to a household, but we will see in Chapters Five and Six that this change does not alter the concept in any way. The result of integrating the various models of vulnerability is a Conceptual Model of Vulnerability (see Figure 2.6) which relates a household and/or a community to its wider context at the same time as relating it to those factors that are unique to its own structure. This gives us a notional estimate of a household's vulnerability.

If we want to *predict* vulnerability and potential recovery then we can apply the process we saw in Equilibrium Theory to the notional estimate of a household's or communitiy's vulnerability as below:

SHOCKS
(Characteristics)

HOUSEHOLD'S VULNERABILITY

LOSSES
(Impacts)

PATHS OF ADJUSTMENTS TO RECOVERY

How does this model of vulnerability assist the most "vulnerable" sections of society and why should we use it? First of all, the model identifies a household's vulnerability to a range of shocks by its investment levels and risk strategies. Secondly, the model relates these characteristics to the interface between the political economy and the cycle of production, exchange and consumption. And thirdly, the model provides an early-warning system of low-asset households and predicts their likely adjustments to a range of internal and external shocks, so that asset losses can be measured in terms of *relative losses* within the context of the phenomenon of differential vulnerability.

3

The Study Area and the Fieldwork Programme

We saw in Chapter One how government cyclone mitigation policies represented by the Conventional View relied on a concept of vulnerability based on exposure measured by losses. In Chapter Two we presented an Alternative View which gathered together a wide range of views mainly deriving from social-science research, and a conceptual model of differential vulnerability which consisted of three components (i) the processes and interrelationships between climate, physiography, development policies and the social relations of production; (ii) the relation between production, exchange and consumption and the accumulation or depletion of assets; and (iii) risk-reduction strategies. This model widened our concept of vulnerability. In this chapter we will first describe the study area and the physical, social and economic features of Divi Seema as they relate to the components in the first part of that model, and then go on to describe the fieldwork programme and the methodology.

3.1 DIVI SEEMA: LOCATION AND DESCRIPTION

The empirical data come from a fieldwork area in Divi *taluk* in Krishna District in the Krishna delta (between latitudes 15°30′N and 16°N). The Krishna delta, created by deposits of sediment from the River Krishna which have extended the coast by about 40 km into the sea, lies on the flat Coromandel coastal plain of Peninsula India, one of two deltas that protrude like carbuncles from the arched curve of the eastern seaboard.

Divi *taluk* (a *taluk* is the smallest unit of local government) is administered from Masulipatnam where the District Collector has had his office since 1857 and is the most southerly *taluk* in Krishna district. It is divided into two

65

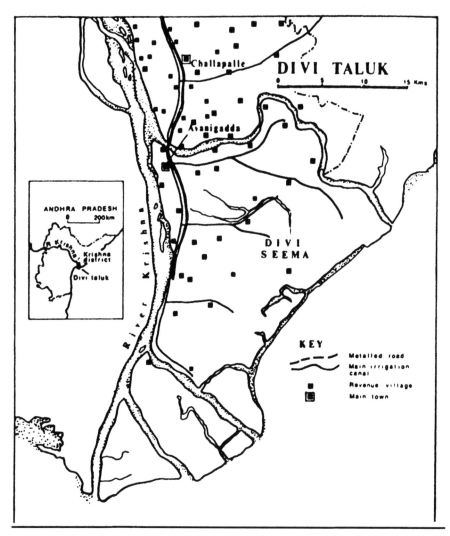

Source: Government of India 1973.

parts, one part is on the mainland and the other is on an island. The study area is the island called Divi Seema. It is triangular and is bounded by the River Krishna on its west side, a tributary on the north and the Bay of Bengal on the east. The island is composed of alluvial soil; 90 per cent of the land is flat and rises from sea level at the coast to about 3 m at the apex of the island. There are many tidal creeks some of which extend inland about 12 km. There were dense mangrove forests along most of coast before the 1930s but now only two small islands have such a natural barrier. The island has an area of 736 sq km (Government of India 1973: 98).

The island has two distinct geographical areas. The low-lying *coastal area* stretches 22 km along the Bay of Bengal and extends about 12 km inland. It is largely unprotected from flooding and high winds as a result of clearing the jungle and vegetation for cultivation and settlement. There are slight but crucial variations in ground level and soil conditions. The low lying areas are prone to waterlogging but are used by the poorer villagers for cultivation (encroachment land) and for settlements. The tidal flats in the eastern part of the island are full of salt-water creeks and backwaters and the south-west corner of the island is veined with creeks and backwaters but these are partially protected by two islands with mangrove forests. In the coastal area about 30 per cent of the land is officially classified as waste land and about 60 per cent is irrigated. In 1977 approximately 60,000 people lived there. The *inland area* is roughly triangular in shape and about 20 km in depth. It is also low-lying and flat but contains two long islands of higher ground on which most of the villages are situated which are well protected by trees. The inland area is more fertile than the coastal area with an abundance of well-irrigated land (80 per cent) and only 10 per cent is classified as wasteland. In 1977 approximately 90,000 people lived there. (Government of India 1973: 100, 102, 104).

3.2 RELATIONSHIPS AND PROCESSES AFFECTING VULNERABILITY IN DIVI SEEMA

In Chapter Two we introduced the Political Economy Model of vulnerability, the components of which were the processes and interrelationships between climate, physiography, development policies and the social relations of production. We shall now look at these in some detail as they affect Divi Seema, to which we will add a section on risk-reduction strategies.

3.2.1 Climate

Climatically, the Krishna delta is within a drought-prone area (Subrahmanyam and Malini 1978). The climate of the area is characterised by an oppressive summer and a good seasonal rainfall and the year can be divided into four seasons. The first, from mid February to the first week of June, is the summer season with temperatures reaching a mean daily maximum for May of 37.4°C and a mean daily minimum of 27.7°C, and a total rainfall of 125 mm. The second period is from mid June to the end of September, when two thirds of rain falls over the Krishna district. This is the period of the south-west monsoon, with a rainfall of 610 mm. The third period, from October to

November, is the period of the retreating north-east monsoon, during which time the rainfall of 382 mm is highest for the year in the coastal areas. The last period, from December to the middle of February, is generally fine weather with the lowest temperatures. Between December and January the maximum daily temperature recorded at Masulipatnam is 28.2°C and the lowest minimum mean daily temperature is 19.0°C, with a rainfall of 51 mm. Humidity exceeds 60 per cent on average in the coastal areas. The average annual rainfall for Divi *taluk* is 1,168 mm (A.P. Government 1977b: 23–25).

Climatic variations include the incidence of cyclones of varying severity and extremes of rainfall (see Table 3.1) and both have different short- and long-term effects. When extreme rainfall variations occur, crops and livestock are the most vulnerable, whereas cyclones and surges damage roads, railways, irrigation networks, public services, all buildings and crops and livestock (Table 1.1). Excessive rain at harvest can do almost as much damage as a severe cyclonic storm whereas excessive rain at planting is less damaging because the paddy fields can be drained to some extent.

In the reports of the Government of Madras, excessive rain was defined as sufficient to ruin the crops, but their definition has to be somewhat qualified after 1935 because cyclone- (and excessive rain) resistant paddy strains were introduced and crops were less likely to be ruined. Nevertheless, we see that over the 78 year period, extreme variations of rainfall at harvest (the main season for cyclones) have occured approximately twice as often as severe cyclonic storms (SCS), and SCS and cyclonic storms (CS) have together not

TABLE 3.1: *Incidence of cyclones and other climatic variations in the Krishna delta and Krishna district since 1870*

Climatic variation	Incidence (100 years)[a]	Frequency in years	Incidence (78 years)[b]	Frequency years × s.d.		Rank[c]
Cyclone (CS)	22	1:4.5	6	1:10	5.7 2.3	(3)
Severe cyclone (SCS)	5	1:20	5	1:12	16 4.0	(4)
Severe cyclone and storm surge (SS/SCS)	3	1:33	2	1:30	32 1.5	(7)
Climatic variation at planting:	Rain failure		7	1:8.4	5.6 2.0	(2)
	Rain excess		14	1:4.2		
Climatic variation at harvest:	Rain failure		14	1:4.2	3.8 0.3	(1)
	Rain excess		14	1:3.5		

[a] Map 0.2, A.P. Government 1980a.

[b] Government of Madras, 1870–1948; Reports of the Irrigation Branch of the Public Works Department, Madras Presidency.

[c] The additional frequencies of combinations of events are ranked in order of the probability of their occurrence: (5) Rain failure or excess at harvest and CS = 1:22 years; (6) Rain failure or excess at planting and CS = 1:32 years; (8) Rain failure or excess at harvest and SCS = 1:61 years; (9) Rain failure or excess at planting and SCS = 1:90 years.

occurred as many times as excessive rain. These figures indicate clearly that climatic variations are indeed the major risk in this area especially as the whole economy depends on the harvest.

3.2.2 Physiography

Geomorphology

The major landforms recognised from aerial photography in the Krishna delta are flood plains, ancient channels, natural levees, ancient beach ridges and swales, mangrove swamps and tidal flats. The delta is covered by a mixture of calcareous and non-calcareous black clay soils together with sandy soils that become saline nearer the coast. Most of the delta is made up of rich alluvial deposits formed in lobes (Nageswara Rao and Vaidyanaham 1978) and also black regar and red ferring mines soil varieties. About 30 per cent of the soil in the delta area is saline due to seasonal marine flooding on extensive areas of low-lying land near the coast. This low-lying land is also frequently waterlogged by flooding from water courses from excessive rainfall due to the poor drainage of the clay soils. Soil salinity, whether due to marine influence or flooding and subsequent waterlogging in some low-lying areas, considerably restricts the capability of the land. Even areas that are covered by a single soil unit have variations in salinity (Government of India 1977b: 7–14).

Vegetation

There are two types of general vegetation in the coastal parts of the Krishna delta, mangrove swamps and coastal flora and forest types of the transition belt (A.P. Government 1977b: 14). The extent of the mangrove forests is determined by the amount of flow of the River Krishna and the nature and extent of the deposits of silt and the extent of clearance. The area of the seaboard in the delta is a monotonous stretch of either swamp or sand with a network of salt creeks or irrigation channels, and supports a distinct type of coastal vegetation referred to as dry evergreen. The combination of the climatic and edaphic factors and the incidence of very high grazing over the years, with other biotic factors such as man and fire have made the land generally incapable of producing anything but forests of medium size or scrub type. The scrub type has been further degraded in the forests at the edges by man and other biotic factors. The Krishna district part of the delta is generally devoid of trees. Banyan (*Ficus bengalensis*) and Peepul trees (*Ficus religiosa*) are trees generally found in villages, around temples and on tank bunds. Trees commonly found in avenues are *Tamarindus indica, Casuaria equit setifolia* and

Enealyptus hybrid. Palmyra (*Borassus flabellifer*) and Date palms (*Phoenix sylvestris*) are found on wastelands and on the edges of the villages. The thorn bush is prevalent on the tidal flats and salt marshes (Government of India 1977b: 12–21).

Landforms

Landforms and other limitations on land use affect the size and spacing of rural settlements which in turn influence the degree of their exposure to cyclones and flooding. Amongst the other variables that affect the location of settlements are landform type, soil fertility, degree and intensity of land use, availability of water and ease of development of transport and communication, so that geomorphology and flooding become the principal determinants of settlement patterns. Within the plains there are subtle variations in land form which can alter the degree of exposure of settlements, for instance the marginally high ground, areas with poor drainage and areas susceptible to waterlogging (Nageswara Rao 1980).

The two types of settlement in Divi Seema are: (1) the nucleated type, which have developed because land is so expensive and cannot be wasted for habitation so that more people live in relatively smaller but scattered sites in the highly fertile inland plain and the less fertile coastal flat; and (2) the linear type of settlement, which have developed along the boundaries between the plain and the levees, and along two islands of higher ground on Divi island. The composition of villages and their physical form is largely determined by caste groupings (discussed later) the effect of which is that the villages are collections of hamlets grouped around a main village. The poorest live on the lowest lying lands in the most exposed areas – i.e., on the fringes – while the richest households live on the highest grounds in the villages, usually in the centre and close to the main roads (Nageswara Rao and Prasad 1979).

3.2.3 Development policies

Historical development of Divi Seema

The study area was not irrigated until 1907 mainly because it was remote and flood-prone (earliest projections show a canal and a pumping station in 1882). It was also known to be hazardous, "the Kistna delta" writes the District Collector in 1871 "is not thickly populated, it having been liable to inroad from the sea and freshwater floods in past times, particularly the coastal areas". When irrigation was introduced into Divi Seema in 1907 in the form of a main canal fed by water from the River Krishna through a pumping station, an infusion of cultivators (*Kapu* and *Kamma* castes) from the mainland resulted. They took over the common lands previously used for grazing, herding and dry-land farming from other non-scheduled castes (*Gouda*, *Golla*, *Kumaru* and others – see below) and pushed them towards the sea. In 1933 the British Administration carried out a huge public-works programme in the deltas and as part of that programme an aqueduct and a road bridge were built across the Puligadda arm of the River Krishna in 1937 linking Divi island to the rest of the Krishna East Bank canal system which replaced the Divi pumping station.

The completion of the aqueduct and extensions to the canal network resulted in a further expansion of the population with the further loss of common lands and keener competition for living space. Between 1907 and 1937, the population increased from 67,466 to 100,080 and common lands had shrunk from 40,476 acres to 31,000 acres (Government of Madras 1901–02; 1907–08; 1937–38). By 1937, half the cultivable land on the island was irrigated and three quarters of the irrigation system was complete (Government of Madras 1901–02; 1907–08; 1937–38). The population influx also resulted in the extensive destruction of the mangrove forests along the coasts. The Survey of India maps printed in the 1930s show a stretch of dense jungle extending 40 km along part of the Divi coastline and a further 15 km of mangrove swamp forming a natural barrier against cyclonic winds and sea surges (Government of India 1932). By 1977 except on two small islands, the jungle and mangrove swamps had all disappeared "because of new settlements and through neglect" (Raghavulu and Cohen 1979: 11); this diminution of the mangrove swamps by population encroachment was a crucial factor contributing to the high death tolls in the 1977 cyclone. By the time of the 1977 cyclone, approximately 150,000 people lived in Divi Seema, a 250 per cent increase in the population since 1907, and the common lands had shrunk further to 10,350 acres (A.P. Government 1977b: Annexure 10).

One of the results of the development was the uneven social and economic balance between the mainland and the island parts of Divi in terms of the provision of electricity and water supply. Although the island was known to have areas of "sweet water", the absence of well water for the bulk of the population on the island meant that they relied on tank water for drinking, which is always contaminated (animals bathing, people immersing themselves and so on), thus ensuring permanent epidemics of gastro-enteritis and other water-borne diseases. The lack of electricity had less effect on the population than the absence of clean drinking water, but it ensured the continuing isolation of the remoter villages. Table 3.2, showing the differences in the provision of facilities and amenities in 1971, gives us some idea of the backwardness of Divi Seema compared with mainland Divi. There is little anecdotal evidence to suggest that there were any changes by 1977.

The difference in the level of facilities and amenities tends to bear out the perception by government officials and mainland people that Divi Seema was a

TABLE 3.2: *Comparison between the facilities and amenities in the villages on mainland Divi and Divi Seema, 1971*

| | Villages | Households | Facilities and amenities | | | | |
			Roads	Schools	Medical facilities	Drinking water type	Electricity
Mainland	66	39,005	37 PR	250 P	8 Disp	84 Well	53 E
			29 KR	28 M	1 Phc	17 Tank	4 Ph
				20 H	– Hosp		
Island	33	21,802	5 PR	82 P	4 Disp	21 Well	7 E
			28 KR	16 M	1 Phc	6 Tank	1 Ph
				3 H	– Hosp		

Source: Government of India 1973: 20–23; 1983: 16–19.
Roads: PR = Pucca road; KR = Katcha road.
Schools: P = Primary; M = Middle; H = High.
Medical: Disp = Dispensary; Phc = Pharmacy; Hosp = Hospital (overnight accommodation).
Electricity: E = number of villages with electricity; Ph = telephone.

remote and therefore dangerous area. These perceptions were heightened by tales that the population were prone to violence and drinking (fishermen, toddy tappers and tribals) and it was said that "mainland people would not give their daughters in marriage to Divi people" with the result that there were high levels of inbreeding and subsequent medical problems.

3.2.4   Forces of production

The agricultural calendar

The agricultural year starts when the canals are opened in mid May to let water down into areas for the paddy seed-beds, but the agricultural year in Divi starts in mid to late June with the onset of the south-west monsoon. The paddies are ploughed and puddled and work on bunding is completed by the end of July when the rainfall increases and transplanting the seedlings can take place. Men and women share this work. Excessive rain at this time is the first threat to the agricultural economy and can affect the paddies in the low-lying areas by submersion. Weeding in August is the main job, carried out by the women, but heavy rainfall at the time can damage the growing crop. If there has not been sufficient rain by October then the likelihood of pest attack increases and this can have disastrous consequences on yields; it also makes the crop increasingly vulnerable to climatic variations.

The north-east monsoon sets in about the middle of October and rainfall gradually diminishes. However, rainfall is erratic and heavy rain can reduce the yields by up to 25 per cent by submersion. The paddy crop is harvested in mid November although the date varies and depends on when the large farmers decide "to cut". Once the decision has been made everybody starts the harvest and since mid November is the period of the highest probability of a cyclone strike the smaller farmers have to decide whether to cut their own crop first or go and work for the large farmers. There can also be heavy and continuous rainfall in December which will slow down or ruin the harvest, and the paddy stored in the stacks will go rotten if it is flooded or saturated by rain. Threshing takes place from the end of December to the end of January.

At the end of January the people from Divi migrate to the mainland for up to six weeks to work on the second crop of paddy (45 per cent of the sample survey) when the wage rates are the highest of the year. Brickmaking takes place in odd corners of harvested fields and housebuilding is an additional activity from the end of February until early April. In April there is work for men repairing paddy bunds, building new ones and clearing the canals ready for the first water and the start of the next agricultural year (A.P. Government 1977b: 32–38).

The agricultural calendar (Table 3.3) is divided into two parts. The first comprises work on Divi Seema and the second is work on the mainland. The significance of the second crop on the mainland is that it provides the crucial insurance for the island's inhabitants against cyclone damage to their own and other people's crops and a subsequent disastrous loss in employment.

Between the periods of concentrated agricultural work there were two- and three-month gaps when large sections of the population were unemployed or "self employed". The pattern of employment created by a monoculture and the dependence on it for food and employment and the timing of the harvest were significant factors in creating widespread economic vulnerability in these areas.

Crops

The principal food crop grown is *paddy* (rice). In the sample area only two cyclone-resistant strains are grown; 68 per cent of households cultivate *Akkulu* and 32 per cent cultivate *Masuri*, both introduced by the British in the 1930s (DSSSS 1978). High-yielding varieties (HYVs) are not grown by the majority of the population, mainly due to water stagnation, poor drainage and before 1977 the scarcity of inputs such as fertiliser and insecticides. Less than 10 per cent of the farmers cultivated HYVs and they were the same ones who cultivated two crops because they could afford the inputs, and because they had the facilities to sell their produce. Paddy is intercropped with pulses. Some sugarcane, betel and chilis are grown on lanka lands but not nearly as extensively as on mainland Divi.

TABLE 3.3: *Employment calendar for adult male and female agricultural workers on Divi Seema, 1981*

Type of work	Time of work	Number of days worked	Daily wage in Rs	Possible earnings in Rs
Local employment				
Sowing				
Planting nursery beds, ploughing, puddling and bunding; applying natural manure. Pulling up paddy nursery, transplanting and watering	June–July	M-28[a] F-28[b]	15 6–10	420 210
Weeding (M, F), applying chemical fertilisers	August	M-10	10	100
	September	F-28	10	280
		(paid on a half-day basis)		
Sowing pulse crop				
Harvesting				
Cutting (F), bunding and stacking	mid November December	M-20 F-20	10 8	200 160
Threshing	December January	M-20	15	300
Sub-totals			M 78 F 76	M 1,020 F 650
Migration to mainland for second crop				
Sowing				
Transplanting (M, F)	Jan–Feb	M-20	15–20	350
Sowing pulsecrop		F-20	10–15	240
Harvesting				
Cutting, bundling and stacking	April	M-15	7.5	12.0
Repair work				
Repair bunds, field-levelling, canal-dredging and clearing	April–May	M-10	10	100
Sub-totals			M 45 F 20	M 560 F 240
Totals for year including migration				
		Days M 123 F 96		Wages M 1,580 F 890

Source: Fieldwork 1981–82.

[a] M = male.

[b] F = female.

TABLE 3.4: *Crops grown in Divi Seema, 1981*

Crop type	Acres cultivated	Percentage of total[a]
Paddy	66,096	65.0
Blackgram	16,750	16.5
Greengram	14,220	14.0
Sugarcane	1,200	1.2
Total (including twice-cropped)[b]	101,584	

Source: Kumar 1982: 4.

[a] Other crops grown amounting to 3.3 per cent of cultivated area are: chillies, vegetables, gingelly, groundnut, banana, cotton, turmeric, castor and fodder crops.

[b] The cropping intensity is 144 per cent.

There are two main harvesting seasons, *kharif* (autumn) and *rabi* (spring). The *kharif* crop of paddy is sown at the start of the south west monsoon and harvested in November, the principal cyclone season. The *rabi* crop of blackgram and greengram is sown just before the paddy crop is harvested. The traditional methods of agriculture are widely practised. Ploughing is carried out using oxen or water buffaloes yoked by wooden yoke to a wooden plough. Bullock carts are the most widely used form of transport. Modern implements such as blade harrows and iron ploughs are being introduced and, increasingly, tractors. Broadcasting of seeds and transplantation are the popular methods of raising crops besides sowing the seeds through a seed drill (*gorru*) (A.P. Government 1977b: 36). Water buffaloes are the most common milch and traction animal. The richer farmers also have plough teams of oxen which are in effect the Rolls Royces of the agricultural world.

3.2.5   Social relations of production

The term social relations of production is widely used in the literature to describe the relationships that exist between workers and those who employ them. The term has ideological connotations because it is used in Marxist analysis of labour relations and we use it here because it is a useful device, although no ideological inferences are intended. The social relations of production can be said to "encompass and relate together the relations of production, appropriation, distribution and utilisation of the social product" (Bernstein 1979:422). In the analysis we will take three key features of these

75

relations: occupations; power relations; and loans, because they indicate some of the most relevant relationships that existed in Divi Seema before the cyclone.

Occupations

With the introduction of irrigation, the main occupation of grazing and some dry-crop cultivation was replaced by intensive paddy cultivation. Many of the cultivating castes (*Kamma* and *Kapu*) also settled on the island, displacing the herders (*Golla*), who were forced to use the forested and unproductive marsh areas for grazing their animals and encroach on the land that the fishermen (*Pallecarlu*) were also cultivating after a fashion.

With the construction of the Puligadda aqueduct and an assured water supply the cultivable lands in Divi passed from the small cultivators to the larger landlords who controlled the land under the local *zamindar*, the Raja of Challapalle (see Map 3.1). With increasing population, the competition for land became intense. The forests on which the villagers had previously depended for firewood and protection from cyclones were taken over as Government reserves and in due course cut down.

The gradual loss of local forests and village-held wastelands and common pasturage narrowed the subsistence options for the majority. As cash became increasingly required through the extensive cultivation of paddy and cash crops on the *lanka* lands (land that was submerged in riverine floods and therefore rich with silt) households became more vulnerable to price fluctuations. The loss of free gifts of nature (common lands) undermined the independence of the poorer households resulting in a higher dependence on hired labour. These households who had only their labour to sell became even more vulnerable to the effects that rainfall variation and cyclones had on agricultural productivity, as they were pushed to the geographical margins of the area. The traditional risk insurance in the villages where all villagers were guaranteed a minimum subsistence in so far as resources controlled by the villagers made this possible, were reduced, drastically.

The marginalisation process – i.e., the process of pushing people to the margins of society both physically and economically – that had begun in the first decade of the century, continued after Independence. The post-Independence re-distribution of *lanka* lands and the formation of the Land co-operatives reinforced the process inadvertently. The land was distributed to small and marginal farmers (description later) but they lacked the means and credit to cultivate it and the co-operatives were quickly taken over by the large farmers who had private and institutional credit and the small farmers became wage labourers on their own land. In the process of economic expansion the larger landlords became less susceptible to the demands of the poorer villages and failed increasingly to respond to the traditional cultural imperatives, whereby the richer members looked after the poorer members in times of crisis.

The result of this was that the villages along the tidal flats and at the tail end of the irrigation network and in most of the fishing villages had become acutely vulnerable to market forces by the 1960s and 1970s, mainly because they had no alternative sources of income that would supplement crop failure or price fluctuations. There was in effect a monopoly of large landlords who held the most fertile lands and a myriad of small land-holders each with pocket-handkerchief size holdings that were insufficient to meet their subsistence requirements.

On the eve of the cyclone, the major occupation in Divi Seema was in agriculture which was dependent on irrigation and subject to the vagaries of the climate. Although most households had other occupations including caste-specific occupations, such as sea fishing (20 per cent of the population), the non-specific-caste occupations such as canal fishing and casual labouring did not compensate for the large gaps in the employment calendar (see below). Times of agricultural employment were bunched and the accumulation of annual income from agricultural wages was sporadic and to some extent uncertain in Divi (see also Table 3.1).

Before leaving occupation we should place it and agricultural labour specifically in relation to the climate and cyclones. Figure 3.1 illustrates the

FIGURE 3.1: *Employment calendar in Divi Seema and the incidence of cyclones*

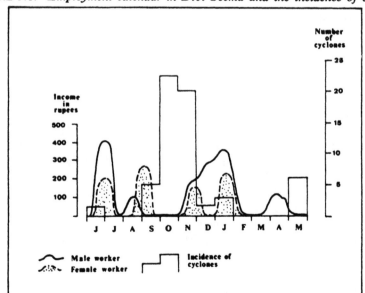

Sources: Tables 3.1 and 3.3.

precariousness of agricultural employment relative to cyclones and highlights the uncertainty surrounding it; the two maximum likely incidences of cyclones (October and May) occurring just before the two peak periods of agricultural employment pose an ominous and recurring risk.

In the Government of India Census of 1971, "main workers" are classified into four main groups. These are: cultivators; agricultural labourers; household industry; manufacturing; processing; servicing and repairs; and other workers. These classifications are based on the principal occupations from which income is derived. Of the 57,095 people classified as "main workers" in Divi Seema in 1977, 29 per cent were cultivators, 49 per cent were agricultural labourers, 19 per cent were other workers and 3 per cent were in the service industries (Government of India 1973: 100, 102, 104).

Power relations

Irrigation

A particular feature of Divi Seema before the 1977 cyclone was the extent to which the economy was dominated by the relationships between the local power-brokers and the politicians in the state capital Hyderabad and the government functionaries 500 km away. The local power-brokers were the large landlords (whom we shall describe in more detail later when we dicsuss caste and faction), the elected village presidents, the chairmen of the Co-operative Banks and the hereditary but appointed officials in the villages, the *muncifs* (village headmen) and the *Karnams* (village accountants). The power-brokers in Hyderabad were the Members of the Legislative Assembly (MLAs), some of whom had very close political ties with the area.

Most of the benefits of the limited rural development programmes were not distributed at random but resulted from the connections between the local power brokers and the politicians, and none more so than the allocation of water from the irrigation canals. These connections enabled the politicians to use the direction of benefits at the local level to build up local followings for vote-catching purposes at state level, but, delicate relationships between the two levels could sometimes be upset, temporarily, by direct intervention on a personal level. This was alleged to have been the case after the cyclone in Divi Seema when larger amounts of money and relief aid arrived than would normally have been expected. Since water availability is the crucial and leading input in the economy in Divi we will take its distribution as an example of power relations in action (Figure 3.2), although the principles underlying these relations are applicable to any other scarce and potentially lucrative resource anywhere in India.

The amount of water "let down" into the local irrigation canals – i.e, let in from the river at the barrage 70 km upstream – is decided impartially in Hyderabad by government officials, advised by the Chief Engineer, who pass

FIGURE 3.2: *Links between power-brokers*

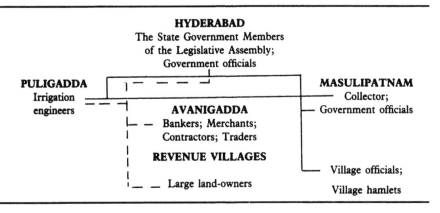

Official links ———; unofficial links – – –.

on the figures to the District Collector, the *de facto* "ruler" in the district, who together with the District Engineer is responsible for the distribution of water locally. But, the specific allocation into particular canals in Divi Seema is decided at local level by the Area Engineer at Puligadda, working with the District Engineer in Masulipatnam.

Engineers at all levels in the Major and Minor Irrigation departments have close contacts which they need to maintain their positions *vis-à-vis* their own internal "arrangements" (Wade 1982, 1984) with the local power-brokers – i.e., the large landlords and the merchants. These contacts can result in obtaining more water than allocated, if, firstly, there are shortages at the start of the agricultural year, and, secondly, if there is a shortage of water for the second crop, the principal insurance device in Divi Seema. Similar power relations concerning the allocation and distribution of resources exist all over India, but relations commanding water resources are the most important and are a virulent feature of life in the deltas. They can have particularly punitive effects in backward areas like Divi Seema and can totally undermine the benefits of other rural development and cyclone mitigation programmes.

Loans and assets

Loans
A particular feature of the social relations of production in Divi Seema which differed from those on the mainland was the long-established *Kartika* loan system (*Kartika* being the month *before* the harvest in the Telugu calendar, corresponding to the last two weeks in October and the first two weeks of November) whereby the large farmers who had the surplus and the storage facilities charged two bags for every bag of rice loaned during the year and

called in the loans immediately after the harvest when the prices were lowest. By August nobody except the large farmers had any food stocks and everybody had to borrow rice from them. It could be argued that in the absence of any other system of distribution of scarce resources (e.g., Government fair-price shops) the large farmers and the moneylenders who made these loans, often the same people, were providing a necessary risk-aversion mechanism within the society by being an assured source of food and guaranteeing a right of subsistence for everybody. On the other hand, it could be argued that the *Kartika* loan system was simply a device through which a small minority controlled the majority and prevented them from ever acquiring the resources to break or lessen that control and was thus a perfect mirror of the social relations of production.

Due to the scarcity of credit from the banks (i.e., formal credit) the bulk of the population were in the grip of the "moneylenders", the large farmers and the *Vaishyas*, a trading caste who owned shops in some of the villages. Table 3.5 shows the scope and structure of the credit market in pre-cyclone Divi and the wide discrepancy between the formal (bank) credit market and the informal (moneylenders) market. Formal loans at going rates of interest of 5 per cent per year were used ostensibly for production purposes – i.e., for agricultural production. In many cases the recipients, the large farmers (officially classified as having 5 acres of land or more), would turn these loans into informal loans for those who were considered uncreditworthy by the banks and would charge between 25 and 100 per cent interest. Informal loans were used for "consumption purposes", a general term that included paying back other debts, paying bribes to officials, buying food and clothing. The large farmers would use the profits from turning bank loans into informal loans for paying bribes to government officials for permissions and for paying

TABLE 3.5: *Formal and informal loans taken in a 202-household sample, classified by occupation, 1977*

Occupation	Households in sample (N)	Formal sector		Informal sector	
		Households with loans (N)	Size of loan (Rs)	Households with loans (N)	Size of loan (Rs)
Cultivators[a]	18	14	1,550	18	2250
Cultivators[b] and agricultural labourers	108	13	550	104	1100
Others[c]	76	7	–	56	750

Source: Fieldwork 1981–82.

[a] Large farmers.

[b] Small and marginal farmers.

[c] Fishermen, mixed occupations, landless.

the irrigation engineers for water allocation, amongst other things, thus tightening their stranglehold on the majority of the helpless population.

From our sample of 202 households (Table 3.5) only 34 households (less than 20 per cent) were favoured by the banks, whereas 178 households (85 per cent) had to rely on the moneylenders in the informal market. The remaining 15 per cent were not considered credit-worthy enough to get loans in the informal market which meant they had no collateral whatsoever (i.e., jewellery), in other words they were destitute. These households were therefore borrowing from within similar households or working as tied labourers. The ability to raise loans from either market was considered an asset in itself which brings us to the subject of assets.

Assets

The most vital asset in this society is land, the best being fertile and irrigated; the next most precious assets are draught animals and farm equipment, and then, milch animals which are crucial but only for some households. On the eve of the 1977 cyclone, the cultivators (10 per cent of the population) owned about 30 per cent of the land, all of it fertile and irrigated, and over 50 per cent of the plough teams and about 30 per cent of the milch animals. The cultivators and agricultural labourers (50 per cent of the population) owned approximately 60 per cent of the land and 48 per cent of the plough teams and 50 per cent of the milch animals. The category of "others" who were by and large the non-cultivating group (40 per cent of the population) owned less than 10 per cent of the land, almost no plough teams and about 30 per cent of the milch animals. We will see what happens to these households in more detail later.

3.2.6 Castes and factions

To understand the intricacies of the social relations of production and power relations in Divi Seema and the unexpected effects which outside interventions may have on the cultural context of rural life, it is important to have a picture of the caste and faction dimensions of village life, since these dominate what happens inside the villages and to a large extent what happens to the outside interventions by government and/or the NGOs.

The majority of the population in Divi belong to the fourth category of the Hindu caste system known as the *Sudra* castes. *Sudras* were classified as "labourers" (i.e., cultivators) who became polluted by work in the fields. *Sudra* castes, known as "non-scheduled castes", are the most numerous of all caste groups in Divi Seema (65 per cent of the population) and are mainly cultivators but include trade and service castes. The next most numerous castes are the "Scheduled castes" (30 per cent of the population) who used to be called "Untouchables" and were outside the caste system; and the least numerous are the "Scheduled tribes" and "Others", such as Christians and Muslims, comprising the remainder of the population.

Among the non-scheduled castes, the *Kamma* (originally soldiers by profession) are the principal cultivating caste in the Krishna delta but are less numerous in Divi Seema than on the mainland where they are the dominant landlord caste. Their intense rivals are the *Kapu* who are also a major cultivating caste related to the *Reddis* who were dominant in the Telegu districts of the old Madras Presidency. While there is rivalry between the *Kamma* and the *Kapu* there is more competition within the castes which the fluidity of local elections illustrates. The *Kamma* tend to be a more heterogeneous group of self-cultivating farmers while there is more economic variation within the *Kapu* and not all the members of the dominant caste are accorded the same deference by other villagers. In Divi *taluk* villages, caste lines are more important than lines of class and this was one feature that helped to perpetuate the traditional imbalances between the various occupations.

Among the non-cultivating castes the most dominant in Divi Seema are the *Idiga* (18 per cent of the population). They are the Telegu *toddy*-drawers whose hereditary occupation is the extraction of the juice of the date and palmyra palms and the concoction of the powerful *toddy* liquor. The *Idigas* were once employed as soldiers but are now also cultivators. They are known in Divi as *Gouda*. Next in number comes the the fishermen's caste of the east coast in the Telegu-speaking areas called the *Pattanaram* but known in Divi as *Pallecarlu* and comprising 12 per cent of the population. The last major scheduled caste in Divi Seema is the *Kummaru*, the potters in the Madras Presidency and still the potters of the Telegu areas. *Kummaru* in Telegu derives from the Sanskrit word *Kumbahakakara* – pot maker (*ku* – earth). Socially they are considered to be superior to the *Sudras* but also work as cooks and now as cultivators. Economically they are definitely inferior to the *Kapu* and *Kamma* because they own very small pieces of land. The last caste in this section is the *Gollalu* caste who comprise approximately 10 per cent of the population of Divi Seema.

There are two main castes within the "Scheduled castes" group: the *Madiga* and the *Mala*. The *Madiga* are the best-known leather-working caste of Telegu-speaking areas of the east coast. For this work they are considered by the other castes to be lowest of all menial castes and contact with them is considered to be polluting. They make drums and are the traditional drummers at caste feasts. Many *Madiga* are Christians in the Krishna delta and as a result are more literate than the other castes. The chief occupations of the *Mala* are weaving and working as agricultural labourers although some are now cultivators. They are also musicians but are considered by caste people to be inferior to the *Madiga* to whom the *Mala* consider themselves to be superior. *Mala* act as messengers for caste people at weddings and funerals.

The majority of members of the "Scheduled tribes" in Divi Seema are

Girijans who are known as "Tribals". They are renowned for their ability to catch rats and snakes, the latter without bruising in any way so that they can sell their skins. *Girijans* are normally nomadic but since the destruction of the forests they have been forced to live in permanent settlements. The last group, known as "Others", comprise Christians and Muslims who together make up less than 3 per cent of the population. The Muslims observe the Mohammedan *gosha* system whereby women are kept in seclusion, although in Divi Seema the women will work outside – but only in their husband's fields. The Godavari and Krishna deltas were the battleground for highly competitive prosetylising campaigns by factions of the Christian church in the late 1880s (see Washbrook 1976) with the result that there are considerable numbers of Christians in the deltas, noticeably among the "Scheduled caste" communities.

A description of caste implies a neat and visible hierarchy of power and privilege within the economic and cultural system and to some extent that is correct. The caste system is a hierarchical system worked out for economic reasons but no brief glimpse at the undercurrents of social relations can be complete without reference to the phenomenon of faction which is simple in concept but can be just as perplexing to the outsider as caste. The term "village politics" is often a synonym for faction and can be used to explain some of the bewildering and seemingly illogical actions of villagers. Thus an explanation of the relationship between caste and faction is needed and the best description to date has come from Elliott (1970).

At the risk of over-simplification, caste and faction possibilities may be viewed along two dimensions. Caste solidarity is the horizontal dimension and factional mobilisation is the vertical dimension. The basic structures for both horizontal and vertical mobilisation exist in the traditional village society. Every villager is a member of several groups in the village which may be ranged schematically along the same two dimensions of a smaller scale. As a member of family and caste he interacts with persons of a similar social status, participating in relationships of ritual, kinship and group regulation. As a member of an occupational group in a village he interacts with persons of different caste and occupation, conducting relationships based on economic exchange, deference behaviours and political status. These relationships between castes constitute vertical ties which connect persons of differing social status . . . . The village society is marked by cross-cutting alignments, providing different bases for conflict, integration and authority. Similarly, village leaders use their position in the hierarchies of both caste and class to maintain their dominance over village affairs . . . . Current political groups, factions and parties build on these patterns of structures to win elections and to gain access to government benefits. (Elliott 1970: 131, 132.)

Political power of the dominant castes is increased more by the numbers of followers that can be rallied for competition than the possession of resources or power in other arenas. Kin and caste ties are two of the important means of rallying support so the leader of a large caste group has more potential followers than the leader of a small caste group. However, elections for office have made it imperative to recruit all potential members, thus providing the many occasions for manoeuvring and bargaining which reveal the fluid nature of the factions and village politics and which are so bewildering to non-Indians. Elections have also increased the opportunities for subordinate groups to express their problems but they have also revealed the differences between groups which were previously implied and vague.

Elliott describes the wider relationships within the caste and faction arena as follows.

> Politics outside the village are carried on by the same dominant caste persons and the political relationships between villages are often uneven in breadth and direction. Usually several villages (or hamlets with 1,000 people) are grouped as a cluster around a particularly dominant village and function more or less like single villages depending on the nature of the caste, economic and political relationships between the units. The most integrated units are those which consist of a main village with hamlets of only service castes living outside the village, because of caste restrictions, but who are wholly dependent on the inhabitants of the main village for employment and representing them with the outside authorities. Such clusters of hamlets can be considered to be one village. Among the hamlets with more than one caste group there are lesser degrees of integration, particularly in the hamlets containing members of the dominant caste. The dominant caste people would have social and political relationships that were quite independent of the main village and would only have weak ties of allegiance with it. (Elliott 1970: 136).

Dominance usually centres on one large family which has extended its influence throughout a region of villages through land-holdings, money-lending, arbitration between villagers and villages and by representations to the administration. Improved communication and increasing monetisation of agriculture (cash wages, cash crops, disaster relief) have increased mobility and larger and larger circles of dominant families have been formed and ties have been expanded creating district élites whose basic structures emanate directly from their cohesion and who can influence government policy to a greater extent than in the more traditional societies. These families are called "the large landlords" by the people of Divi or "large farmers" in the literature, and they dominate the daily life in Divi Seema.

3.2.7 Risk-reduction strategies

In Chapter Two we outlined the theory and practice of risk aversion. Here we should be more specific and explain in detail some of the responses of the people in Divi Seema, to the range of risks with which they were faced. Risk strategies are based on choices which are largely governed by the priorities that people have and their perception of the constraints or opportunities inherent in deciding priorities. We found early on in the fieldwork that peoples' priorities varied according to their economic status (see Table 3.6) and that there was a certain cut-off point at which priorities changed quite dramatically from being focused on trying to guarantee a bare subsistence to improving their overall positions.

We shall see these priorities more clearly as we go through some of the major risks likely to be encountered and some of the strategies devised to counteract them.

Cyclone risk

The cyclone risk is of course the largest and most devastating risk people in Divi Seema have to face. However, cyclones only occur once every 5 to 10 years whereas other extremes of climatic variation occur more often as we have seen (Table 3.1) and we shall mention below the principal strategies devised to counter such extremes. In the face of a cyclone warning, before 1977, people could either stay in the villages or "go to the high ground". These decisions were largely constrained by their own assessment of the probabilities of the cyclone strike hitting them *and* their assessment whether their belongings would be stolen while they were away (Winchester 1990: 103). If there was extensive flooding then their only options would be to scramble onto the roofs of the rich people's houses (sturdily constructed with flattish tiled roofs) whose owners would probably have left, leaving only retainers behind, or go into the temples and schools. If there was no flooding and just screaming winds, then they could sit tight in their own huts and pray for the cyclone to pass them by. (An accidental risk strategy, that is only worth mentioning because it is sometimes used, is when the roof of the huts become rafts, the mud walls having eroded in about 12 hours; most people would still prefer to get on the rich man's roof.)

Since the 1977 cyclone, the choices have been widened in some villages by the construction of "durable houses" and cyclone shelters. However, over the years the risk strategies have widened. Since 1977 when the government found itself in the position of having to increase relief costs more and more, mainly for political reasons, the villagers have turned to more sophisticated risk reduction strategies, the basis of which is to be first in line for the handouts. Either the villagers return as quickly as they can after being evacuated or they stay close and send a representative to Hyderabad, at the *first cyclone warning*, to lobby for favours amongst the competing politicians. These last strategies could backfire.

Agricultural risks

We mentioned above that in Divi Seema the technical arrangements in relation to risk strategies included the use of varieties of rice strains, developed in the 1930s, to withstand the effects cyclones – i.e., *Masoori* which is wind-resistant and has a short stem and *Akkulu* which can withstand long periods of immersion. Other technical arrangements included the adoption of planting techniques, the timing of planting and harvesting developed by trial and error over many generations, and shared labour, expertise and inputs.

However, since the cyclone, the technical arrangements – even the use of traditional varieties – have been threatened by the increased costs and use of fertilisers and other agricultural inputs. With increased cultivation costs the income of cultivators now varies within much wider limits, and costs can absorb two thirds the value of the crop yield (Winchester 1986) so that a difference in yield due to the effect of cyclones and other climatic variations can produce wide income variability and harmful consequences for those households with the lowest incomes. Agricultural specialisation such as monoculture can produce differential vulnerability to exogenous forces of which the market is one; yield variability due to soil variation is another.

Individual risk-reduction strategies

Individual household risk-reduction strategies are closely linked to their priorities (see Table 3.6). Education (i.e., educating a son) as a strategy was given only by the most affluent group – the large farmers, whose priorities consisted of improvements to what seemed an already secure lifestyle. Better medical facilities and improved health care was considered as a viable risk-reduction strategy by the small and marginal farmers, the fishermen and the petty shop owners and small traders. Paying a dowry for a good marriage for a daughter was put forward by the large farmers, who could afford to "marry on to the mainland", whereas the small farmers put a marriage onto the mainland as a priority and a secure risk-reduction strategy. Paying off debts was regarded as a high priority by the least affluent – i.e., the marginal farmers and the landless, whose risk-reduction strategies centred on obtaining credit to keep themselves alive. Obtaining more credit was considered to be a top priority by all groups although its use would vary from improving land (large and small farmers) to bribing officials (marginal farmers, the landless and the small traders) performing ceremonies and giving gifts (large and small farmers). Only the small farmers seemed to think that durable housing was a realistic risk-reduction strategy.

Social arrangements were based on traditional patterns of reciprocity, work-sharing and the use of common lands – i.e., the moral economy (Scott: 1976) – but these had been eroded to some extent by 1977 by a mixture of absentee landlordism and the take-over of the common lands, although people claimed that caste and factional loyalties, acting as shock absorbers, had balanced these to some extent. The principal risk-reduction arrangement that was widely practised in Divi Seema before the 1977 cyclone, and since, has been temporary migration.

TABLE 3.6: *Priorities of households according to occupations, 1981–82*

Occupational household group	Number of households	Priorities
Cultivators		
Large farmers	18	Beautiful village[a]; beautiful house[b]; good marriage; better animals and farm equipment; easier credit from banks; education.
Cultivators and agricultural labourers		
Small farmers	72	Veterinary services; production credit from banks; money for dowries; minor infrastructure improved environment for health reasons; safer community buildings; stronger houses; marriage to mainland family.
Marginal farmers	36	Crop loans; credit for carts and milch animals; better and cheaper fertiliser; lavatories; medical services; money for clothes; paying off debts.
Others		
Fishermen	27	Credit for boats and nets; credit for carts and milch animals; better and cheaper fertiliser; better roads to villages; lavatories.
Small cultivators; petty traders; minor government officials	11	Formal credit for business; better houses; better medical services; education.
Landless	38	Credit for milch animals; another job; extra income for food; credit from money lenders; opportunities for wage labour; paying off debts.
Total	202	

Source: Fieldwork 1981–82.

[a] "Beautiful village" did not mean aesthetically beautiful but one where the houses of the poorest could not be seen.

[b] "Beautiful house" meant a large house, probably a new urban-style concrete house with added status.

Migration

We mentioned in Chapter Two how migration strategies are a response to collective risks and how they are one of the ways of reducing the risk of destitution by earning extra income. In many parts of India remittances sent from a family member who had migrated permanently or at least for a number of years are an additional source of income, but this pattern did not exist in Divi Seema. There were few towns on the mainland to which people could migrate that would offer any better prospects of employment than existed in Divi Seema because the industries in the towns were primarily engaged in processing cash crops (sugarcane and fruits) and competition for employment was eager and yielded few job opportunities for outsiders.

The only way to minimise the risks of climatic variability in Divi Seema and dependence on the large landlords was in temporary migration to the mainland (see Table 3.3). This was not such an acute response to collective risks as permanent migration but was considered to be the "traditional way". The phenomenon of temporary migration was widespread in the coastal areas of the Krishna delta and had become part of the agricultural life-cycle ever since the completion of the canal irrigation network and the expansion of paddy-growing land in the late 1930s, and a small but changing army of workers would follow the harvest down the coast every year because one area would "cut" two weeks after another area and so on. People from the mainland would migrate to Divi Seema for the main harvest, and in January, Divi people would migrate to the mainland for the second crop, working until April or May, by which time they would have to return to start work on the main crop on the island.

Migration was an economic necessity for at least 60 per cent of the population, extending the average working year for a male agricultural labourer from 78 to 123 days (a 50 per cent addition to his wages) and a female agricultural labourer from 76 to 96 days (a 25 per cent addition to her wages) – see Table 3.3. People tended to migrate as households but often only the women or just the men would migrate and they would travel and live in groups in makeshift huts beside the fields for up to three months at a time, leaving the children in the care of elderly relatives

3.3 DIVI SEEMA ON THE EVE OF THE CYCLONE

According to government officials and people who lived in Divi Seema before the 1977 cyclone, the main characteristics of Divi Seema were its backwardness and remoteness and we can begin to see why. Divi Seema shared the same climatic and physiographic characteristics as other areas in the Krishna delta but its unique characteristics of backwardness had undoubtedly arisen from the way it was developed. Development policies had produced a physical, social and economic imbalance; much of the land had lost its natural cover and was pathetically exposed to cyclones, and the British and later Indian governments did little to protect the people living in the most exposed areas. (In 1966 a 3 m-high earthen tidal bund was built 2 km back from the coast which may have reassured some people, but in the event gave them no protection.) The richer paddy-growing areas were connected to Avanigadda by good roads and from there via the aqueduct and road to the mainland. Only the inland plain farmers were capable of producing any surplus which was easily taken to the markets on the mainland. The roads in the coastal flat were washed away every year in the rainy season which meant that the coastal villages were cut off every year from August to December.

Health and education facilities lagged behind those of the mainland; health was poor for reasons already stated. In the rainy seasons, cholera and other diseases reached epidemic proportions. The uneven development had resulted in uneven social relations of production with a dependence by the majority on the minority (many of whom were absentee landlords). Apart from agriculture the range of occupations was minimal and there was little to do except migrate for a short spell and wait for the start of next year's agricultural work. No wonder "Mainland people would not marry their daughters into Divi" (personal communication with K. R. Naghabushanam, *tahsildar* of Divi Seema 1970–76 (government official in charge of a *taluk*)).

3.4   FIELDWORK PROGRAMME AND METHODOLOGY

The Andhra cyclone ("the worst in living memory") has already been introduced (Chapter One, section 1.1.3) and we know that it became the watershed for present-day cyclone mitigation policies (Chapter One, section 1.2.2) and that it was the most publicised cyclone event in India's history. Part of the widespread attention this cyclone received was reinforced when it was presented as a case-study at a conference on *Disasters and the Small Dwelling* (Davis 1981b) held in Oxford in May 1978, which I attended as an observer. In August of that year, I attended another conference about the Andhra cyclone, in Vijayawada, Andhra Pradesh, on the subject of the post-disaster operations (Winchester 1979). The general view of the conference was that the relief operations and the rehabilitation and restoration programmes had been successful. The most contentious issue to emerge, however, was the decision by many NGOs and the government to provide individual protection in the form of the pucca concrete-housing programmes. This became one of the subjects that initially drew me to undertake the research on which this book is based.

Over the next two years, I made three more reconnaissance trips to the area before deciding to make a study of the storm-surge affected area only and setting up the fieldwork programme to which we now turn. By the time I started the fieldwork I was becoming aware that the subject of post-disaster development was very complex and I had sensed that simplistic housing solutions may not be the most appropriate way of tackling the underlying issues of cyclone vulnerability.

3.4.1 Fieldwork

The fieldwork programme and the methodology were designed specifically to find the links between vulnerability, cyclone impact and recovery. The view held by government (represented by the Conventional View) suggested that recurrent exposure to cyclones increased vulnerability and that it would only decrease if the impact of cyclones could be reduced. The view held by social scientists (represented by the Alternative View) suggested that some people were more vulnerable than others to cyclones because their everyday conditions made them susceptible to shocks of all types, irrespective of cyclones, and that their vulnerability stemmed from the historical development of the area and the resultant power relations. These contrasting views and their underlying assumptions made it necessary to develop a methodology that could disentangle and identify the causes of cyclone vulnerability.

The fieldwork programme was set up to test the hypotheses that underpinned both views; for the Conventional View, that **Cyclone vulnerability is caused by exposure to cyclones** and for the Alternative View, that **Everyday conditions make people vulnerable to cyclones**. In testing both sets of hypotheses it was essential to have data from which the effects of cyclones could be clearly distinguished from the effects of other variables. Data were required as follows:

1. An economic profile of representative households living in a strip stretching back from the coast to as far inland as reliable data could be gathered, making the spatial variable a major stratification, and which would take into account the height of the storm-surge wave and the varying degrees of exposure.
2. A representative distribution of castes and occupations.

Initial information was gleaned from a socio-economic survey of 4,132 households carried out by a Catholic relief agency, the Divi Seema Social Service Society (DSSSS) with whom I stayed for nine months altogether while carrying out the fieldwork programme. Their socio-economic survey (DSSSS 1978) subsequently became the core of my sample frame. The survey covered the area that had been agreed by government and the other NGOs in which DSSSS could operate. Data in the DSSSS survey made the identification of the social and economic features of the population much quicker than would otherwise have been the case and probably saved me six months' work.

The overall fieldwork programme was carried out in three stages. Stage One began in October 1981, coinciding with the period of maximum likely incidence of cyclones and the climax of the year, the harvest, and ended a year later in September 1982, coinciding with the period between transplanting and the harvest and the "dull season" of *Kartika*. This provided the data for the immediate pre- and post-cyclone periods (the pre-cyclone data based on claims and the post-cyclone data based on claims but partly substantiated by the DSSSS survey) and also for the agricultural year 1981–82. Stage Two was carried out a year later after preliminary analysis of the data had suggested that I was on the right track but needed more information about the vital aspects of recovery. This provided data for the agricultural year 1982–83, and seen in retrospect, was also the peak of the development perod in Divi Seema. Stage Three was carried out in 1988 and provided a 10-year transect.

3.4.2 Methodology

The storm surge affected 19 of the 25 revenue villages (85 per cent of the total area) on the island of Divi Seema (a revenue village is a collection of hamlets and small villages grouped together for tax purposes and usually within 5 km of a larger village from which the revenue village takes its name). Of those affected I decided to construct a sample frame of villages and hamlets from within the three revenue villages of Kammanamolu, Mandapakala and Lingareddipalem in the DSSSS survey area and within the revenue villages of Ganapeswaram and Etimoga in the area adopted by the Salvation Army (see Map 3.2).

Since the revenue villages were the administrative centres outside the urban areas, my first action, on the advice of DSSSS, was to meet the elected officials of the revenue villages which I had chosen for the sample frame. I met the village presidents, the *muncifs* (the village headmen) and the *karnams* (the village accountants), as a matter of courtesy before meeting anyone else, to ask them for their permission to work in their villages. I explained the aims and structure of my fieldwork programme and the mystifying (to them) process of taking a stratified random sample of households (which they didn't think was necessary because they knew everything about the villagers anyway). I told them that I wanted to ask the villagers questions about what had happened to them in the cyclone and about their families and the things they owned. I explained to the village leaders that I was not an aid-worker or a government spy and that I had nothing to give them. They were so used to outsiders coming in with offers of aid that they were not unduly disappointed to find out that I wanted to ask questions because I was writing a book. I knew enough about India by then to know that, by first meeting the people who were considered to be the most important in the villages, I had cleared an important political hurdle and when I met the villagers they would know that I had been

MAP 3.2: *Divi Seema: revenue villages and hamlets in sample frame*

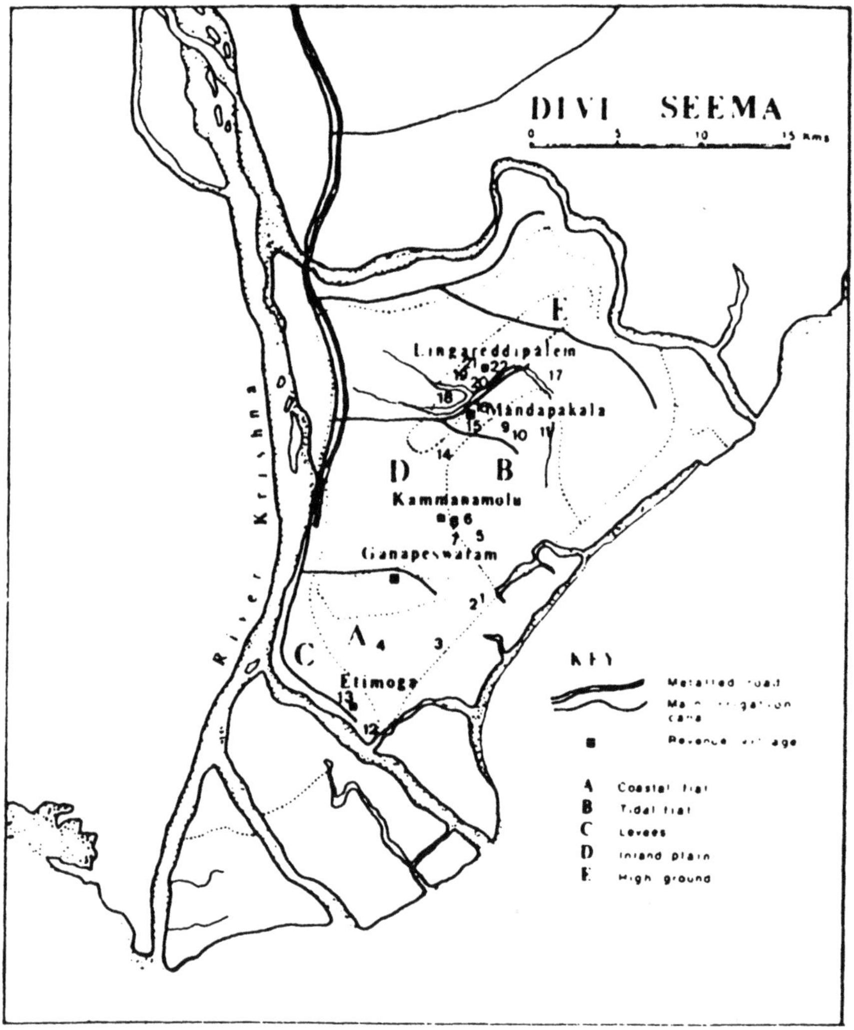

Sources: Government of India 1973; topography after Nageswara Rao and Vaidyanaham 1978.

vetted and also what I wanted. The language problem was minimised by having a DSSSS field officer as my interpreter with whom I had briefly worked on two previous reconnaisance visits in 1980 and 1981. The other purpose of going to the revenue villages first was that I could also make a preliminary survey of likely hamlets in which to carry out the interviews.

The revenue villages selected themselves; the next stage was to select hamlets that were representative of all the hamlets in the revenue villages within the storm-surge area according to:

1. the height contours of the storm surge correlated with varying degrees of exposure;
2. the death tolls recorded (to counterbalance the numbers killed according to storm-surge contours because high death tolls were recorded inland at lower contour heights than at the coast);
3. general topographical classifications; and
4. different housetypes.

Having calculated that it would be possible to acquire data from 200 households within the nine months available for fieldwork, the next task was to make a sample frame that spread the households equally between the coastal area and the inland area while incorporating the previous stratifications suggested by the storm-surge contours and numbers killed. Having done this, I then met the caste and village leaders in all the hamlets and repeated the explanations I had already given in the revenue villages.

Taking topographical variation as the principal criterion for the spatial distribution of the sample, I decided to take 100 households from the unprotected hamlets in the coastal flat, divided into three areas (coastal flat, tidal flat and levees), and 100 households from the more protected hamlets in the inland plain, divided into two areas (inland plain and high ground – after Nageswara Rao 1980).

In the coastal flat, I selected 13 hamlets: in the coastal flat – *Nali* (1), *Francispuram* (2), *Sorlagondi* (3) and *Mulapalem* (4); in the tidal flat – *Ramanthapuram* (5), *Gollapalem* (6), *Girijanawada* (7), *Peddavarem* (8), *Goudapalem* (9), *Gunniahgarudibba* (10) and *Bellamkondadibba* (11); in the levees – *Gullamodu* (12) and *Etimoga* (13).

In the inland plain, I selected nine hamlets; in the inland plain – *Potumeeda* (14), *Mandapakala* (15), *Mandapakala Harijanawada* (16) and *Jerungivanipalem* (17); and on high ground – *Kummaripalem* (18), *Chinagodimodu* (19), *Peddagudumotu* (20), *Lingareddipalem* (21) and *Lingareddipalem Harijanawada* (22).

Altogether, these hamlets comprised 18 of the 24 hamlets within the DSSSS socio-economic survey and four in the area of influence of the Salvation Army which were later taken into the DSSSS programmes (see discussion in Chapter Five).

I was ready to meet the villagers, but first I had to find a way of taking a random sample (using the grid method) that corresponded to the facts on the ground. This method required village plans, but, since no intelligible (to me) plans existed, we had to produce them ourselves from surveys. The 12 largest village hamlets were surveyed and 2,186 houses were recorded in detail, of which 1,165 were concrete houses (815 in the coastal area and 350 in the inland area) and 1,021 were traditionally built in the traditional villages and housing colonies (248 in the coastal area and 773 in the inland area). The concrete houses were re-surveyed in 1983 for a structural and conditional

MAP 3.3: *Divi Seema: villages and hamlets in sample frame and topography*

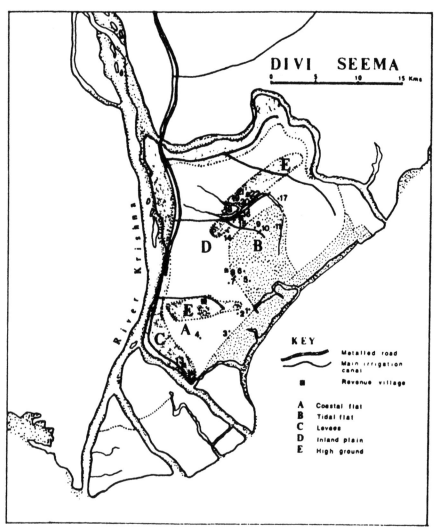

Sources: Government of India 1973; topography after Nageswara Rao and Vaidyanaham 1978.

analysis and revisited in 1988.

Village plans were drawn in diagrammatic form to an approximate scale (see Figure 3.3) showing the spatial relationships between the houses, the location of the major and minor roads, public spaces for haystacks and other uses, tanks, irrigation canals, public buildings, the principal contours, special features, cyclone shelters, and marshy or waterlogged ground. Each house was numbered on the plan and with my interpreter's detailed knowledge of the villages and the DSSSS socio-economic survey we were ready to start.

Having come to this study from an architectural and planning background it was inevitable that my initial research interest was in the role that housing played in post-disaster development and the effects that housing provision had had on the economic improvement of the poorest sections of the population. However, ever since the Vijayawada conference and other conferences that I had attended in India, I had had doubts about the value of housing even in a cyclone-prone area and my interest switched early on in the programme when it became quite apparent from the pilot study of 51 households that housing was indeed a very low priority for the vast majority of the population (see also Table 3.6). My research interests expanded to take into account those forces that underlay the socio-economic structure that influenced economic recovery, which in fact interested me far more and which are the subject of this work.

The easiest and simplest method to chart vulnerability and recovery of the people was to *measure their assets and resources over time*. This entailed no value judgements but relied to some extent on the accuracy of the observations and on the claims made by the people we interviewed. The claim figures were later subjected to a sensitivity analysis (Winchester 1986: 217) but were checked on the ground at the time, either by asking nextdoor neighbours and others in the village how accurate the claims were or by checking them with the DSSSS village workers who by then had extensive knowledge of the villages.

The assets chosen were houses, land holdings, plough teams, carts, milch animals, household goods, food and fodder stores and specialised equipment for caste occupations. Data about the more obvious risk-aversion strategies such as decisions to migrate, to diversify employment and so on, and the less visible but none the less subtle decisions affecting cultural imperatives, such as who to bribe, who to marry, which ceremonies to pay for and so on, were also collected, together with data about household structures and composition.

At the end of the 1982 data collection period I had enough data to satisfy the requirements of a PhD thesis, but a grant from the Royal Institute of British Architects produced the funds to consider another season. Subsequently I undertook the second season of data collection with two supremely able field assistants, without whose work in 1983 much of this book could never have been written. With the funds and time available and with the advice of English academic colleagues we decided that the best strategy was to go deeper into the economic and social situations of fewer households; consequently we reduced the number of households in the sample frame from 202 to 42, which we called case-study households, and which were selected on the basis of being the most representative spatially and socio-economically of the larger sample. The advantage of reducing the frame to 42 households was that with limited time we could go much deeper into what was happening to households and it also gave us more time to check the claims that they made. There were numerous difficulties in collecting data of an economic nature and these will be explained later (Chapter Five, section 5.2) when we test the empirical data against the model of vulnerability (already discussed in Chapter Two, section 2.6). In

FIGURE 3.3: *Village plans and stratified random sample. (a) Linga reddy palem.*
(b) Gouda palem

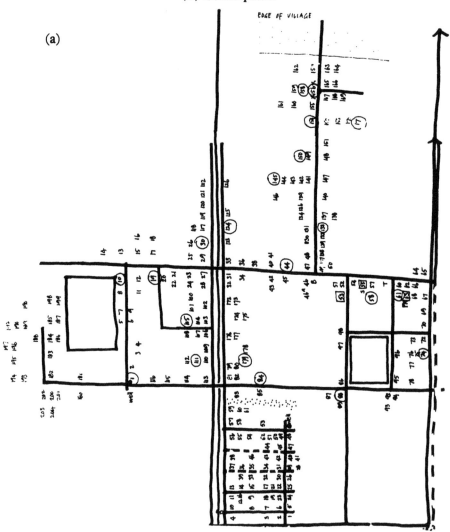

1988 I was able to return to the field area and, with the same interpreter, I
carried out a further two-month interview programme, which fortuitously gave
me a 10-year longitudinal study.

There was some difficulty in keeping the same households throughout the
10 years. In the 1988 survey, three households had disappeared since 1983 but
we had a number of reserve households that we had interviewed in 1983 so we
were able to retain consistency for 42 households which may have led to a less
than a perfect match with the previous 202 households, but was none the less
still a representative one. Using terms which we shall explain shortly, we had

96

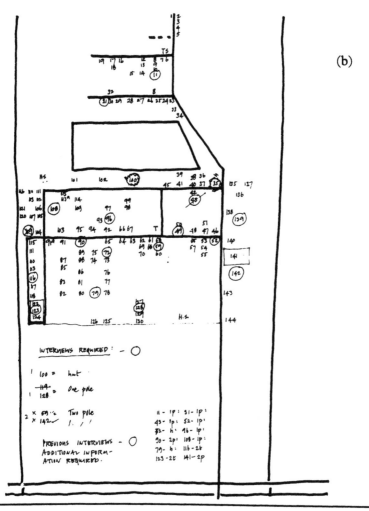

(b)

Source: Fieldwork 1981–82.

in the 42 case-study sample : four large farmer households (in the 202 household sample we had 18); 10 small farmers (72); five fishermen (27); two petty shop-owners and/or non-cultivators (11); 14 marginal farmers (36) and seven landless (38). A number of households changed their main occupation (as classified by criteria we will also explain shortly) over the period: three fishermen in 1983 had become small farmers by 1988; three marginal farmers in 1977 had become landless by 1988 and two landless households in 1977 had become marginal farmers by 1988. However, we have retained the same classifications throughout because the differences in occupational classifications are fairly arbitrary, except for those that are clearly quite different, and consistency of classifications is less important than consistency of identification of households.

97

The Cyclone of 1977 and Changes in Divi Seema, 1977–88

4.1 THE CYCLONE EVENT

The cyclone struck the coast of the Krishna delta at dusk on the 19th November 1977 with windspeeds of 150 kmph and a storm surge 5 m high at the coast. The storm crossed the coast of Divi Seema at 1630 hours (Subbaramayya *et al.* 1979) and the surge waters reached the first villages at 1700 hours. By the time they reached the more densely populated inland villages it was dark and the combination of shrieking winds and a wall of water must have added to the terror and confusion of the villagers and may also partly explain the high proportion of women and children's deaths.

The most detailed account of the storm and the surge is by Subbaramayya – see Subbaramayya *et al.* 1979 – who carried out a survey of the storm-surge-affected area two weeks after the event and traced the times and heights of the surge from discussions with survivors. Another social scientist made a survey of the area and collected survivors' accounts in his study (see Raghavulu and Cohen 1979). Both accounts point out that the storm surge came as a surprise to the villagers, including the fishermen, and suggest that the time of its arrival was a major contributory factor to the high death toll. According to Raghavulu and Cohen (1979: Appendix A) 62 per cent of the deaths on Divi Seema were in the area where the storm surge was up to 3 m high, 28 per cent of the deaths were in the remaining area covered by the surge waters and 10 per cent in the inland areas not affected by the surge waters (see Map 4.1), so we can infer that perhaps up to 90 per cent of the deaths were caused by drowning. Of the total number killed (estimated at 6,892), 19 per cent were adult males, 28 per cent were adult females and the rest (53 per cent) were children (Raghavulu and Cohen 1979: Appendix A).

Topography was a significant factor in accounting for the extent and spatial distribution of deaths; the highest death tolls occurred among the hamlets in or adjacent to the low-lying coastal areas and tidal flat in the eastern part of

MAP 4.1: *Storm surge contours and sample frame*

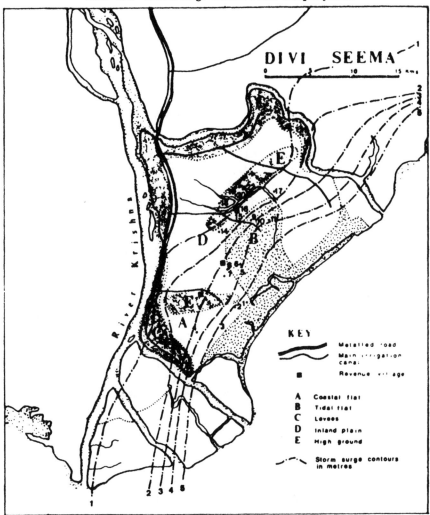

Divi Seema and in the central section where the tidal flat penetrates inland up to 10 km. The highest concentration of deaths was at the eastern end of the island which is low-lying and full of creeks and backwaters; here some villages lost between 40 and 68 per cent of their populations (Raghavulu and Cohen 1979: Appendix A). The south-west corner of the island is also veined with creeks and backwaters and was the first area to be swept over by the storm surge; high casualties were recorded here also; in one hamlet in the south-west portion of the coastal flat (Sorlagondi: No 3, Map 4.1) 50 per cent of the population was drowned; in another (Nali: No 1, Map 4.1) 30 per cent of the population was drowned. In the four hamlets within the revenue village of Kammanamolu in the tidal flat (Nos 5–8, Map 4.1) 25 per cent of the population was drowned, whilst in the five hamlets within Lingareddypalem revenue village in the inland plain (Nos 17 and 19–22, Map 4.1)) only 2 per cent of the population were killed.

4.1.1 The aftermath

In the darkness the villagers fled to the large *pucca* houses in the villages or tried to get to higher ground. Many were trapped in the thorn bushes and debris that the surge had gathered. When morning came, people were wading about waist-deep in water dotted with corpses and carcases. Many people were stranded far from roads and bodies floated across an 80 sq km area. The survivors were in a state of shock. The suddenness and fury of the cyclone and surge had terrified them especially since many had ignored the weather warning signs and the government's warnings. According to Raghavulu and others this shock gave way to depression at the sight of ruined fields and then to feelings of acute anxiety and guilt because of their failure to save their wives and children. Raghavulu and Cohen (1979: 32–33) paint a grim picture:

> Some individuals were stranded in tree tops for over fifteen hours; a large number died there and corpses draped the palms in many acres of Divi and Bandar. For those on the "ground" which was a sea of silt, filth and slime and debris, the situation was no better. Their lush, ripe paddy fields were turned into a vision of hell. Corpses and carcasses were strewn everywhere; under rubble, in the mud, across the paddy fields (all to be discovered as days or even weeks passed); other corpses lay jammed in temples, houses and schools, often by the dozen. Thousands were caught in thorn bushes and along the canal bunds . . . . All the stricken area was silent, except for the weeping; all birds had been swept away, vermin and rats were drowned, only a few dogs remained gorging.

It took until the next morning before the government officials became aware of the scale of the catastrophe because all telephone communications had been destroyed. All the roads had been washed away or blocked with debris so it took another 30 hours for relief supplies to get into the stricken area, by which time it is claimed (by some relief agencies) that hundreds of survivors had died from exposure. When the scale of the tragedy became apparent the Government alerted the central Government and the outside world. Divi Seema became the focus of international media attention. Supplies poured in; the main roads were jammed with people leaving the inundated villages and the NGOs going towards them.

Among the NGOs who rushed in were the Indian Red Cross Society, TATA Relief, EFICOR, Lions and Rotary Clubs from various cities and towns in the state, the Andhra Pradesh Red Cross Society, the Citizens' Cyclone Relief

Committees from Maharashtra and Karnataka (Raghavulu and Cohen 1979: 45, 46) and a contingent from the Society of Jesus from the Catholic Diocese of Vijayawada, DSSSS, whom we will discuss in greater detail later. Among the foreign NGOs to come to the aid of the stricken population were the International Red Cross, OXFAM, CARE, the Salvation Army, CARITAS, Save the Children Fund and representatives from charities in EEC countries (*ibid.*). Many of these NGOs created confusion, and, in due course, this confusion made the Government include powers to exclude NGOs from future disaster areas, if they so wished (A.P. Government 1988b: 11–12).

The relief phase lasted six weeks. The Government, with experience of previous disasters, acted quickly and organised emergency relief measures for the survivors which consisted of giving 10 kg of rice to each household, providing temporary shelters for the survivors, supplying free clothing and medical assistance, giving *ex gratia* sums of Rs 1,000 to the next-of-kin of anyone who died over five years of age, providing blankets and clothes, providing household goods to the value of Rs 150 and providing Rs 150 worth of free building materials for the survivors to rebuild *katcha* (mud and thatch) houses (A.P. Government 1977a: 11–15). As well as the emergency relief measures the Government's other immediate priorities were the disposal of the dead (which was difficult because Hindu custom required that bodies should be cremated and waterlogged bodies were hard to burn), clearing debris from the roads, starting the public-works programmes to inject cash into the shattered economy and supplying drinking water which was brought in by tanker for the next three months. Five high-ranking Indian Administrative Service (IAS) officers were appointed as Special Officers to assist the District Collector to ensure that the relief operations were carried out effectively.

After six weeks, the rehabilitation and restoration programmes were underway. The rehabilitation programmes consisted of providing assistance to fishermen by way of replacing their boats and nets, to weavers by replacing their looms and materials through 50 per cent subsidies and 50 per cent grants, to artisans by way of grants and subsidies through the Khadi and Village Industries Board, and to the farmers by giving them subsidies for paddy seedlings, fertilisers and land reclamation at varying rates – 25 per cent subsidy to small farmers and 33⅓ per cent subsidy to marginal farmers for seedlings and fertiliser; and 50 per cent subsidy to small and marginal farmers for land reclamation (A.P. Government 1977a: 15–17). Rehabilitation programmes were co-ordinated by the District Collectors. The restoration programmes consisted of rebuilding roads, bridges, schools and other public buildings, clearing out major and minor irrigation canals and drinking wells and tanks, and restoring electrical installations (A.P. Government 1977a: 17). The intention of the rehabilitation and restoration programmes was to "return the area to normality" (A.P. Government 1977a: 3) and the programmes were more or less completed within six months of starting, so that by early June 1978 (the opening of the agricultural year) the major infrastructure of the storm-surge and cyclone-affected areas had been repaired and rebuilt, and planting the main crop could begin. Losses had been extensive (see Chapter One, Table 1.2) but the energy and enthusiasm of NGOs and the efficiency of the relief, rehabilitation and restoration programmes, and a good north-east monsoon in May and June restored confidence in the people and took their minds off the trauma and the tragic losses they had suffered.

Before we go further we should look at the distribution of these losses within our sample survey and at the same time make our first test of the hypotheses underlying the Conventional and Alternative Views.

4.1.2 Losses correlated with topography

Our first task is to test the government's hypothesis – i.e., that casualties and losses were positively correlated with topography; this was summarised in the Conventional View (Chapter One, section 1.5), The Conventional View centres on the topographical characteristics of coastal areas, which are generally exposed, low-lying, poorly drained and prone to flooding, as the principal causal variable. The climate is all-pervasive, but there are sufficient physiographical variations within the coastal areas which we have to recognise in order to test the hypothesis rigorously.

The two areas of Divi Seema mentioned previously contain a variety of topographical features. The coastal area contains three sub-areas – the coastal flat; the tidal flat, and levees (high banks along the River Krishna) – and the inland area contains two distinct areas – the inland plain and high ground (Nageswara Rao 1980). These distinctions are referred to in Table 4.1. We would expect the majority of casualties and losses to have occurred in the coastal flat and perhaps in the tidal flat, with considerably less in the inland areas. Table 4.1 more or less confirms our expectations.

Undoubtedly, the topography was a major factor in the distribution of casualties and losses. Deaths and losses were highest in the most exposed areas of the coastal and tidal flats accounting for almost 90 per cent of all the people killed. In the coastal and tidal flats, 88 per cent of all asset losses were recorded (66 per cent of plough teams and carts; 82 per cent of milch animals and 83 per cent of the houses). These findings substantiate Government's perceptions of the close relationship between losses and vulnerability, and vulnerability and exposure.

However, in the light of the scepticism expressed in Chapter Two and illustrated in the Alternative Model (Chapter Two, section 2.2), we might argue that these findings are not sufficient to conclude that exposure was necessarily the major variable affecting the distribution of casualties and losses. Since we described a process of marginalisation in the historic development of Divi Seema which was mirrored in the nature and types of occupations we

TABLE 4.1: *Distribution of casualties and numbers of assets lost in the 1977 cyclone in a 202-household sample, stratified by topography*

Topography	Number of households	People killed N (%)	Plough teams lost N (%)	Carts lost N (%)	Milch animals lost N (%)	Houses destroyed N (%)
Coastal flat	30	33 (25)	4 (100)	17 (100)	38 (100)	30 (87)
Tidal flat	63	77 (26)	18 (88)	39 (91)	111 (96)	60 (89)
Levees	18	5 (7)	1 (100)	3 (75)	14 (70)	16 (89)
Inland plain	29	7 (6)	2 (44)	16 (73)	38 (75)	25 (89)
High ground	62	11 (4)	4 (33)	9 (31)	55 (73)	43 (73)
Totals	202	133	29	84	256	177

Source: Appendix 2.

should add occupations as a variable and combine it with topography and test the distribution of casualties and losses accordingly. In order to carry this out we need to briefly describe the main occupations in Divi Seema.

4.1.3 Losses correlated with topography and occupations

For anyone investigating a rural community in India, it is crucial to know that most people have more than one occupation. The terms "Cultivator" and "Agricultural labourer" which are used in the Census are too general for detailed analysis and other classifications are therefore required to describe the population more accurately. In the Government of India anti-poverty programmes the agricultural groupings are based on size of land holdings; these classifications are large, small and marginal farmers and landless and these are used also in other publications such as the ones we have referred to above.

In rural India there are two distinct groups which are quite visible to the outsider and which represent the two extremes of agricultural wellbeing; these are the large farmers and the landless. Other groups between the two are less well-defined because their fortunes tend to change rapidly and permanent classifications are difficult to make. The most difficult group to identify is that of the small farmers; one year they may be almost on the verge of becoming large farmers, the next year they may be marginal farmers. Since the crucial determinant of economic survival in Divi Seema and elsewhere is the *number of occupations* a household can muster we will use this criterion as well as landholding size to classify the sample population within our version of the

103

TABLE 4.2: *Distribution of principal occupations in Divi Seema, 1981–82*

Classification[a] and number of occupations	Description of activities	Households in sub-group	Households in main group	Percentage of total sample
Cultivators				
More than three occupations	*Large farmer*: Own cultivation[b] employing others, combined with business interests inside and outside village		18	9
Cultivators/agricultural labourers				
Not more than three occupations	*Small farmer*: Own cultivation/ agricultural labour and animal husbandry	26	72	36
	Own cultivation/agricultural labour and caste occupation[c]	46		
Not more than two occupations	*Marginal farmer*: Own cultivation/ agricultural labour		36	18
Others				
Not more than three occupations	*Fisherman*: own cultivation and agricultural labour		27	13
	Government official: own cultivation and agricultural labour	5	11	5
	Petty shop-owner or tradesman: own cultivation and agricultural labour	6		
One or less occupations	*Landless*: No cultivation, mainly agricultural labour or dependent on others		38	19
Total households			202	100

Source: Fieldwork 1981–82.

[a] Classifications as used in Appendices and Tables in Chapters 5 and 6.

[b] Cultivation of own land not necessarily employing others.

[c] Includes Herders = 8; Potters = 5; Service = 2; Tapper = 13; Goldsmith = 1; Leather-workers = 4; Dhobi = 3.

Government of India Census classifications (Government of India 1973). In Table 4.2 we bring these two classifications together with our classification of households by the numbers of occupations.

In Divi Seema only the *large farmers* can provide for their own subsistence requirements from their own land and do not have to work for any one else. The size of landholdings in our sample of large farmers averaged five acres but the important point to note as far as landholding *size* is concerned is that it takes at least three acres of irrigated fertile land to produce enough rice to feed an average-sized household for a year. Large farmers have at least two *other* means of earning income such as money-lending, selling produce and non agricultural activities and are the only group placed in the classification of "**Cultivators**" because they do not undertake any agricultural labouring. In our sample population 9 per cent of the households were in this classification.

The next group of **Cultivators and Agricultural Labourers** consists of two sub groups; these are *small farmers* who own more than 1 acre of land and less than 3 acres and generally have no more than two other income-generating occupations, and *marginal farmers* who own less than 1 acre and have one other subsidiary occupation. Both groups work as agricultural labourers on other peoples' land to make up income to meet their subsistence requirements and comprise 54 per cent of the sample population.

The last group classified as **Others** combines the "Industry", "Manufacturing", "Services" and "Other workers" classifications and consists of subgroups of *fishermen* who sometimes own small pieces of cultivable land and labour for other people, *mixed occupations* who are small traders (petty shopowners) who do not labour and occasionally have their own land; caste trades, most of whom labour on other people's land and sometimes have small pieces of land, and the *landless* who own no land and work almost exclusively as agricultural labourers. The group comprises the remaining 37 per cent of the sample population.

Deaths correlated with topography and occupation

An indication that occupation might be a significant variable in explaining differential vulnerability is provided in Table 4.3. The highest casualties occurred amongst the two major groups in the coastal area, amongst whom the landless, marginal farmers and fishermen suffered most (Appendix 2). It is difficult to draw firm conclusions from these simplified classifications of occupations (we are trying to reduce the extent of data and simplify the presentation), because we have the second and fifth groups ranked by economic measures, i.e., the small farmers and marginal farmers, in the same overall classification. There is some indication, however, that occupation was more positively correlated with the number of deaths in the inland area than in the coastal area because the marginal farmers and the landless had the highest

TABLE 4.3: *Distribution of casualties and numbers of assets and resources lost in the 1977 cyclone in a 202-household sample, stratified by topography and occupation*

Occupation	Topography	Households	People killed	Plough teams/carts lost	Milch animals lost	Houses lost
Cultivators	Coastal	6	3	10	29	4
	Inland	12	–	9	23	6
Losses as % of pre-cyclone totals			3	28	50	50
Losses as % total losses			2	17	20	6
Cultivators and	Coastal	59	56	53	110	57
agricultural labourers	Inland	49	11	34	51	40
Group losses as % of pre-cyclone totals			19	92	94	94
Losses as % total losses			51	77	63	55
Others	Coastal	45	55	1	24	40
	Inland	31	8	1	19	30
Group losses as % of pre-cyclone totals			21	100	100	95
Losses as % total losses			57	2	17	39
Total losses			133	113	256	177
Losses as % of pre-cyclone totals			14	62	85	88

Source: Appendix 2, where Coastal = Topographies 1–3; and Inland = Topographies 4–5.

absolute and relative numbers of casualties in the inland area (Appendix 2), suggesting some differential vulnerability on account of occupation – but not enough to be statistically significant (Winchester 1986: 191).

Asset losses correlated with topography and occupation

Asset losses were highest again in the Coastal area, as expected, but the relatively lower figure of losses amongst the **Cultivators'** plough teams (28 per cent) and milch animals (20 per cent) compared with the asset losses of the **Cultivators/Agricultural labourers'** plough teams (92 per cent) and milch animals (94 per cent) indicates some degree of differential vulnerability most likely as a function of protection. Asset losses spread between the two areas suggest some differential vulnerability on account of occupation but again not enough to be statistically significant (*ibid.*).

Conclusion

Exposure and topography played a major part in accounting for the extent of death and devastation. Variations in losses within the same degrees of exposure suggest varying degrees of protection, and also that protection was a significant factor in reducing the relative numbers of losses and *vice versa*. The high casualty and asset losses among the weaker economic groups suggest that they had little or no protection for themselves or their animals and we could conclude that the steady marginalisation process and the lack of development in the area were major factors contributing significantly to the extent of the devastation of assets and the tragedy of high casualties. This could lead us to think that protection was the key to reducing losses in cyclone strikes but we shall see later that, in fact, the people who suffered the most losses – i.e., those with insufficient relative protection – recovered the quickest and the best, suggesting that recovery was based on other aspects of vulnerability as well as the need for protection (see also Chapter Six, sections 6.1.1 and 6.1.2).

Our criticisms of the Conventional View might not have been proven by these findings but equally there are some clues, particularly in the findings of *occupations* correlated with losses and topography to suggest that it might be worthwhile to look at possible contributory causes of differential vulnerability other than location and exposure.

4.2 PANORAMIC VIEW OF DEVELOPMENT IN DIVI SEEMA, 1978–88

The development in Divi Seema following the cyclone created a number of changes in the society which had some passing effects on the *social relations of production*. The changes occurred in two fairly clear phases corresponding broadly with the development of the area; the first one starting with the relief and rehabilitation programmes and ending in 1983 when the government restoration and development programmes were complete and the influence of the NGOs was at its peak; and the second phase which lasted until the last collection of field data in 1988.

4.2.1 Phase One: 1977–82

By the end of May 1978 the public-works programmes which had provided work for about 25,000 men (a quarter of the male population of Divi Seema), consisting of clearing and repairing the main irrigation canals, making new roads and rebuilding the sea wall, had been completed. By the start of the agricultural year in early June all those employed in these programmes had returned to their own fields to start work on preparing for the main crop. However, the minor irrigation network had not been cleared entirely and many of the small and marginal farmers in the tail-end areas could not get water to their fields and so were unable to plant anything for the next harvest. With the roads repaired, the government and NGOs were able to start the concrete housing and cyclone shelter construction programmes, with over 40 NGOs providing funds on a "matching grant" basis (A.P. Government 1980c). Unfortunately these provided little employment for local people, apart from levelling the sites, since the programmes entailed the use of skilled labour mainly brought in from the mainland (A.P. Government 1982d).

The pause in farming activity should have given many people the time to rebuild their houses; but, many villages (about 80 per cent – the remaining villages having been excluded on political grounds) had been promised *pucca* concrete houses so many people preferred to remain in their flimsy temporary bamboo and thatch sheds and wait for the free gift of a concrete house, which they regarded as status symbols. Instead of building houses, the unemployed labourers spent their money, squirrelled away from the relief handouts, going to the three cinemas (five shows a day) in Nagayalanka, two of which had opened since the cyclone (personal communication with a senior IAS officer, 1982). The relief agencies complained that it was impossible to get people to work for them clearing the minor irrigation canals and the salt-covered land because they were all either "in the cinemas" or "standing around waiting for voluntary organisations to give them free handouts" (personal communications with a senior official in a voluntary organisation, 1980).

During this phase of post-cyclone development, significant improvements were made in the level of the provision of facilities and amenities in Divi compared with previous levels. Some idea of the improvement in the standard of provision of facilities and amenities in Divi Seema *provided by the Government* before and after the cyclone can be seen in Table 4.4. All-weather (*pucca*) roads connected all the revenue villages to which electricity was also taken and the drinking water supply was improved by installing wells in many villages. These wells reduced the villagers' reliance on the village *tanks* (small earth-bunded reservoirs), which were always contaminated, but, in the rainy season the wells too became contaminated as a result of human excreta seeping into the ground water.

As well as improving the facilities and amenities in the area, the Government also expanded its long-term development (anti-poverty) pro- grammes mainly by increasing the supply of rural credit through the banks. This was the central plank of Government policy which some of the NGOs took as the cue for their own longer-term development programmes and we shall examine the effects of these interventions later.

By the end of 1978 most of the voluntary agencies had departed because their budgets were geared for short periods of assistance and only 15 NGOs remained of the 100 or so that had come originally. These NGOs, encouraged by the Government, "adopted" villages, and in some cases "adopted" large areas with several villages in them. As well as supplying temporary housing,

TABLE 4.4: *Changes in the provision of facilities and amenities in the 13 storm-surge affected revenue villages in Divi Seema, 1971–81*

			Facilities and amenities				
Year	Households	Households per village	Roads (type)	Schools (N)	Medical (type)	Water supply	Electricity (N)
1971	11,998	923	5 PR	48 P	3 Disp	10 Well	2E
			8 KR	5 M	– Phc	4 Tank	1 Ph
				2 H	– Hosp		
1981	12,671	974	13 PR	47 P	5 Disp	8 Well	13 E
			1 KR	5 M	1 Phc	7 Tank	4 Ph
				3 H	3 Hosp	4 Hp	

Source: Goverment of India 1973, 1983.
Roads: PR = *Pucca* road; KR = *Katcha* road.
Schools: P = Primary; M = Middle; H = High.
Medical: Disp = Dispensary; Phc = Pharmacy; Hosp = Hospital (overnight accommodation).
Electricity: E = number of villages with electricity; Ph = telephone.

the NGOs also set up small-scale employment projects and credit schemes.

Among the plethora of NGOs working in the storm-surge affected area, only two took the trouble to undertake socio-economic surveys into the needs of the survivors, before plunging into projects; these were DSSSS (DSSSS 1978) as previously mentioned, and the Salvation Army. In their "targeted" surveys they found that the majority of households had only very small pieces of land (less than half an acre) and few assets other than cooking utensils, some jewellery, some gold (particularly the fishermen) and specialised equipment (nets, potters' wheels). Less than 10 per cent owned animals (DSSSS 1978: 14). As a result of their surveys, both DSSSS and the Salvation Army concentrated their main efforts on getting the banks to provide loans to those people whom they had previously ignored so that the beneficiaries could increase the productivity of their land (through crop loans) and the number of their assets (through animal and other loans).

The targeted people were the marginal farmers, landless, artisans, and fishermen who comprised about 80 per cent of the population. Initially the DSSSS and the Salvation Army provided the financial collateral through their own credit-union schemes, but later, as the credit unions became trusted by the banks, the DSSSS and the Salvation Army ceased providing collateral and diverted their funds elsewhere. The DSSSS, with more funds, started education and mother- and child-care programmes; set up and stocked four dispenseries and six nursery schools in the remoter coastal villages and also started alternative employment-training programmes (rickshaw-plying, petty vending, sewing and other small trades). They had also set up a small non-profit-making agri-business providing subsidised agicultural inputs and animal services for the small and marginal farmers (Kumar 1982).

Sadly, in late 1982, the Salvation Army pulled out of its area by the coast due to internecine bickering over the leadership of the project and, although the DSSSS were able to take over some of the programmes, most of the people in the three villages (10,000 people) were left without support. The Salvation Army programmes collapsed as soon as the banks had regained their outstanding loans and within six months of leaving, it seemed as if the Salvation Army had never been in the area; the only evidence being a few cross braced huts in a compound overrun by vegetation and thorn bushes.

The presence of the NGOs and the large quantities of goods and money that came into the area following the disaster had little effect on the existing power relations, but it did alter (temporarily) the vice-like grip of the moneylenders. Other changes occurred as well. The villagers were taught to become aware of their civic and legal rights *for the first time* by the DSSSS and the Salvation Army through "conscientisation" programmes, as a result of which a number of "village committees" were formed (*only* in the DSSSS and the Salvation Army areas) which temporarily altered the hold of the large landlords (from now on called large farmers) on employment and the supply of informal credit (see Table 3.5). The village committees could not alter the social relations of production in any substantial way but their presence was a visible sign to the government, and the banks in particular, that illiterate uneducated people were capable of organising themselves for their own good in a manner that did not overtly challenge the government or the people they relied on in the villages. As a result, people in villages with village committees received substantially more loans than people in villages without such organisations.

The scale of the DSSSS and the Salvation Army work never at any time threatened the dominance of the large farmers mainly because the DSSSS and the Salvation Army were even-handed in their work, not restricting their services to any one particular group but offering them to all, and also because the help they gave was relatively small-scale. The large farmers were not interested in the small loans that the DSSSS could arrange through the banks (up to Rs 1,500) or in the relatively small amounts of fertiliser and other agricultural inputs that the DSSSS could supply (on a rationed basis for people with up to 2 acres) because the large farmers were looking for loans of Rs 10,000 and fertiliser for 5 acres or so. As a consequence, the large farmers (the power-brokers) remained relatively uninterested in the activities of the DSSSS and the Salvation Army, and tolerated their presence.

NGO programmes are usually very small in scope and geographical extent and benefit only a very small percentage of populations, usually just one village or perhaps a small group of villages. Where the programmes become larger in scope and extent and cover populations of 25–50,000, they tend to encounter hostility from the ruling groups, unless they are as politically adroit as the Jesuits. But even political skill does not guarantee success, since village and local politics are so fluid and political allegiances and affiliations constantly change. One NGO (an atheist organisation) 25 miles up the river and working in villages of scheduled castes, solved this problem by its chief members marrying into local political circles, but this is unusual and provoked considerable hostility from the other NGOs who accused them of "selling out".

Some of the NGOs were skilful in attracting publicity to the area, especially the Jesuits whose work benefited all groups (not just the target groups) and articles on the "Miracle in Divi" became a regular feature in the local Press. Every month or so a new project involving "joining the people to the banks" was initiated and ministers and officials came down, had their photographs taken with the recipients, attended the official lunch, made a few more speeches and left in a flurry of promises. As long as the NGOs were in the area the villagers knew that they had a link to the outside world and could put some pressure on the government to improve their conditions, which the DSSSS encouraged through their "conscientisation" programmes. One possible outcome of the presence of two such positive NGOs in the area was that for the first time ever, water for a second crop reached the tail-end lands. This might have been the result of the attention the area was then receiving in the Press. But neither the innovation nor the attention lasted. Perhaps the most important change in the pre-existing power relations were the new links forged between groups of villagers with the banks (Appendix 2.1) which temporarily changed the political and factional allegiances.

The quantum leap that occurred in the numbers of assets being owned from before the cyclone to the end of 1982 and the increase in the number of households owning assets (80 per cent of the sample) is partly reflected in Table 4.5; the increases being due to the massive infusion of bank credit into the rural areas as part of Government policy through the IRDP schemes, *and the vigorous intervention of the DSSSS and the Salvation Army.*

By the end of 1982 the efforts of the Government and the NGO schemes had resulted in bringing more land into cultivation and although the dominant group of cultivators had not increased the average size of their land holdings, the other two groups had. Through the conduit of animal loans all three groupings had increased the average number of their assets, the cultivators by about 10 per cent, the cultivator/agricultural labourers by about 15 per cent and the others (mainly the fishermen and landless) had increased theirs by about 25 per cent. These changes in the first phase of development can be seen in Table 4.5.

4.2.2 Phase Two: 1983–88

In March 1985 the DSSSS left the area. Their attitude all along had been that the "people must stand on their own feet" (Kumar 1982: 1), but unfortunately

TABLE 4.5: *Changes in the mean distribution of assets and resources in a 202-household sample, classified by occupation, 1977–81*

Occupation	Size of household		Land holdings		Plough teams and carts		Milch animals	
	1977	1981	1977	1981	1977	1981	1977	1981
Cultivators[a] (18)	6.1	6.3	4.9	5.1	3.4	3.9	3.5	4.1
Cultivators[b] and agricultural labourers (108)	4.6	4.2	1.5	1.3	0.5	0.6	1.3	1.6
Others[c] (76)	5.1	4.2	0.4	0.5	0.1	0.1	0.6	1.3

Source: Appendix 2.
[a] Large farmers.
[b] Small and marginal farmers.
[c] Fishermen, mixed occupations, landless.

their premature withdrawal had not allowed time for the village committees (replicas of the society) to stand on their own feet and become established. The result of the DSSSS withdrawal was the swift collapse of the village committees. Only those village committees with outstanding group loans from the banks continued to operate and when the loans had been repaid the committees collapsed because the banks refused to give further credit to the village organisations without the "moral collateral" of the DSSSS. The banks claimed that without the DSSSS the loans would not be repaid. This was a dubious claim but difficult to refute. Repayments by beneficiaries (marginal farmers, fishermen and landless) had been recorded as being over 95 per cent (Kumar 1982: 19) when the DSSSS were still acting as the conduit, but evidently the banks felt happier lending money to the large farmers who regularly defaulted on their loans (personal communication with senior IAS officer, 1991). However, there was another cogent reason why the banks were becoming increasingly reluctant to extend loans to the small and marginal farmers and artisans. By the mid 1980s it had become a custom in state politics for a political party, when elected, to cancel outstanding loans, and the banks claimed they were losing millions of crores of rupees as a result.

At about the same time as the withdrawal of the DSSSS, new men came into the area. They were entrepreneurs from the coastal districts (mainly Kammas from the mainland) and supporters of the ruling political party in the State, (Telegu Desam Party) who, lured by the development that had taken place (all-weather roads and electrification) bought up large tracts in the coastal flat for fish- and prawn-farming. This same land had previously been given as *patta* (freehold) to the marginal farmers and fishermen in the 1960s. In the inland plain the new men bought up land from the small and marginal farmers (cultivator/agricultural labourer households) and took over almost all the remaining common lands, turning them over to coconut-palm cultivation. The result of the introduction of non-labour-intensive "cash crops" was a decline in agricultural employment for the marginal groups (marginal farmers, fishermen and landless) and unfavourable competition for the traditional fish market. In 1985 new political allegiances were formed between the new men and the established Congress (I) parties temporarily changing the old pattern of power relations.

In November 1987, Divi was again struck by a cyclone but not as severely as in 1977. The resulting flooding and considerable damage to the crop, reduced the harvest by 10 to 25 per cent depending on the degree of exposure. The widespread lack of recovery as recorded in the 1988 interviews could have been partly attributable to this cyclone and may have contributed to the pre-1977 cyclone socio-economic conditions observed in a number of households.

4.3 CHANGES: 1977–88

Since we are focusing on change over the 10 years we should now briefly look at how the numbers of vital assets changed over the years without classifying them in any way beyond their numeric values. We will start our examination with land, the most important asset in a rural society.

4.3.1 Landholdings, 1977–88

The overall impression from Table 4.6 is that the situation regarding land has not changed much in 10 years. The number of people not owning land is about the same in 1988 as in 1977 and so are the numbers of people owning land of less than 3 acres. The principal changes are the number of households owning more than 3 acres and the size of their holdings. Within the overall picture we see some interesting changes over the 10 years. Perhaps the most dramatic was the increase in the numbers of households owning land (i.e., the decrease in landless households) and then that increase reversed sometime after 1983.

Table 4.6 shows the gradual increase in the amount of land in cultivation over the 10 years by about 50 per cent (53 acres to 76 acres) in the 42-household sample. The increase was due to factors mentioned above – i.e., more credit aviable in the rural banks and the intervention of the NGOs until the mid 1980s. The decline in the number of households owning land occurs sometime after 1983 which broadly corresponds to the withdrawal of the NGOs.

TABLE 4.6: *Land ownership classified by numbers of owners and extent of landholdings in acres in a 42 case-study household sample, 1977–88*

Year	Nil	Landholding sizes in acres						Total area
		0.1–0.99		1.00–2.99		≥ 3.00[a]		
		n[b]	x̄	n	x̄	n	x̄	
1977	10	14	0.56	14	1.74	4	5.25	53.2
1981	5	19	0.52	13	2.02	5	5.00	61.4
1983	3	18	0.47	15	1.68	6	5.12	64.53
1988	8	12	0.58	13	1.72	6	6.14	76.62

Source: Fieldwork.
[a] The key landholding size is 3 acres which is the minimum amount of irrigated land required by an average household to meet its annual subsistence requirements of 15 bags of rice (75 kg of paddy per bag).
[b] n = number of owners.

The most crucial aspect of the change was the *increase in the extent and amount of landholdings* which were the result of three interdependent factors: (i) more types of land coming under cultivation – i.e., previously uncultivable land given by the government to the economically weakest sections (EWS) in the coastal flat; (ii) a 1,000 per cent increase in the number of crop loans given to all sections *for the first time*; and (iii) the increased use of agricultural inputs (fertilisers, herbicides and insecticides). According to the fieldwork interviews the major reason for the relative decline in the fortune of the poorest households was the withdrawal of the DSSSS. The secondary reason was the failure of the government programmes to benefit groups other than those with resources to take advantage of the ensuing development. The third reason, which hit the poorest groups the hardest, was the 1987 cyclone and its effect on agricultural productivity and lost agricultural employment. The data in Table 4.6 suggest that there was a gradual build-up of households owning land until the mid 1980s and then a decline. In Table 4.7 we shall see the shifting pattern of land ownership more clearly and the inexorable increase of landholdings in those households owning more than 3 acres.

Changes in patterns of land ownership

In Table 4.7 we see that the average size of landholdings held by the group with over 3 acres has increased from 21 acres to 36.84 acres and that this group has increased the area of land under its control from 39 per cent of the total in 1977 to 55 per cent in 1988. We also see a steady decline in landholding ownership in the two other categories, with perhaps the more dramatic being

TABLE 4.7: *Land ownership classified by size and percentage of total in a 42 case-study household sample, 1977–88*

Year	Nil	0.1–0.99	1.00–2.99	≥3.0	Totals
			Landholding size in acres		
1977	–	7.84 (15%)	24.36 (46%)	21.0 (39%)	53.2
1981	–	9.88 (16%)	24.36 (43%)	21.0 (41%)	61.24
1983	–	8.46 (13%)	25.22 (39%)	30.72 (48%)	64.53
1988	–	7.54 (11%)	22.36 (34%)	36.84 (55%)	76.62

Source: Fieldwork.

the 12 per cent drop in land ownership in the group holding between 1.00 to 2.99 acres.

4.3.2 Changes in other assets, 1978–88

Next to land, the other major assets, or investments, in this society are labour – i.e., how many workers in a household – and moveable assets – i.e., farm equipment and animals. Table 4.8 gives a general picture of the changes in the numbers of investments in the 42-household sample over the 10-year period, and we will briefly discuss these changes, starting with the most widely used investment – labour.

Changes in the numbers of workers in households

The livelihood and survival of most households depends on how many people of all ages in the household can go out to work. The first point of interest in Table 4.8 is not the number of people killed in 1977 (just over 25 per cent of the sample) but how rapidly the numbers picked up again by 1981. This came about directly as a result of the many quick marriages that took place soon after the disaster. Men who had lost their wives quickly re-married to make up the lost labour-power and provide a mother for their children, where they survived. In many cases the men re-married and started new families, but women were not so fortunate; those who had lost their husbands did not remarry. Marriages were entirely restricted to the poorer and lower castes. The richer households could afford to wait.

The point of interest about the numbers of workers per household is the overall decline in the *numbers* of workers but *not* the decline in the *average*

TABLE 4.8: *Numbers of investments in a 42 case-study household sample, 1977–88*

	Number of workers in household[a]		Plough teams[b]		Carts		Milch animals	
					Investments			
Period	n[c]	x̄[d]	n	x̄[e]	n	x̄[e]	n	x̄[e]
Pre-cyclone	92	2.4	17	1.4	18	1.1	38	1.6
Losses	24	0.6	11	1.5	17	1.5	38	1.6
1981	91	2.3	11	1.5	20	1.1	41	1.4
1983	90	2.3	19	2.1	19	1.2	50	1.9
1988	81	2.1	18	2.0	16	1.2	42	1.7

Source: Fieldwork.

[a] Numbers of workers are transcribed to a labour-power equivalent as a simplified measure of earning-power units. An adult male is the equivalent of 1.0 units, an adult female or an adolescent male is the equivalent of 0.5 units and an adolescent female is the equivalent of 0.25 units.

[b] Plough teams are pairs of oxen which work as traction animals both for preparing the ground for planting and for transporting produce.

[c] n = total number of workers in 42 households.

[d] x̄ = average labour power estimate per household.

[e] x̄ = average number of investments per investment-owning household.

number of workers per household. The similarity between the average number of workers in 1977–81 and the average number of workers in 1988 indicates that whole households disappeared in the cyclone rather than all households declining a little. According to the interviews the reasons for the decline in numbers of workers since 1983 was a combination of the effects of age and illness in some households and permanent migration in others – we have already noted that three households have disappeared – due to new patterns of employment and the subsequent decline in job opportunities for some (discussed later).

Changes in ownership of farm equipment and animals

It took until 1983 for the *numbers of plough teams* to reach pre-cyclone levels although by then the average size of plough team had increased by 50 per cent on the pre-cyclone levels. Once re-established, the numbers and average size have remained more or less constant indicating a degree of prosperity amongst the large farmers. The *numbers of carts* increased steadily from the drastic loss in 1977 until 1983 when numbers dropped off again, which suggests heavy selling. The reasons for the decline in cart numbers (through selling) are difficult to pinpoint other than to suggest that the cyclone of 1987 affected the small farmers (the majority of cart-owners) worst, many of whom had over extended their credit and diversified into fish-farming. Carts are part of the "fixed assets" of a farm so it is possible that the change in agricultural practices in Divi Seema between 1985 and 1988 is reflected in these figures.

The notable feature about the figures for *milch animals* is the surge in their numbers until some time after 1983 and then their collapse after that time. The 20 per cent drop in numbers is quite serious in terms of asset accumulation, especially since milch animals are the most cost-effective assets that poor people can have and the provision of milch animals through loans was the principal thrust of the Government's anti-poverty programmes, supported whole-heartedly by some NGOs, as we have noted. The decline in numbers in milch animals could be attributed to the two major NGOs pulling out in 1983 and 1985 but milch animals are traditionally "fluid assets" which are bought and sold continually as part of traditional risk-reduction strategies for paying off debts and meeting marriage expenses so the decline in their numbers could be less serious than it might appear. The other traditional risk reduction mechanism for able-bodied people in an agricultural society is migration to which we now turn.

4.3.3 Changes in migration, 1977–88

The most revealing feature of Table 4.9 is the steady decline in migration as affluence spreads until sometime after 1983, and then a reversal back to pre-cyclone levels. Until sometime after 1983 there had been a 30 per cent reduction in the total number of days worked by households migrating for extra work and the total number of days on migration and the average number of days on migration per household had also decreased. The differences in the standard deviation of the mean numbers of days on migration per household between 1977 and 1983 suggests that not so many entire households (two people or more) were migrating for work in 1983 as they had been in 1977. However, these figures show a fairly dramatic reversal of fortunes, which in all likelihood accurately reflects the effect of the 1987 cyclone more than any other factor. This would appear to suggest that cyclone vulnerability measured economically was not far removed from the levels of 1977, but we shall be returning to this in later chapters.

4.3.4 Changes in availability of loans, 1977–88

Before the cyclone all the households in the sample took informal loans (i.e. loans from individuals who lent money) and some had formal loans (i.e. loans from banks) for reasons we have discussed previously (Table 3.5). After the

TABLE 4.9: *Number of households migrating for work and number of mandays per year in a 42 case-study household sample, 1977–88*

Year	Number of households	Number of days	Mean number of man days per household	Standard deviation
1977	30	990	31	8.5
1981	26	738	28	13.2
1983	22	618	28	15.1
1988	28	870	32	9.6

Source: Fieldwork.

cyclone that situation changed, for a while. The presence of the NGOs together with the government's revitalised rural banking policy in the field area resulted in a three fold increase in the number of households with formal loans over the post cyclone period to 1983. At the same time the number of households taking loans from moneylenders decreased (from 42 to 35 and then down to 32) and the amounts declined but not to the extent to show that the grip of the moneylenders had been broken (Table 4.10). The decline in the number of informal loans was directly attributable to the availability of loans through the DSSSS Credit union.

Between 1983 and 1988 the numbers of households with bank loans decreased. After the DSSSS pulled out those households with DSSSS loans were forced to return to the clutches of the informal market, so that by 1988 the position vis a vis the number of households with informal loans was the same as before the cyclone despite 10 years of development.

TABLE 4.10: *Changes in the distribution of formal and informal loans taken in a 42 case-study household sample, 1977–88*

Year	Formal loans		Informal loans	
	Number of households	Average size of loan	Number of households	Average size of loan
1977	11	1135	42	1480
1981	28	925	35	1375
1983	32	985	33	1635
1988	17	1325	42	1750

Source: Fieldwork.

4.4 DIVI SEEMA IN 1988

By 1988 Divi Seema had only partly changed its outward appearance since the cyclone. In late summer, the inland plain would still be a sheet of emerald green criss-crossed by the irrigation canals reflecting the bulging clouds in the blue skies, heralding the rainy season. In late November, after the harvest the plain would be covered by golden stubble, becoming gradually paler as the summer wore on, interspersed with fat haystacks, The only visible changes since 1977 were the intrusion of rows of coconut saplings standing in plantations beside the roads and canals. In the coastal flat things had changed less. The feeling of remoteness and desolation under the vast skies remained and the chequered pattern of the concrete housing colonies in the monotony of the salt marsh were broken only by the presence of the fish farms with their low grassed bunds.

According to those who had lived in Divi before the cyclone the differences between the situation in 1988 and 1977 were very substantial, on the outside at least. Compared with pre-cyclone days, the degree of affluence was the most noticeable change. Better road communications had resulted in the expansion of the markets in Nagayalanka, Kodduru and Avanigadda. Since the disaster the amount of money circulating had increased by at least 500 per cent, mainly as a result of the expansion of the credit market and the demand for agricultural and consumer requirements. The general affuence was more evident; most people wore better clothes and almost every male wore a shirt. There were five cinemas on the island and there were also tea shops in the remote coastal villages which would have been unheard of before 1977 when there were no shops at all in the coastal areas and tea had been a luxury only available in Avanigadda.

From the comments made during the interviews and from the findings themselves, a picture emerged. The main feeling among the respondents was that there had been a return to the *status quo* of 1977 manifested mainly by a decline in wage-labour opportunities resulting from the alternative land uses and the increase in minimally labour intensive cash-crop activities. The economic and spatial marginalisation of the landless and small and marginal farmers appeared to have continued, claimed by several interviewees to be the result of the influx of entrepreneurs taking over the previously uncultivable land (i.e., common grazing and forestry land) for cash crops (fish farms and coconut plantations).

From the interviews and the analysis of the findings, there would appear to have been a return to the high levels of dependence on moneylenders' credit, despite the 10-year presence of the banks, during seven of which they were working closely with the DSSSS. We discovered that the banks were unwilling to make loans to the small agricultural and artisan groups for a variety of reasons, mainly from fear of defaults, and the poorest households said they found it easier and more convenient to go to moneylenders in any event, and in their case, it was no more costly, taking into account the time wasted waiting outside offices and the payment of bribes (*moomulu*: the word for custom in Telegu) at each step of the procedure.

A distressing find, borne out in the detailed figures of the 42 case-studies presented in the next chapter, was the continuingly exhorbitant costs of medical treatment despite the presence of government clinics and the increase in the number of para-medical personnel on the island since 1977. The proportional cost of medical treatment per year had remained about the same – i.e., in many cases the poorest households could still spend about 50 per cent of their annual income (Rs 3,500–5,000) for treatment of illnesses and ailments requiring medical attention and minimal hospitalisation.

There had been little overall change in the standards of road communication to the villages in the coastal flat since 1977 although there had been an improvement for two or three years after they had been constructed. Ever since the bus companies had changed from being state run to privately run in 1986 the buses had only operated on the metalled roads. The poor state of the non-metalled (*katcha*) roads in 1988 suggested that plans to evacuate coastal populations in the event of future cyclones, especially if the need arose after a prolonged rainy period, might be problematic.

There was a general feeling among all but the better off households that there had been an increase in risks associated with agricultural activities, the reasons given being the decline in productivity as a result of the increasing costs of fertiliser and other inputs. Another example of the increase in agricultural risks for all but the better-off was the perennial dependence on irrigation water, its distribution still being governed by the powerful sections in the community. However, the villagers felt that these risks were to some extent offset by the migration of poorer households for work on the mainland, equivalent in their estimation to the number of days they used to go for work on the mainland before the 1977 cyclone, although in the mid 1980s the incidence of Divi people migrating had declined. The risks associated with agricultural activities were further reinforced by the general decline in wage labour in agricultural production, although wage rates had doubled since 1977, due to more land being cultivated by tractor and more land being used for the cultivation of cash crops (growing coconuts and fish- and prawn-farming).

The risks associated with non-agricultural activities for the less well-off groups were also felt to have increased. For instance the fishermen in the sample claimed that the traditional dried fish market at Nagayalanka (where the fishermen brought their fish) had been undermined by the people who owned the new fish and prawn industry, because the new men had the money to use refrigerated lorries and had skills in marketing that the traditional fishermen were unable to match. The land that had been given to the landless groups in the 1960s and 1970s had been taken over by these new groups (who were also leasing land from the large farmers), because the government failed

120

to supply additional inputs for the development of the land (credit, training, equipment etc.) and this was claimed to be another reason why migration had increased again to the 1977 levels.

It was also felt that the less-advantaged groups in the population were as physically vulnerable to future cyclones as they had been in 1977 and many households cited the 1987 cyclone as proof. They pointed to the deteriorating roads, and the fact that the sea wall had been breached in several places meant to them that if another storm surge occurred and the sea flooded the land then the remaining sections would hold back the retreating waters and flood the land for longer. (In fact this is what happened in 1990). Some villagers claimed that the underprovision of health services and the increasing cost of medical attention was a serious threat to their economic vulnerability, and their feelings about this underprovision were made more bitter by memories of the four DSSSS health clinics they had attended for several years.

The marginal value of housing provision was made quite evident during the course of the 1988 interviews. The aims of the concrete housing programmes had been durability and safety but there was little evidence of this in at least 50 per cent of the houses in the housing colonies that we observed in 1988 and little to suggest that their provision had made any contribution to the economic recovery of their owners. The power of symbolism and imagery in housing was still in the minds of the people after 10 years and most of those interviewed still wanted *pucca* houses *for status reasons* although the villagers could see many of them in a state of collapse all round them.

The community cyclone shelters had proved to be a mixed blessing in the 1987 cyclone. Thirty-two of the 42 households used them, but some were excluded on caste grounds (as predicted in 1978), and the others could not get in because there was not enough room. In one case (*Mandapakala*) the shelter was not used because the villagers thought it was unsafe. By and large the shelters served their purpose and justified the claims made by the government and the donors who provided the funds for their construction.

4.5 SUMMARY AND REASONS FOR CHANGE, 1978–88

Having broadly traced the events in Divi Seema over the 10 years since the cyclone and having seen a moving picture of a very small number of households, we are left with a number of questions, two of which are more germaine to the discussion than perhaps some others. These two questions are: what effect did the government interventions have on the population? And what effect did the NGO interventions have?

On the whole, it would appear that the government's interventions had reinforced the social and power relations of the pre-cyclone days. The aims of the government had been to attract more investment into the area by making it and its population safer than they had been in 1977. And they had succeeded in this to some extent. But it would appear that they had not altogether thought through the consequences of their policies, because, the groups that seemed to have benefited from their protection policies (infrastructure and physical protection) had been the larger farmers, the new men from the mainland, shopkeepers and traders but **not** the small or marginal farmers, artisans, fishermen and landless. In effect their policies were repeating the same patterns that we saw in the historical development of the area, which we concluded was the principal cause of the widespread vulnerability which the cyclone had uncovered in 1977. Judging from the large gaps in the working year claimed by the majority of the interviewed households, the government had not been able to introduce any alternative employment either.

What effect did the NGOs have, and the DSSSS in particular? In the first place they had raised the living standards of thousands of people, perhaps only marginally, but enough to make the people feel that life could indeed be better than it had been before the cyclone. It is impossible to prove but it is extremely likely that without the vigorous and whole hearted intervention of the two major NGOs the standard of living for these thousands would **not** have improved, however temporarily, and so their interventions had been positive. They had given the people hope and taught them that they could stand up for their rights; they had offered an alternative to oppression, exploitation and destitution and dependence on the large farmers, albeit temporarily, but, after they had packed up and left the memories they left behind were mixed. The better off households who had had the least to do with them, did not miss them although they were appreciative of the work they had done for the other villagers. The poorer households were bitterly disappointed at the departure of the DSSSS, having become quite dependent on them, although of course that had not been the DSSSS's intention. They were pathetically grateful for the programmes that the DSSSS had initiated and they wished they would come back.

To conclude the chapter, we will summarise the reasons that seem to have affected the changes we have recorded here; in the next chapter they will become variables. The aim of the subsequent analysis is to find out which of these variables are the most relevant in explaining differential vulnerability but at this stage they are not ranked.

The reasons for the INCREASE or DECREASE in asset levels (land, other assets and household numbers) were attributable to:

1. the benefits or penalties of **location** and whether households lived on high or low ground and the extent to which their village or house site was protected from high winds, sea and/or land flooding;
2. the benefits or penalties of **area improvement** in the form of new and improved roads and irrigation, electrification and the provision of amenities and facilities;

3. the benefits from the extent and nature of **Government intervention** in the form of subsidies and housing provision and the penalties associated with their withdrawal or diminution;
4. the benefits or penalties attached to the availabity of **credit** from the formal and informal markets;
5. the benefits from the extent and nature of **NGO interventions** in the form of loans, training, health care, education, awareness-of-rights programmes and housing provision and the penalties associated with their withdrawal or diminution;
6. the opportunities for expansion and diversification in **employment**;
7. the benefits of **household changes** in terms of health, the numbers of people working, labour-power and worker-dependent ratios and the penalties arising from misfortunes within households through natural cycles, the incidence of illnesses and the subsequent cost-penalties of reduced labour power, increased expenditure on medical treatment, lower worker-dependent ratio, permanent migration and in some cases the breakdown of households through divorce or desertion.

Testing the Model

5.1 THE MODEL

In this chapter we will be focusing on individual households and their characteristics, and the key relationship between those characteristics and the context in which households live. This relationship largely determines the vulnerability of households to all internally or externally generated shocks. Since the discussion centres on the Conceptual Model of Vulnerability we present it again to illustrate this relationship (Figure 5.1).

Until this stage we have described the fortunes of the 42 case-study households by tracing the total numbers of their assets and how they changed over

FIGURE 5.1: *A conceptual model of vulnerability*

	CLIMATE	
PHYSIOGRAPHY	SOCIAL RELATIONS OF PRODUCTION	DEVELOPMENT POLICIES
PRODUCTION		CONSUMPTION
	EXCHANGE	
	↕	
	HOUSEHOLD CHARACTERISTICS	
	Investments	
Assets	Claims	Stocks
RISK-REDUCTION STRATEGIES		RISK-DIFFUSION STRATEGIES
	HOUSEHOLD VULNERABILITY	

time. Now we test our conceptual model of vulnerability by looking in more detail at the 42 case-study households in terms *of all their assets* and we relate the patterns of accumulation or depletion, if possible, to their household characteristics and see if particular characteristics or combinations of them can they tell us more about vulnerability. The data and the reasons why they were collected have been described before but now they are classified as variables and grouped according to their explanatory or descriptive power. The variables that might tell us why some households fare better than others and which focus on the *characteristics of households* are called **explanatory variables** (or dependent variables). The variables that describe what households have by way of the value of their *Investments* – assets, claims and stocks (according to the model outlined in Chapter Three) – are called **response variables** (or independent variables).

The **explanatory variables** that have been chosen reflect some of those household characteristics that affect the economic well-being of a household over time and its position in society. They are as follows:

HOUSEHOLD CHARACTERISTICS

Location

Family type
Caste
Occupation
Housetype (see below under "Assets")

Numbers of workers in household
Number of non-workers to workers (worker-dependent ratio)
Numbers of deaths in the cyclone and since
Number of illnesses since cyclone
Size of dowries

Some of these variables are coded by category (location, through to housetype), some by numbers (numbers of workers, worker-dependent ratio, number of illnesses) and some by size (dowries).

The **response variables** that have been chosen have been grouped according to the definition of investments in our model (Assets, Claims and Stocks) and are measured in Rupee income-equivalents (discussed shortly). They are as follows:

ASSETS
House
Landholdings
Main and second occupation
Migration
Assets generating income
Assets supplementing income

CLAIMS
Government intervention (subsidies, housing)
NGO intervention (loans, housing, training)
Credit from banks and informal market

STOCKS
Bank accounts
Surplus from cultivation
Jewellery
Food stores

The classifications in Figure 5.2 are arbitary to some extent because some variables can appear under two or even three headings (e.g., housetype) and we would not claim that the classifications represent more than a convenient way of linking the larger-scale conceptual model to the specific detail of an individual household (for instance, the variable "credit" is a direct reflection of creditworthiness which is as much a function of the production/exchange/consumption relationship as it is a function of the social relations of production). Figure 5.2 ties the explanatory and response variables into the overall conceptual model.

FIGURE 5.2: *Relationship between explanatory and response variables and the conceptual model of vulnerability*

Model	Explanatory variables	Response variables
Climate and physiography	Location: exposure to wind, sea and ground flooding; environmental improvement	
Social relations of production	Occupation	Credit; NGO intervention
Development policies		Government intervention
Production/exchange/ consumption		Main occupation; secondary occupation; credit
Household characteristics	Family type; caste; numbers in house; numbers of workers; life-cycle changes; illnesses	
Investments		House; land; assets; stocks
Risk-reduction and risk diffusion strategies	Dowry costs	Migration

5.2 MEASUREMENTS OF DIFFERENTIAL VULNERABILITY

Having grouped the variables, the next most important decision was how to measure *differential* vulnerability, not how to measure vulnerability for which there is a wide choice. The more conventional methods of measuring vulnerability ignore **differential** vulnerability and simply measure physical and economic vulnerability in terms of the value of property losses, the value of damage to buildings, the numbers of people killed and so on. Although the differences in the scale of losses will point up differences between groups and households the effects of losses will remain submerged. From these measurements, losses can be predicted according to degrees of exposure, proximity to a hazard, the strength of the hazard and so on and are easy enough to calculate. The more conventional methods of measuring vulnerability also depend on classifications of populations according to socio-economic groupings using occupation, housetype, caste (in India) and location (particularly in urban areas) amongst others as the principal criteria. The main drawback of these measurements is that they give little idea of the *relative impact* of losses and therefore vulnerability. There is no difficulty in finding classifications *separately*; the difficulty lies in combining classifications in such a way that households who do not fall conveniently into any one classification are not missed out in development programmes – as well as finding a method of measuring the differential impact of losses.

There are several techniques of risk mapping and impact assessment currently used in disaster studies (UNDRO 1978; 1979a, *inter alia*). Most of them are technically biased and depend for acceptance on their capability of measuring physical phenomena. These techniques often have the deceptive blandness of a jet fighter's wing and as a result ignore the fundamental complexity of life and in so doing simplify reality. The task here is to try and present a picture of reality and some of its complexity while at the same time trying to keep such an exposition simple.

5.2.1 Income-equivalents

One way of combining all assets, claims and stocks into one measureable unit is to measure them by their *income-earning capacity* and convert them into **income-equivalents**. There have been few if any analyses based on income-equivalents in disaster studies, probably because calculating incomes is hazardous in itself and also because income estimates require long periods of time for verification and the nature of disaster research and the relative infrequency of a disaster in the same place tends to preclude long-term studies.

In this case we have been fortunate enough in having had the time to confirm which were the most relevant indicators of incomes to use and to verify income-equivalents. Notional and real incomes and income-equivalents are widely used by economists when they want to show the relationship between households and poverty measures – for instance, the Economically Weakest Sections (EWS) in India are defined by income, and they also provide a picture of the *overall* economic state of a household which can indicate the value of such intangibles as skills, education and so on which reflect the subtleties of everyday life that an inventory of assets may not. Income-equivalents also provide a means of comparing the overall conditions, economic status, strengths and weaknesses of different households; another advantage is that income-equivalent losses can be estimated from asset losses; for example the loss of productivity of two acres of land by sandcasting after a storm surge and the death of a wage-earner can both be calculated in income-equivalents and in this way the effect of the losses and the relative vulnerability of a household can be assessed quickly. All income-equivalent calculations have been based on wage rates and prices prevailing in October 1981.

The use of income-equivalents is essentially an attempt to estimate the income capacity of an asset. The process is one of *conversion* and there are a number of problems, which we discuss shortly. We want to make it perfectly clear that we have converted the earning capacity of assets and other resources into income-equivalents, **not** actual incomes, for the sake of getting as total a picture of households as possible. The income measures that are notoriously difficult to estimate are real incomes, not least because they can be difficult to confirm and also because many assets do not produce money as such and therefore have to have an income-equivalent applied to them. Providing it is clear that we are using income-equivalents to represent investments then the reader should only be further aware that claims about investments were double and treble checked in the field. Double-checking in rural India is much easier that one might suppose. First of all, Indian official statistics are of a very high order of accuracy; secondly, the standard of Indian academic research is of the highest order; thirdly and probably more relevant, it is relatively easy to get information about a household's investments from immediate neighbours, village elders, caste leaders and sometimes the village officials, since nothing is secret in an Indian village and exaggerations one way or the other can be ironed out, as well as running sensitivity tests on the data (Winchester 1986: 217).

5.2.2 Household groupings

Having decided to use income-equivalents as the measure of the extent of households' investments, our next decision was how to group the households to achieve our aim of finding out if we could measure vulnerability using the conceptual model, and, if so, if we could then predict vulnerability. Vulnerability would be ascertained first by measuring the effects of a range of losses on households and secondly by measuring the recovery of households over a period and we decided to use two criteria by which to gauge the effects of losses and recovery measured by income-equivalents. The criteria were (1) the *relative differences in the income-equivalents of their investment* over the whole period or between specific dates; and (2) the *total income-equivalents of all their investments* over the whole period or for specific dates. Both criteria are needed because relative differences would provide a picture of change which is a vital clue to past and future vulnerability, and totals would provide an economic hierarchy (EWS, for example) from which other groups could be identified.

The first method was to group households over the whole period according to the relative differences in their total income-equivalents from all investments from before the cyclone to 1988, and secondly according to the total value of their investments in 1988. These households are discussed at some length later in this chapter. Using the two criteria we also decided to look at other households that had commonly perceived characteristics of vulnerability such as those with a high incidence of ill-health, low asset numbers, low labour-power (Chambers 1983: 108–34), and also those households living in the most exposed positions, those provided with free concrete houses, those with the highest absolute losses in 1977, those with the highest relative losses in 1977, and those whose assets have declined since their peak in 1983. These households are discussed in Chapter Six. Our aim throughout has been to find out if some groupings of households had particular characteristics in common which could help us predict vulnerability and if these characteristics could be traced to internally-generated causes (accidents of birth or location, illness, life cycle demands) or externally-generated causes (cyclones, area development, policy changes).

We considered a number of parametric and non-parametric statistical procedures to test degrees of association between the explanatory and response variables, but decided not to use them for two reasons. First, the sample is too small to produce a normal distribution and secondly the data were not precise enough due to their very nature and also because the data set is based on conversions from observations of numbers into a common measure of income-equivalents. Results from sophisticated statistical procedures are only as good as the quality of the data that are used and apart from some correlations we present the findings in cross-tabulated form with a few tests for probability. The analysis uses rudimentary economic measures and descriptive statistics to present the more detailed picture of what has happened to the 42 households over 10 years.

5.2.3 General problems in collecting data on households

The first difficulty in gathering and assembling data for households lies in identifying households as separate measurable economic entities and in identifying what investments they own or share or have claims to. These difficulties more or less revolve around what sort of family type the household is. The second difficulty lies in putting a value on those investments and centre on how to convert assets (owned or shared) into income-equivalents.

We discussed family types briefly in Chapter Two (section 2.4.3), but identifying family type is an important factor in data collection and we should remind ourselves of them again. The two types of family in rural India are the *extended* family (co-parcenary) and the *joint Hindu* family. There is a third family type which we in the West would call the *nuclear* family, where a family lives on its own and not in the same village as its other family members, but this is a rare occurrence in the rural areas and we found none in the 1981 survey of 202 households.

In our survey we found that all the interviewed households had family members living in the same villages, and the strength of the household unit was often directly reflected by its physical proximity to other family members. Being aware of the problems of measuring households that shared assets and labour, we would first try to establish the family type of the household. If it was an extended-family type household we would ask questions which would focus onto the aspects of sharing assets and so on. In all cases, the other family members were only too keen to be included in the discussions and in this way we were more or less able to fix a value on the assets the particular household owned and had claims to.

The most common family type in the villages was the extended family, which reflected the custom of living in single-caste hamlets or villages. In these villages, clumps of relatives all live close to each other forming a more or less homogeneous support group. When one interviews one household in a row of houses in which say four other brothers have their houses it is difficult to know whose investments you are counting. An extended family is not so different from a family that has all its immediate family members in the same village but live apart from them, so care is needed to find out just what investments a family has. It is often difficult to measure the economic status of a household in an extended family because the network of its economic and social relationships is very complex and has no hard-and-fast boundaries. A household in an extended family is generally regarded as the strongest household economically and is identified here as a household where family members, such as parents or siblings, live next door or close by, sharing entitlements to land or other assets. The households live separately and own separate assets but share some of them among the other households in the extended family.

A joint Hindu family is one household in which two families live as one under the same roof and sharing the same food, because in many cases they cannot afford to live separately. A joint family is not always less well-off than a household in an extended family; in some cases two families live as one household because there is not enough land to put up a house nearby for the second family (usually a son or daughter). A joint-family household is generally less strong economically than an extended-family household but it can also benefit from the common use of family labour and investments. Family type is used as an explanatory variable but in the event it had little significance on the changes we recorded (see Chapter Six).

Households also change from being households in an extended family to being one in a joint family as a result of internal events (life cycle) and external events (a cyclone can destroy the house of a family member who then moves in with its kin), which further complicates the possibilities of establishing the economic well-being of a particular household over time. Many households radically alter their internal structure over time and the following examples may indicate some of the complexities of classifying households. A household in 1981, living separately but part of an extended family, composed of a husband and a young wife (replacing the one killed in the cyclone) with a 12-year-old son and 8-year-old daughter had changed into a joint household by 1988 as a result of the son marrying and bringing his wife to live with his parents and the unmarried daughter – a change from two workers in the household to four workers. Another household in 1981 composed of an elderly man and his elderly wife living with their nephew in their own hut (their sons and daughters being married and living nearby or elsewhere) had changed radically by 1988 as a result of the old man dying and his widow going off to live with her son next door and leaving the house to the nephew with his new ailing wife and baby. The household was still virtually an extended-family type household but had changed its economic base from three workers to one and a half.

In all cases we recorded what had happened to the household – i.e., the people living in the house. People rarely sell up and leave a house unless it is to get married, so that even if the composition of the household changes over time one is still tracing the fortunes of the *same family*. Where we discovered (in three cases) that a household had moved away from the area entirely by 1983 we abandoned the case study and chose another household.

5.3 TESTING THE MODEL

At the beginning of the chapter we outlined the criteria by which we would group households according to the relative differences in the income-equivalents of their investments and the total income-equivalents of their investments. From the analysis of the *relative differences* in the income-equivalents of investments, two clear categories of household stood out; (i) those that had *substantially increased* their income-equivalent in rupees from all their investments by over 50 per cent in the 10-year period (15 households); and (ii) those households that had increased the income-equivalent of their investments by not more than 10 per cent in the 10-year period (11 households). Allowing for some degree of error in the data and in its conversion, this amounts to a probable *decrease* in equivalent incomes so we have classified these households accordingly. The remaining 16 households have been excluded from the analysis.

From the analysis of the total income-equivalents from all investments, two clear categories stood out: (i) those households standing at the lower end of the range (median of 42 household sample Rs 38,500) whose total income-equivalents from investments from pre-cyclone to 1988 were below Rs 35,000 (14 households); and (ii) those households who were clearly at the other end of the range whose total income-equivalents in the four years taken exceeded Rs 50,000 (nine households).

5.3.1 Explanatory variables

HOUSEHOLD CHARACTERISTICS

Location
Family type
Caste
Occupation
Housetype (see below under "Assets")

Numbers of workers in household
Numbers of deaths in the cyclone and since
Number of illnesses since cyclone
Size of dowries

Location:
The place where a household lives is often the key factor in shaping its economic well being. Location in Divi governs the degree of a household's exposure to winds and flooding, and, to some extent location governs the availability of employment opportunities and the provision of facilities. The reader will remember the argument underlying the government's cyclone policies: that **exposure** to winds and flooding largely determines cyclone vulnerability. Since exposure is a function of physiography, we consequently

classify location according to three measures of **Environmental risk** that take physiography into account – its susceptibility to (i) sea-flooding, (ii) wind damage and (iii) ground flooding. The estimate of the value of these measures is calculated on principles used by UNDRO (1978) and others, i.e., each of them is given a coefficient corresponding with the author's judgement (and government estimates) of the proportion of that measure to the total damage likely to be caused by cyclones which is then applied to a figure on a scale of 1–10 that reflects the physical relationship of the household to that measure.

The reader will also remember that a major thrust of cyclone policies is on reducing physical and economic risks by improving the environment and we include three further measures that reflect these policies within the Location variable (improvements to roads, irrigation and electrification and water supply) which we collect under the heading – **Environmental improvement**. The same procedure of evaluating each measure as above is followed except that the coefficients relate to the economic improvement of the area.

The extent of **sea-flooding** is determined by the distance from the coast and the height above sea level. For instance there is a long tongue of land (Tidal Flat – Map 3.2) which runs 12 kilometres inland at the end of which some of the highest casualties occurred. Sea flooding creates the most damage to crops due to sand casting and salinisation of the ground. A 3 metre high tidal bund was in place before the 1977 cyclone but its breaching was a major cause of the extent of casualties and destruction that followed, as we have noted previously (Chapter 4.1). The tidal bund was subsequently rebuilt to five metres in height in 1978 but severe erosion was noted in 1983 and likely points of breaching were recorded in 1988. Most households in the Coastal and Tidal flats are nominally protected by this bund but its deterioration has been taken into account in the calculations. Sea flooding (storm surge or tidal flooding) has been calculated at causing 60 per cent of all damage in a cyclone (coefficient 0.6).

Wind damage is less extensive than sea flooding but it occurs more often. High winds with cyclones cause extensive damage to houses and animal shelters and many animals are injured during a cyclone when their shelters are blown away. Protection from the wind is almost non-existent in the coastal areas whereas some of the inland villages are quite well protected by the bunded roads and most villages are surrounded by stands of broad leaved trees. Subsequently asset losses are significantly lower in the inland areas except that once again the poorest households live on the edges of the villages or in hamlets beyond the sheltering trees. Wind damage has been calculated as causing 20 per cent of damage (coefficient 0.2).

Ground flooding after heavy rains is widespread, with or without a cyclone, due to the high water table and the susceptibility of the soil to waterlogging (Chapter 3.2). Ground flooding is more frequent than the incidence of high winds and sea flooding and causes more damage to houses and animal sheds and less to crops than wind or sea flooding. The exception is that the poorest people have access only to low lying encroachment land that always floods rendering their crop useless in many instances and in many cases they live on encroachment land as well. Ground flooding has been calculated as causing 20 per cent of damage (ceoffecient 0.2).

An overall value reflecting the relationship between the physical location of each household and the three measures of exposure to environmental risks has been calculated in two steps. First the relationship is identified and a value given on the basis of the relationship between the physical location of the household and the environmental risk as an inverse ratio of exposure to risk, i.e. the higher the risk the lower the value of the measure. This value is then multiplied by the damage coefficient. For example a household in the Coastal Flat with high exposure to sea and ground flooding and high winds would have a value of; $2 \times 0.6 + 3 \times 0.2 + 3 \times 0.2 =$ a total of 2.4; whereas a household in the Inland Plain with the low exposure to all three would have a value of $7 \times 0.6 + 6 \times 0.2 + 8 \times 0.2 =$ a total of 7.0. These calculations are made for each of the time periods.

The three major measures of **Environmental Improvement** are those that take into account the **construction of new roads, the expansion of canal irrigation and the supply of drinking water and electricity.** The calculation for the value of a household in relation to Environmental improvement is different to the one above for Environmental risk, in so far as we have calculated a value for each household on the basis of its economic relationship with the three measures of environmental improvement and not its physical relationship. The household is given a value on a sliding scale up to 10 on the basis of the extent to which it has benefited from the measure of environmental improvement, i.e. the more it has benefited the higher the value of the measure, which is then multiplied by a coefficient which reflects the estimated proportional impact of the measure on the economic improvement of the area, i.e. improvement to the roads is taken as being worth 30 per cent of the general improvement to the area (coefficient 0.3), irrigation as being worth 50 per cent (coefficient 0.5) and the provision of drinking water and electricity supply as being worth 20 per cent (coefficient 0.2). For example a household in the Coastal Flat which has not benefited economically from the improvement to roads and irrigation but has from electrification and the supply of drinking water would score say, $2 \times 0.3 + 2 \times 0.5 + 6 \times 0.2 =$ a total of 2.8; whereas a household in the Inland Plain which had benefited from all three might have a score of $6 \times 0.3 + 6 \times 0.5 + 8 \times 0.2 =$ a total of 6.4. The calculations for Environmental Risk and Environmental Improvement are added up for each date and make up a grand total for location.

In many cases improvements to the roads and irrigation system in the Coastal areas had had little beneficial effect on many of the households since they had little land and nothing to sell. One advantage of course was that better roads would make evacuation easier but even by 1983 most of the all weather

TABLE 5.1: *Means of the measures of location of households with least and most differences in total income-equivalents, 1977–88; and lowest and highest total income-equivalents, 1988*

Variable	Households with least differences[a] (11)	Households with most differences[b] (15)	Households with lowest totals[c] (14)	Households with highest totals[d] (9)
Location	45.8	40.1	52.3	41.2

Mean of 42 households: 42.8; median: 41.2; standard deviation: 16.63; range: 24.4–67.9.

Source: Appendix 4.

[a] Households with the least differences (≤ 10%) in total income-equivalents from investments, 1977–88: Households 8, 9, 10, 11, 18, 31, 33, 34, 37, 40, 41.

[b] Households with the most differences (> 50%) in total income-equivalents from investments, 1977–88: Households 1, 2, 3, 5, 14, 16, 17, 19, 22, 24, 29, 30, 32, 36.

[c] Households with total income-equivalents from investments, 1977–88 (below Rs 35,000): Households 3, 8, 9, 10, 22, 29, 30, 33, 34, 35, 36, 37, 38, 40.

[d] Households with total income-equivalents from investments 1977–88 (above Rs 50,000): Households 1, 4, 6, 7, 16, 18, 25, 26, 31.

roads had collapsed and were unuseable after a few days rain. We found that the totals for Location as measured by susceptibility to damage from sea flooding, ground flooding, high winds and environmental improvements correlated negatively with total income equivalents from assets (corr = − 0.242) suggesting that the *absence* of environmental improvement had something to do with high income equivalents from all investments but not enough to be significant. Some idea of the relationship between Location (as measured by environmental improvement) and total income equivalents from all investments and relative differences can be gathered below but the findings suggest Location measured by exposure to environmental risks and environmental improvements seems to have had little effect on economic improvement or otherwise. Depending on their exact location within the village, households in coastal villages scored around 35 and those inland scored around 60. There is considerable difference between the households with the lowest and highest totals, suggesting that those households with the highest totals were spread out between the coastal and inland areas (shown by the large standard deviation) whereas those with the lowest totals appear to be concentrated in the inland areas.

Family type

A third category of family type has been added to the two main ones of extended family and joint family to acknowledge that many households had changed family type over the years as a result of the cyclone. This does not

TABLE 5.2: *Number of family types in households with least and most differences in total income-equivalents, 1977–88; and lowest and highest total income-equivalents, 1988*

Variable	Households with least differences[a] (11)	Households with most differences[b] (15)	Households with lowest totals[c] (14)	Households with highest totals[d] (9)
Family type				
Extended	4	7	7	3
Joint	7	8	7	6
Changed[e]	6	5	5	3

Source: Fieldwork.
[a]–[d] as for Table 5.1.
[e] To take account of changes in households over the period.

appear to have had any significant effect on the fortunes of the household types, as Table 5.2 suggests, and we have excluded family type from the subsequent analysis.

Caste

Caste is an integral part of the social system and some of the complexities of caste associations were discussed in Chapter Three (section 3.2.6). It does not follow that all members of the higher-ranking castes (*Kapu*) are better-off economically than their opposites numbers in other castes and *vice versa*; of the 11 households with the least difference in their income-equivalents, three were *Harijans* (group total 8) and of the 15 households with the most differences in their income-equivalents three were *Kapu* (group total 7); in the 14 households with the lowest total income-equivalents from investments, eight were *Harijans* and two were *Kapu*, and, in the nine households with highest total income-equivalents from investments, four were *Kapu*. The numbers of *Harijans* in the lowest-totals category suggests that caste is significant and we will note caste differences where appropriate later.

Occupation

Occupations were discussed in Chapter Four (section 4.1.3). The six classi-fications (large farmer, small farmer, fisherman, petty shop-keeper or non-cultivator, marginal farmer, and landless) are based on the main occupations in the household and related also to size of landholdings. Occupation associated more positively with income-equivalents of total investments than caste. Of the 11 households with the least difference in their income-equivalents, seven were marginal farmers (group total 16), in the 15 households with the most

TABLE 5.3: *Means of total numbers of workers overall in households with least and most differences in total income-equivalents, 1977–88; and lowest and highest total income equivalents, 1988*

Variable	Households with least differences[a] (11)	Households with most differences[b] (15)	Households with lowest totals[c] (14)	Households with highest totals[d] (9)
Total number of workers	8.6	10.1	8.4	12.0

Mean of 42 households: 10.2; median: 10.0; standard deviation: 3.1; range: 4–17.
Source: Fieldwork.
[a]–[d] as for Table 5.1.

differences in their income-equivalents, six were small farmers (group total 12) and five were marginal farmers; in the 14 households with the lowest total income-equivalents from investments we found eight marginal farmers and six landless (group total 6) and in the nine households with highest total income-equivalents from investments, three were large farmers and four were small farmers (group total 4). These figures suggest that occupation is significant in accounting for differences and we will note occupations in the subsequent analysis, but will not use them as a key variable.

Number of workers in household

The number of workers (labour-power) in a household is generally considered to be a crucial variable in determining a household's economic well-being. Measures of labour-power vary considerably. Here we have recorded the numbers of male and female workers in the household, without ascribing a value to them. Later, when we measure occupation by wages we differentiate between male and female workers and adults and adolescents by the wages they earn which also takes age into some account. There is a positive correlation between the numbers of workers in a household and the total income-equivalents from investments of households (correlation = 0.389) and some association between the numbers of workers and the households ranked highest in both groupings, and we will use this variable in the subsequent analysis.

The number of non-workers related to the number of workers (worker-dependent ratio) has been calculated by dividing the number of non-workers by the number of workers and the overall mean was found to be 0.50. We recorded each household's worker-dependent ratio at the four dates and the average over the 10 years, but there was insufficient evidence to suggest any positive correlation between the worker-dependent figure and improvement and decline, high and low totals. The mean value for households with totals below the median was 0.53 and for those in the highest rank the median was

0.46; the mean value for households that had not improved their relative position was 0.53 and for households that had improved most, relatively, the mean was 0.51. Because this is generally considered to be an important measure, we have retained it in the subsequent analysis.

Number of deaths

The number of deaths has been recorded in two categories; the first is the number of deaths resulting from the cyclone; and the second is the total number of deaths over the 10-year period. The number of cyclone deaths does not appear to have had any significant effect on the economic status of the households as shown in Table 5.4, nor does the number of deaths overall. However, we have retained it in the subsequent analysis because the reduction

TABLE 5.4: *Means of cyclone deaths and other deaths, 1978–88, in households with least and most differences in total income-equivalents, 1977–88; and lowest and highest total income-equivalents, 1988*

Variable	Households with least differences[a] (11)	Households with most differences[b] (15)	Households with lowest totals[c] (14)	Households with highest totals[d] (9)
Cyclone deaths[1]	1.2	1.1	1.1	1.0
Other deaths[2]	2.1	1.4	1.1	1.7

Mean of 42 households: 1.7; median: 1.0; standard deviation: 1.5; range: 0–7.

Source: Fieldwork.

[a]–[d] as for Table 5.1.

[1] Cyclone deaths: mean of 42 households: 1.24; median: 1.0; standard deviation: 1.5.

[2] Total deaths: mean of 42 households: 1.71; median: 3.0; standard deviation: 1.6.

of cyclone deaths is an important feature of government policy and it has considerable bearing on labour-power.

Number of illnesses

The number of illnesses after the cyclone have been classified as any health conditions that prevented someone working for more than one agricultural season and include endemic-type illnesses such as "village fever" and chronic gastro-enteritis. Illnesses have also been classified as conditions of disablement that prevented people from working (in many cases having developed as a result of the wrong treatment or no treatment at all).

There is some association between the numbers of illnesses and differences in equivalent incomes from investments and some between illness and total

TABLE 5.5: *Means of number of illnesses overall in households with least and most differences in total income equivalents, 1977–88; and lowest and highest total income equivalents, 1988*

Variable	Households with least differences[a] (11)	Households with most differences[b] (15)	Households with lowest totals[c] (14)	Households with highest totals[d] (9)
Total illnesses	4.5	2.1	3.6	2.9

Mean of 42 households: 2.8; median: 3.0; standard deviation: 1.7; range: 0–6.
Source: Fieldwork.
[a]–[d] as for Table 5.1.

income-equivalents from investments (see Table 5.5). The low mean ascribed to the households with the most differences suggests at this stage that the low incidence of illness in these households may have been significant in creating their relative improvement and we shall discuss this later. Numbers of illnesses did not correlate positively with any of the response variables; the most positive correlation being between numbers of illnesses and NGO intervention.

One difficulty in trying to look for a causal link between the number of illnesses and economic standing is the fact that the richer households report a higher number of illnesses requiring treatment (because they can afford to have them treated) than poorer households. What a richer household will perceive to be an illness requiring medical treatment would not be considered such by a poorer household, illustrating that perception is dominated by choice. Costs of illnesses were recorded but have not been included in the analysis because there was no way of reliably checking the figures.

Size of dowries

Number and size of dowries appears in Swift's model and has been included as an *explanatory* variable because the giving and receiving of dowries indicates to some extent the mechanisms of one of the risk-diffusion strategies we discussed before and to that end might explain certain patterns of economic behaviour. The size of dowry is a direct reflection of a household's economic standing in society and generally the higher castes can command higher dowries than other castes, but there are considerable variations within the same castes, reflecting economic differentiations precisely and these often cancel out the differences in dowry sizes between castes. The size of dowry to some extent also indicates the social ranking of the household as regards taking part in rites-of-passage ceremonies (births, weddings, funerals). We recorded differences in dowry sizes from Rs 1,000–20,000 (includes land). Not surprisingly, we found that dowry-giving followed predicable patterns and that dowry-giving was positively correlated with total income-equivalents from investments (corr = 0.827) and with caste and occupation.

5.3.2 Response variables

ASSETS
House type
Landholdings
Main and secondary occupations
Migration
Assets generating income
Assets supplementing income

CLAIMS
Government intervention (subsidies, housing)
NGO intervention (loans, housing, training)
Credit from banks and informal market

STOCKS
Bank accounts
Surplus from cultivation
Jewellery
Food stores

The main difficulty in establishing the economic profile of a household by its investments is finding a way to account for the complexity of the occupational relationships, barters and swaps that characterise rural households which do not involve money. The three investments that can be most directly measured in terms of the income-equivalents are: (i) wages from occupations, (ii) assets that generate an income-equivalent from their hire or sale; and, (iii) land which produces an income-equivalent by way of its product that can be used by the household or sold or exchanged. Other investments classified here as producing income-equivalents are loans from the formal and informal credit markets and bank accounts. (The latter are rare, only two households in the original sample of 202 said they had bank accounts.) These can be transformed into income-equivalents but there are conversion problems with other claims such as government and NGO intervention and with houses, gold and jewellery, which we will discuss in more detail.

In the following tables, income-equivalents will be presented in abbreviated form – i.e., a value of 4.4 is the income-equivalent of Rs 4,400. In all cases mean income-equivalent figures are used instead of medians because in most cases the households have been grouped more or less as quartiles or tertiles. The means are a more accurate representation than they would otherwise be if the whole sample range was taken and should be read with the standard deviations and the ranges.

Assets

Housetype

The income-equivalent of a house stems from three possible sources: (i) as savings for one year in the case of the free provision of a concrete house (i.e., the savings of the replacement of a one-pole house costing Rs 1,000 at 1981 prices); (ii) as rental when part of it is used as a shop or let out as an office (large houses only); and (iii) as savings created for a household by having one house shared by two families in a joint Hindu family.

Housetype has been classified here as a response variable because it is possible to calculate it as an income-equivalent – although it could also be classified as an explantory variable in so far as it relates to the socio-economic status of a household. There are many variations within housetype categories which might confuse the outsider, but a good guide to the wealth of a household is the thickness of the external mud wall. Housetype is used in Chapter Six in the calculation of income-equivalents.

Landholding

The income-equivalent of landholding has been based on the net productivity of the land, the figures for landholding deriving from the respondents and then being checked where possible with the village *karnam* and others (next-door neighbours, village elders, and so on); the net productivity of the landholding being the sum of its yield in 75 kg bags at 1981 prices and taking account of inflation (each bag being worth Rs 1,000), less production costs (hiring labour and agricultural inputs). The productivity directly reflects the quality of land – i.e., fertile land can produce from 25 bags per acre – and its title (*patta* – owned outright), leasehold or encroachment). Income-equivalents for leasehold land have been calculated at half the value of *patta* because the landowner on average takes half the net product of the land; income-equivalents for encroachment land have been taken at one quarter to one half the value of *patta* land (according to location) since encroachment land by its very nature is not continually productive land and often produces low yields due to salinity and/or waterlogging.

Several changes in landholding size were recorded over the 10 years. The reduction in landholding size does not necessarily mean a decline in the economic status of the family as a whole. Nearly always, landholdings are reduced in size as a result of giving part of the landholding as a dowry or splitting part of it while the owner was still alive between sons. Even then the previous owner has some sort of claim on the land and is supported by the recipient – for example, in three cases: a widow being supported by her son, and two sons supporting their parents, and in some other cases, giving the land outright to surviving children and being supported by them. Land sales are very rare, almost negligible in fact, and where land holdings have increased they were due to land coming in as dowries (and the household becoming a

TABLE 5.6: *Mean total income-equivalents from landholdings in households with least and most differences, 1977–88; and lowest and highest totals, 1988*

Variable	Households with least differences[a] (11)	Households with most differences[b] (15)	Households with lowest totals[c] (14)	Households with highest totals[d] (9)
Land	3.0	4.1	1.2	14.2
Percentage of total[e]	13	18	11	58

Mean of 42 households: 4.8; standard deviation: 6.1; range: 0.0–27.0.
Source: Fieldwork.
[a]–[d] as for Table 5.1.
[e] Total income-equivalent from land productivity of total sample = 205.

joint family) or, in the case of the large farmers, acquiring land as debt repayments. The decline in landholding sizes that we noted previously sometimes reflected land going out of productivity due to the increasing costs of agricultural inputs and in four cases the owner of *patta* land leased out land because he could no longer afford to cultivate it.

In Table 5.6 we see a relationship that is obvious to all who know rural India reflected dramatically in households with the lowest and highest total income-equivalents. The standard deviation suggests that many households which show the least differences and the least totals have no land at all.

Main occupation

The total income-equivalent for a household from their main occupation is based on the number of people working, and verified in the villages and elsewhere, and amounts to the total amount of wages earned in the calendar year as the principal occupation of the household members – i.e., cultivation, caste trades (potter, *dhobi*, shop-keeper, and fishing). The total income-equivalent reflects the length of time the household members work and excludes wages from migration which are shown separately although totalled up under Assets. Wages for cultivation are based on the figures for agricultural employment in late 1981 (Table 3.3) and are Rs 850 for an adult male and Rs 550 for an adult female agricultural worker. These figures apply to all occupations including the large farmers who do not work for other people (one of the criteria for this classification), but who employ others (as do some small farmers). The cost of employing others has been included in the calculation of the productivity of land.

Wages from caste trades are more difficult to assess but could nevertheless be calculated from the numbers of days worked and the going rate for such work or from the income-equivalents derived from the products of their work (fish, pots and so on). People whose caste trades are their main occupation also

TABLE 5.7: *Mean total income-equivalents from main occupations in households with least and most differences, 1977–88; and lowest and highest totals, 1988*

Variable	Households with least differences[a] (11)	Households with most differences[b] (15)	Households with lowest totals[c] (14)	Households with highest totals[d] (9)
Main occupation	6.5	7.0	6.0	8.7
Percentage of total[e]	30	20	33	22

Mean of 42 households: 3.9; median: 3.6; standard deviation: 2.1; range: 0.0–12.6.
Source: Appendix 4.
[a]–[d] as for Table 5.1.
[e] Total income-equivalent from main occupations of total sample = 157.

worked as agricultural labourers or on their own small pieces of land and wages for these non caste specific activities are accounted for in secondary occupations.

Other factors influencing the income-equivalent of occupations were the time spent working and the nature of the work. Health is an important factor in assessing length of time working and working ability (i.e., nature of the job). Unless a person was severly disabled or too old they would "go for work" in the fields. We were able to confirm which people could work or not by carrying out two of the three surveys during the harvest by direct observation when all but the very old, very young or crippled were working in the fields (three cases in 42 households).

The income-equivalents from the main occupation do not appear to be significant in accounting for the differences between the household groups, although households with the highest totals have marginally higher income-equivalents than the other groups. However, this would be expected since we saw the positive correlation between the numbers of people working in a household and its total income-equivalents from investments (Table 5.3).

Secondary occupations

Secondary occupations are vital determinants of economic well-being in Divi for everyone including the large farmers. A secondary occupation or even a third one is the best practical insurance device that most families have, and one of the reasons for the poverty and hardship that the cyclone exposed was the lack of alternative employment to cultivation for the vast majority of people in Divi. Calculations for income-equivalents are the same as for main occupations.

The income-equivalents from secondary occupations account for the marked

TABLE 5.8: *Mean total income-equivalents from secondary occupations in households with least and most differences, 1977–88; and lowest and highest totals, 1988*

Variable	Households with least differences[a] (11)	Households with most differences[b] (15)	Households with lowest totals[c] (14)	Households with highest totals[d] (9)
Secondary occupation	3.6	3.7	2.4	6.4
Percentage of total[e]	28	19	27	29

Mean of 42 households: 3.9; median: 3.6; standard deviation: 2.1; range: 0.0–12.6.
Source: Fieldwork.
[a]–[d] as for Table 5.1.
[e] Total income-equivalent from secondary occupations of total sample = 157.

difference between households with least and most totals but do not account for the differences in improvements. The standard deviation suggests that second occupations are widespread. Income-equivalents from secondary occupations are about half the totals from occupations.

Migration

The income-equivalents derived from migration were based on the length of time households were away and were verified with neighbours and sometimes with village elders. Wages earned from migration have been calculated from the figures for agricultural employment in late 1981 and allow for inflation (Table 3.3); they are Rs 560 for an adult male for 45 days' work and Rs 240 for an adult female agricultural worker for 20 days' work; adolescents are usually paid half those rates. Income-equivalents are more difficult to assess for migration than for occupations because wages are often paid in kind (food or

TABLE 5.9: *Mean total income-equivalents from migration in households with least and most differences, 1977–88; and lowest and highest totals, 1988*

Variable	Households with least differences[a] (11)	Households with most differences[b] (15)	Households with lowest totals[c] (14)	Households with highest totals[d] (9)
Migration	2.4	2.4	2.7	0.4
Percentage of total[e]	37	21	45	3

Mean of 42 households: 2.3; median: 3.1; standard deviation: 1.8; range: 0.0–5.5.
Source: Fieldwork.
[a]–[d] as for Table 5.1.
[e] Total income-equivalent from migration of total sample = 112.

cooking oil). The negative correlations between income-equivalents from migration and total income-equivalents from investments (corr $= -0.640$) suggests that those people with the most investments do not need to migrate for extra work (providing 3 per cent of the income-equivalent from main and secondary occupations) as the Table 5.9 bears out.

The mean and standard deviation of the overall sample indicates that migration is slightly higher among the poorer households and suggests their continued dependence on it. The mean of 2.4 (an income-equivalent of, say, Rs 600 in each of the four years) for households with the least differences and a mean of 2.7 (an income-equivalent of, say, Rs 680 per year) for households with the least totals conceals an increase in migration in both groups which reinforces the finding of dependence on migration. Before the cyclone the incomes from migration for both household groups averaged Rs 950; incomes after the cyclone averaged Rs 550 and in 1983 (the peak year of NGO and government intervention) incomes averaged Rs 650; by 1988 incomes from migration had risen to around Rs 850 suggesting the dire necessity of migration even after 10 years of development. Incomes from migration in households with the highest totals amount to less than 5 per cent of incomes from land, main and secondary occupations and other assets.

Assets generating income

These are farm equipment – i.e., plough teams (two oxen and a plough) and carts. Calculations for income-equivalents have been based on the numbers of these assets observed per household, allowing for family type and sharing implications, and on their being hired out to non-family members. Plough teams and carts are also "hired out" to family members but income valuations for these transactions become meaningless in the face of the economic complexities within households which an outsider could never pierce, even with a reliable and well-informed interpreter. The calculations are based on the rates of hire and the length of time the assets are hired out during one agricultural year at rates prevailing in 1981; the amount received for hiring out a plough team for the agricultural year 1981–82 was Rs 1,750 (most large farmers have irrigated land that produces two harvests but not all of them have sufficient numbers of plough teams and some animals are ill, or die and are not replaced); the amount received for hiring out a cart for the agricultural year 1981–82 was Rs 750.

Assets supplementing income

Income-equivalents for these assets are based on the number of observed milch animals per household and are calculated on the basis of productivity. Income-equivalents from herding animals have been excluded (three households) because the figures were impossible to verify. The net annual income from one milch animal has been calculated as Rs 1,000 at 1981 prices, but milch animals are bought and sold on a fairly continous basis so annual incomes are difficult

TABLE 5.10: *Mean total income-equivalents from income-generating and income-supplementing assets in households with least and most differences, 1977–88; and lowest and highest totals, 1988*

Variable	Households with least differences[a] (11)	Households with most differences[b] (15)	Households with lowest totals[c] (14)	Households with highest totals[d] (9)
Assets	3.0	5.2	2.2	13.4
Percentage of total[e]	20	15	17	49

Mean of 42 households: 5.5; median: 3.6; standard deviation: 4.9; range: 0.0–23.1.
Source: Fieldwork.
[a]–[d] as for Table 5.1.
[e] Total income-equivalents, income-generating and income-supplementing assets of total sample = 231.

to verify. The ownership of milch animals to some extent reflects the status of a household and in the poorer housholds the income from milch animals is a significant part of their total annual incomes (30 per cent).

We recorded that most milch animal sales took place as a result of having to raise money quickly (a distress sale) to repay a loan to a bank (to be eligible for further loans), but other sales were made because a household wanted to raise money for a dowry, medical treatment, educating a son (never a daughter!) and so on, and the fluctuating numbers of milch animals in households did not always signify poverty or decline.

Summary

There is a very significant gap in the income-equivalents from assets between households with the least and most totals and a significant one between households with the least and most differences. The figures suggest that the asset accumulation may have been succesful in creating the relative improvements, but they do not appear to have helped those households with the lowest totals. Asset numbers fell off dramatically amongst the poorer households (Chapter Four, section 4.3, Tables 4.5–4.8) after the departure of the NGOs and this has accounted for the low figures in the households with the lowest totals.

Claims

We now come to uncharted waters in which our model could founder – the area in which we transform claims into income-equivalents. The reason we are in these waters at all is to explore the possibilities of including claims within the overall picture of differential vulnerability and to reflect the range of differentiation that exists between households. The key to survival in this area lies in power relations, which we discussed earlier and our inclusion of claims is an attempt to reflect these relations and quantify some of their subtleties.

Government intervention (subsidies, housing)
NGO intervention (loans, housing, training)
Credit from banks and informal market

Government intervention

Before the cyclone government intervention in any shape or form was very patchy in this part of the delta, but, some households claimed to have received subsidies, some of which were later verified with the banks. The income-equivalents of subsidies have been put into the calculations but in some cases there was a payment-in-kind component as well. IRDP subsidies reflect the status of a household and varied in size according to the type of land owned (size, ownership and quality) and were targeted at landowners holding more than 2.5 acres of irrigated land (the large and small farmers). Other groups such as marginal farmers, artisans and the landless only received government subsidies after the cyclone as part of the post-disaster rehabilitation programmes.

TABLE 5.11: *Mean total income-equivalents from government intervention in households with least and most differences, 1977–88; and lowest and highest totals, 1988*

Variable	Households with least differences[a] (11)	Households with most differences[b] (15)	Households with lowest totals[c] (14)	Households with highest totals[d] (9)
Government intervention	4.3	4.4	3.2	9.2
Percentage of total[e]	24	21	21	39

Mean of 42 households: 4.8; median: 4.2; standard deviation: 2.8; range: 0.8–13.6.
Source: Fieldwork.
[a]–[d] as for Table 5.1.
[e] Total income-equivalents from government intervention of total sample = 238.

Income-equivalents for the provision of free housing by government apply to 23 households in the sample and are based on savings possible in one year, and attributed equally to government and NGOs. The effects of government intervention in terms of health and education services could not be converted

147

into income-equivalents by any stretch of the imagination. We recorded claims that a member of the household had gained a job as a result of having received a certain standard of education (a minor village official in two cases) or where the presence of a government health clinic had otherwise saved the cost of an expensive journey to the nearest hospital (Vijayawada – 70 km away, Guntur–130 km by road) and the cost of treatment.

The effects of government intervention were to increase the amount of money circulating in the form of credit and some savings in housing costs as the result of free housing provision.

NGO intervention

NGO intervention was decisive in raising the standards of living and the hopes of many households in the disaster area as the evidence in the next chapter will show. NGO intervention took numerous forms which we have discussed before. Here, for the sake of testing the model, we have tried to attribute income-equivalents to various forms of intervention which focused mainly on providing the means for people to secure loans, providing loans themselves and subsidiary services such as housing provision, education and health facilities, training and the "conscientisation" programmes.

TABLE 5.12: *Mean total income-equivalents from NGO intervention in households with least and most differences, 1977–88; and lowest and highest totals, 1988*

Variable	Households with least differences[a] (11)	Households with most differences[b] (15)	Households with lowest totals[c] (14)	Households with highest totals[d] (9)
Non-government intervention	4.3	4.9	4.2	2.9
Percentage of total claims[e]	35	24	36	13

Mean of 42 households: 4.6; median: 4.9; standard deviation: 2.2; range: 0.0–9.5.
Source: Fieldwork.
[a]–[d] as for Table 5.1.
[e] Total income-equivalents from NGO intervention of total sample = 194.

In some cases the NGOs supplied **loans** and income-equivalents have been calculated on the same basis as with credit (see below). Income-equivalents for free **housing provision** are calculated as above. The effects of training programmes and village organisation have been quantified into income-equivalents on the basis of their proven results. For instance, many people in the villages increased their incomes directly as a result of the training programmes instigated by the NGOs *only*, and also in many cases the conscientising programmes which produced the formation of Village Committees enabled many people to get work or loans that they otherwise would never have received. Income-equivalents attributable directly to NGO intervention have been put half under secondary occupations wages and half under NGO intervention. Income-equivalents deriving directly from NGO intervention in the form of training and village organisation are relatively small compared with the figures for land, occupations and assets.

From Table 5.12 we see that NGO intervention does not appear to have had a significant effect in creating differences between the groups of households. Some idea of the scale of NGO intervention can be seen when we compare the estimates of their intervention with those derived from the other variables which we show in a matrix in Appendix 4.

Credit

Credit falls under two headings: *formal credit* – i.e., bank loans; and *informal credit* – i.e., loans from "moneylenders" who are mainly professional moneylenders but can be other farmers, big men and caste fellows (the expression that the loans had come from "inside the village" meant that they came from these, usually unspecified, people). Credit is placed under "Claims" and given an income-equivalent because loans are treated as income by people and reflect creditworthiness (which their vabiety and interest rates do as well).

The three main types of bank loans, the details of which vary considerably according to landholding size and occupation, are: crop loans, animal loans and loans for other activities. The largest in size are crop loans which vary according to the size of landholding (Co-operative Bank for land-owners with more than 5 acres of land, the Indian Bank for land-owners with more than 1.5 acres, the Federal Bank and the Syndicate Bank give loans to land-owners with less than 2.5 acres). The largest in extent are animal loans and these are more or less standardised at Rs 1,000 per animal at a rate of interest of 4 per cent per annum of which Rs 600 have to be repaid in the first year, after which a second animal can be purchased. Since the cyclone, the banks have made other

TABLE 5.13: *Mean total income-equivalents from credit in households with least and most differences, 1977–88; and lowest and highest totals, 1988*

Variable	Households with least differences[a] (11)	Households with most differences[b] (14)	Households with lowest totals[c] (15)	Households with highest totals[d] (9)
Credit	6.9	8.5	5.5	18.3
Percentage of total[e]	23	19	21	40

Mean of 42 households: 9.3; median: 7.3; standard deviation: 6.7; range: 3.0–34.0.
Source: Fieldwork.
[a]–[d] as for Table 5.1.
[e] Total income-equivalents from credit of total sample = 442.

types of loans available, including those for people wanting rickshaws, potters wheels, fishing nets and boats, stock for petty trading, sewing machines and tools. Loans are also now available for buying sheep and goats, chickens, ducks and, in some cases, plough animals. People who earn their livings as dhobis, potters, tinkers, carpenters and ice-vendors or travelling traders are now also eligible for loans and so also are women. None of these people would have qualified for bank loans before the cyclone (and may not still outside the sample area) without the presence of the NGOs, and the saddest finding in 1988 was that most of these loans had been withdrawn by the banks following the departure of the NGOs.

Loans from the informal market are secured by the status of the borrower. The large farmers get informal credit on the strength of the productivity of their land at rates of interest that are competitive with the banks, whereas marginal-farmer and landless households have to secure theirs with jewellery or items of equipment with interest rates varying from Rs 5 per Rs 100 borrowed per month (60 per cent p.a.) to less about Rs 2 per Rs 100 borrowed (20 per cent p.a.). Both types of loans have been lumped together as one here mainly because it was almost impossible to find out exactly what happened to consumption and production loans in most cases.

The figures in Table 5.13 suggest that credit does not account for differences beyond the fact that those with the most investments get the most credit, so that creditworthiness could be a possible measure of vulnerability.

Other claims

Other claims in Jeremy Swift's model (i.e., claims on kin, caste, landlords and big men) were impossible to quantify beyond tracing whether loans came from such people, in which case they have been subsumed under credit, but such claims were noted. Claims on kin and caste extend to loans of all sorts, help with labour and so on. It is not the purpose here to make any comments on the nature of claims beyond saying that they are difficult to quantify and have been left for others to wrestle with and are consequently omitted from the calculations. One aspect of such claims could be measured by dowry size, which we discussed previously. Other claims are far more complex but ubiquitous. Claims by a family member of one household to be supported by the family members of another household are commonplace but difficult to quantify; for instance, a widow who lives separately from her sons nevertheless has full claims on her sons and is supported by them, although in this sample her household of one is calculated separately. A poor family has claims on kin and caste, but the strength of these claims is likely to be only the same value as their own economic status – but not necessarily – whereas a powerful man has full claims on many more kin and caste fellows, which can be more or less predicted.

Other claims on landlords or influential people (large farmers, merchants, elected village officials – i.e., presidents, chairmen of Co-operative Societies and government officials) were impossible to quantify beyond trying to measure the effects of the "favours" these men could give in terms of the authenticity of other claims about the extent of land they had, how long they worked, who with, and so on. Since there are no restrictions on agricultural work in Divi these claims related mostly to favours ranging from using land, water from irrigation, and preference for work.

Stocks

In his model (Figure 2.6) Swift (1989: 11) suggested three "Stores" which should be taken into consideration in any analysis of vulnerability; these were *"food stores*: granaries; *stores of real value*: such as jewellery or gold; [and] *money or bank accounts"*.

We have transcribed food stores into *surplus from cultivation* and given it an income-equivalent. Surplus was quite easy to see. Any household which owned 3 acres or more of irrigated fertile land would have a surplus of paddy. Bank accounts were difficult to verify and only two households claimed them as such.

Gold and gold jewellery are widely-held assets and are most commonly used as collateral for raising *consumption* loans. Nearly all households possessed some gold in the form of jewellery, as part of one of the innate insurance mechanisms within the society, and gold is the most prized gift in a dowry for marriage (all married Hindu women have a *mangalasutra*). One of the reasons why the fishermen refused to evacuate their villages in 1977 was their fear of leaving their gold behind which they had hidden (personal communication with senior IAS officer co-ordinating post cyclone activities in Krishna district 1977). We have not included an income-equivalent for jewellery in our calculations.

5.4 SUMMARY

Looking now to Table 5.14, we can see that some variables had a greater effect in accounting for differences *within* the two household groupings. Numbers of workers and the productivity of land are the most closely associated with degreees of vulnerability as measured by total income-equivalents from investments in 1988 and differences from 1977 to 1988, which is not surprising; but is is surprising to find that location and occupation are not strongly associated with totals and differences, suggesting that occupation may not be such a good indicator of vulnerability after all. It is sad to see that NGO

TABLE 5.14: *Variables ranked in order of greatest influence in accounting for differences in total income-equivalents, 1977–88; within households with least and most differences, 1977–88; and lowest and highest totals, 1988*

Households with strength of association	Households with least and most differences[a]	Highest and lowest total income-equivalents[b]
Most	Number of workers Land productivity	Number of workers Land productivity
Some	Illnesses	Illnesses Secondary occupation Migration Government intervention Credit
Nil	Location Number of deaths Main occupation NGO intervention	Location Number of deaths Main occupation NGO intervention

[a] Over the period pre-cyclone to 1988.

[b] Over the period pre-cyclone to 1988.

intervention does not seem to have much overall effect in these households. The number of illnesses also played a major role in influencing both totals and differences and a clutch of other variables – i.e., secondary occupation, migration, government intervention, and credit. To round off the summary and to introduce the reader to the data presentation used in the next chapter we should compare the total income-equivalents from investments in the four types of household we have been discussing in this chapter.

From Figure 5.3 we can see that except for households with the highest totals, the other three households improved their positions after the cyclone boosting their claim figures (see also Appendix 5). This was a direct result of government and NGO interventions, mainly in the form of credit, but also through housing provision. However, we can also see that households with the least overall differences and those with the lowest overall totals failed to maintain their recovery as well as the others. We should also note the approximately 5 : 1 difference between households at the top and bottom end of the economic scale.

One disturbing feature emerges from our findings so far (Figure 5.3, notes 1–4). There is a marked increase in the total income-equivalent value of claims in the less well-off households as a percentage of their total income-equivalents from investments. This feature will be more closely examined in the next chapter. For the time being we can say that our search has thrown up some

FIGURE 5.3: *Mean income-equivalents from total investments of households with least (– · –) and most (– – –) differences, 1977–88; and lowest (· · · · ·) and highest (————) totals, 1988 as in Table 5.1. The two points marked for 1977 are pre-cyclone (left) and post-cyclone (right)*

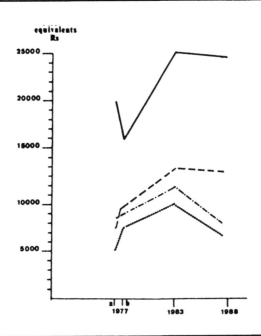

Source: Fieldwork.

Least differences:
  Mean income-equivalents 1977: Assets 5.7; Claims 2.0; Stocks 0.6: Total 8.3.
  Mean income-equivalents 1988: Assets 4.8; Claims 2.8; Stocks 0.6: Total 8.2.
Most differences:
  Mean income-equivalents 1977: Assets 5.2; Claims 2.0; Stocks 0.5: Total 7.7.
  Mean income-equivalents 1988: Assets 7.3; Claims 4.4; Stocks 1.0: Total 12.7.
Lowest totals:
  Mean income-equivalents 1977: Assets 3.8; Claims 1.1; Stocks 0.2: Total 5.0.
  Mean income-equivalents 1988: Assets 3.9; Claims 2.5; Stocks 0.2: Total 6.6.
Highest totals:
  Mean income-equivalents 1977: Assets 11.8; Claims 5.9; Stocks 2.2: Total 19.9.
  Mean income-equivalents 1988: Assets 13.4; Claims 7.9; Stocks 3.2: Total 24.5.

interesting aspects of vulnerability, that might have been passed over otherwise, if we had not included claims as part of total investments, as per Swift, and if we had not used the measure of income-equivalents.

6

The Most Vulnerable Households

6.1 TESTING FOR DIFFERENTIAL VULNERABILITY

In the final stage of the analysis we group households according to three main lines of inquiry which we explain below. In order to know which households are likely to the most vulnerable to the effects of cyclones, we need to be able to forecast the capacity of households to withstand the effects of cyclones by their potential ability to recover from them – and we can estimate this by tracing the recovery of the household groups after the cyclone in 1977 until 1988. In order to predict vulnerability we need to know if households with the least capacity for recovery and the least capacity for improvement have common characteristics. Using the pre-cyclone position as the base line we will see what happened to the different types of household over the period, taking the income-equivalents from their investments as the basic measure, all converted to 1981 prices.

The first line of inquiry focuses on **recovery**. We have chosen four types of households and traced their recovery from before the cyclone to 1988; these were households with the least income-equivalents from assets and households living in the most exposed places before the cyclone, and those households with the highest income-equivalents of asset losses, and the most casualties after the cyclone. We will look for any common characteristics which might indicate a household's ability to recover or otherwise.

The second line of inquiry focuses on **change** and we have taken three groups of households – i.e., those whose income-equivalents increased (i.e., they made gains) within a year of the cyclone, those whose income-equivalents substantially increased from 1983 to 1988, and those whose income-equivalents increased by less than 10 per cent in the same period – to see what, if any, characteristics they had in common.

The third line of inquiry focuses on the **characteristics of vulnerable households** and we have grouped households which would seem to have had the most patent characteristics of vulnerability over the period – i.e., those with the lowest income-equivalents from assets, those with the lowest total income-equivalents in 1988 and the least differences in total overall income-equivalent from 1977 to 1988 – and have compared them with their opposite numbers (i.e., those with the highest income-equivalents from assets, those with the highest income-equivalents in 1988 and the most differences in total overall income-equivalent from 1977 to 1988) to see again, what, if any, characteristics these households have in common.

One household can be put into a number of different groupings and the matrix at the end of each section will illustrate this. For instance, one household might be in a group with the lowest income-equivalents from assets in 1977, the most deaths in 1977, whose income-equivalents increased within a year of the cyclone, with the lowest income-equivalents from assets overall, with the lowest total income-equivalents in 1988 and the least differences in total overall income-equivalents from 1977 to 1988 and in another group with the most illnesses; another household might only be in two groups, say a group whose income-equivalents increased within a year of the cyclone and in a group whose total income-equivalent increased from 1983 to 1988. The purpose of going through these groups is so that at the end of the chapter we can identify the most vulnerable households and describe their characteristics.

We should explain what these income-equivalents mean in relation to living costs. In 1981 the Government of India judged that a household was below the poverty line and belonged to the Economically Weakest Sections (EWS) if its total annual income was less than Rs 3,250 (or 3.25 in the Tables). This would more or less cover the basic costs of living (food, clothing, shelter) but little else. If we add *minimum* medical costs of Rs 250, house repairs of Rs 250 and extras then the income required for a meagre standard of living would have had to have been in the region of Rs 4,000 p.a. (4.0 in the Tables). This sum could not possibly have covered the costs of rebuilding a house after a cyclone or of paying bribes for favours or even of seeing a qualified doctor, so that any attempt to improve the quality of life in terms of better health care, education and the social obligation of taking part in ceremonies and so on would have had to have come from borrowing.

The average income *in a non-cyclone year* in 1981 for an average household whose main income came from agricultural labouring in Divi and migration to the mainland, would have been in the region of Rs 2,500 p.a. with perhaps the income from an animal taking it up to Rs 3,000. If the family had some land then the total income from *all their assets* might have reached Rs 4,000 p.a. but since this was insufficient to pay for any extras or sudden contingencies it explains why the vast majority of the population was permanently in debt. The average size of loans for the lowest-income households in Divi in 1981 was around Rs 1,200 p.a (s.d. 0.58; range 500–2,500) but this could have been increased to around Rs 2,250 if the household had managed to get production loans, so that the total income *including* loans for the poorest households would have ranged from Rs 3,700–5,200 p.a. (3.7–5.2 in the Tables).

From these figures for income and expenditure, we can say that *without loans* the existence of the poorest families would have been precarious. We can broadly group the poorest families into three sub-categories: (i) below the poverty line; (ii) between the poverty line and merely coping; and (iii) able to cope but not able to deal with any outside events such as a cyclone or a poor harvest. Any household with total income-equivalents from *all its investments, including loans*, below the figure of say Rs 4,000 would have been below the poverty line and households with income-equivalents from Rs 4,000–5,500 would have been able to cope with everyday life but would have been vulnerable to any outside shocks. Therefore the income-equivalent figure we want to keep in mind is **Rs 5,500**, but the figure that would signify sufficient resources to cope with the after effects of a cyclone or poor harvest would be in the region of, say, Rs 7,500.

6.1.1   Recovery

Recovery based on income-equivalents from assets, claims and stocks

In Figure 6.1 we examine the recovery of four of the most conventionally vulnerable households by comparing income-equivalents from all their investments from before the cyclone to their position in 1988 in four time periods. The households are (i) those with the least income-equivalents from assets before the cyclone (**least assets** in Figures 6.1 and 6.2; and Table 6.1), (ii) those who lived in the most exposed areas (**most exposed** in Figures 6.1 and 6.2; and Table 6.1), (iii) those who suffered the highest income-equivalent asset losses in the cyclone (**most losses** in Figures 6.1 and 6.2; and Table 6.1); and (iv) those who suffered the most casualties (**most deaths** in Figures 6.1 and 6.2 and Table 6.1).

It is apparent that households who were most vulnerable *physically* (most exposed) were not the same as the ones who were the most vulnerable *economically* (least assets). Households with the most losses suffered approximately a 30 per cent reduction in the their total income-equivalents as a result of the cyclone strike. The other households gained after the cyclone but this was mainly due to doubling the income-equivalents of their claims (see also Appendix 4). Looking at the total income-equivalents from all their investments, it would seem that all groups had improved on their pre cyclone positions, in three cases out of the four reaching their peak sometime around 1983 and declining a little afterwards. This decline could be attributable to the 1987 cyclone but the graphs conceal a number of disturbing trends. One of these is that while the income-equivalent from assets in all groups more or less retained the same relative level, the income-equivalent from claims increased. This suggests a greater dependence by the average size household on government and/or NGO intervention than before.

FIGURE 6.1: *Recovery: mean income-equivalents from total investments of the most vulnerable households, classified by lowest assets (· · · · ·) and highest exposure (– – –), before the cyclone; and highest losses of assets (——) and highest casualties (– · –), after the cyclone. The two points marked for 1977 are pre-cyclone (left) and post-cyclone (right)*

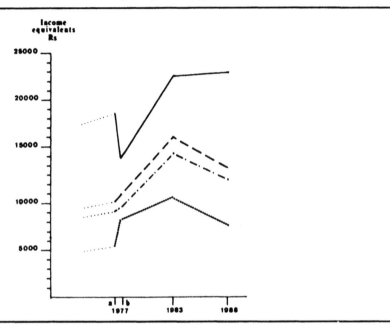

Source: Appendix 3 (Table A 3.2).

Assets: income-equivalents from house, land, principal and secondary occupations and migration.

Claims: income-equivalent from government and NGO interventions and credit.

Stocks: income-equivalent from surplus from land, bank accounts and jewellery.

Income-equivalents from assets of less than Rs 4,500 before the cyclone for households: 3, 8, 15, 19, 22, 27, 28, 29, 30, 32, 33, 34, 35, 36, 37.

Mean locational value less than 30.0 for households: 5, 6, 9; 13, 14, 15, 18, 19, 20, 21, 22, 23, 24, 25, 39, 40, 41.

Income-equivalent losses of more than 30 per cent of total *investments* in 1977 for households: 1, 4, 6, 7, 10, 16, 18, 24, 25.

More than two deaths in cyclone in households: 2, 4, 7, 9, 13, 14, 17, 21, 22, 23, 38, 39, 40, 41.

Lowest assets before the cyclone:

    Mean income-equivalents 1977: Assets 3.5; Claims 1.2; Stocks 0.2: Total 4.9.

    Mean income-equivalents 1988: Assets 4.2; Claims 3.0; Stocks 0.4: Total 7.6.

Highest exposure before the cyclone:

    Mean income-equivalents 1977: Assets 6.8; Claims 2.6; Stocks 0.7: Total 10.1.

    Mean income-equivalents 1988: Assets 7.8; Claims 4.9; Stocks 1.0: Total 13.7.

Highest casualties after the cyclone:

    Mean income-equivalents 1977: Assets 11.3; Claims 5.3; Stocks 2.0: Total 18.6.

    Mean income-equivalents 1988: Assets 13.1; Claims 7.5; Stocks 3.1: Total 24.7.

Highest loss of assets after the cyclone:

    Mean income-equivalents 1977: Assets 6.5; Claims 1.9; Stocks 0.4: Total 8.8.

    Mean income-equivalents 1988: Assets 7.8; Claims 3.7; Stocks 0.7: Total 12.0.

Recovery correlated with household characteristics

The reasons for recovery and improvement are a little clearer in Table 6.1. We saw above that the groups with the highest overall income-equivalents were those who suffered the greatest losses and lived in the most exposed areas, while those with the lowest income-equivalents had the least income-equivalent from assets. One reason for the improvement of the first group and not the second could have been the difference in the numbers of workers in the households over the period. If this is so then it tends to reinforce the findings we presented at the end of the last chapter. There is little to indicate that recovery (measured by an increase in total income-equivalent of investments) is related either with the ratio between workers and non workers or with the number of deaths. The highest income-equivalent group also had the most illnesses which tends to confirm that the better-off households reported more illnesses than other groups.

In terms of vulnerablity being related to exposure we see in Figure 6.2 that nine of the 17 households living in the most exposed places also had the highest casualties, confirming the previous correlation between the number of deaths and exposure. Only one of 11 households with the lowest income-equivalents from assets lived in the most exposed areas, while three of the 11 households with the highest losses lived in the most exposed areas – suggesting, perhaps, that the government's hypothesis that the poorest only live in the most exposed places may be askew.

TABLE 6.1: *Recovery: means of measures of household characteristics of the most vulnerable households, classified by the lowest income-equivalents from assets, and highest exposure before the cyclone; and the highest income-equivalents of losses of assets, and the highest casualties after the cyclone*

Household type	Number of households N	Total workers[a] x	Worker: non-worker[b] x	Total deaths[c] x	Total illnesses[d] x
Least assets	15	9.1	0.55	1.0	3.0
Most exposed	18	10.4	0.51	1.8	2.4
Most losses	9	11.4	0.47	1.5	2.8
Most deaths	14	10.9	0.51	2.7	4.3

Source: Fieldwork.
[a] Total number of workers pre-cyclone to 1988.
[b] Worker-dependent ratio pre-cyclone to 1988.
[c] Total deaths 1977–88 including deaths in cyclone.
[d] Total illnesses post-cyclone to 1988.

FIGURE 6.2: *Recovery: matrix showing relationship between the most vulnerable households, classified by lowest assets, and highest exposure before the cyclone; and highest losses of assets, and highest casualties after the cyclone*

Household type	(N)	1	2	3	4	5	6	7	8	9	10	11	12	13	14	15	16
Least assets pre-1977	(15)		★					★							★		
Most exposed pre-1977	(18)					★	★		★					★	★	★	
Most losses in 1977	(9)	★			★		★	★			★						★
Most deaths in 1977	(14)		★		★			★		★				★	★		

17	18	19	20	21	22	23	24	25	26	27	28	29	30	31	32	33	34	35	36	37	38	39	40	41	42
	★		★							★	★	★	★		★	★	★	★	★	★					
	★	★	★	★	★	★	★	★													★	★	★		
	★						★	★																	
★				★	★	★															★	★	★	★	

Source: Appendix 4.

6.1.2 Change

Change based on income-equivalents from assets, claims and stores

In Figure 6.3 we compare the changes in income-equivalents from investments that have occurred in three groups of households: those whose income-equivalents from all their investments increased within a year after the cyclone (**most gains after cyclone** in Figures 6.3 and 6.4; and Table 6.2); those whose income-equivalents from all their investments substantially increased from 1983 to 1988 (**increase 1983–88** in Figures 6.3 and 6.4; and Table 6.2); and those whose income-equivalents increased by less than 10 per cent from all (**decrease 1983–88** in Figures 6.3 and 6.4; and Table 6.2).

It is noticeable that households who continued to improve after 1983 were comparatively well-off even before the cyclone although they sustained about 20 per cent losses. The households who gained after the cyclone consisted mainly of those who were targeted by the NGOs and they steadily improved

FIGURE 6.3: *Change: mean income-equivalents from total investments in households classified by the most gains after the cyclone* (· · · · ·), *and increase* (——) *or decrease* (– – –) *in investments, 1983–88 as for Figure 6.1. The two points marked for 1977 are pre-cyclone (left) and post-cyclone (right)*

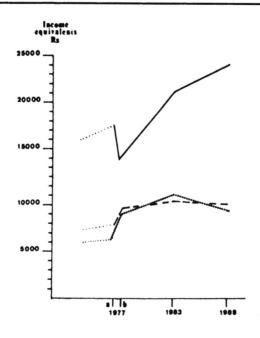

Source: Appendix 3 (Table A 3.3).

Income-equivalents from all investments to have increased within a year of the cyclone in households: 3, 5, 8, 12, 13, 14, 15, 19, 22, 24, 26, 27, 28, 29, 30, 33, 34, 37, 38, 39, 40.

Mean of 42 households: 25.0; median: 21.1; standard deviation: 13.9; range: 5.1–71.21.

Income-equivalents from all investments either to have increased or not to have decreased from 1983–88 in households: 1, 4, 7, 16, 17, 18, 21, 25.

Income-equivalents from all investments to have decreased by more than 20 per cent from 1983–88 in households: 4, 6, 8, 9, 10, 11, 12, 13, 14, 15, 20, 22, 23, 27, 28, 29, 30, 31, 32, 33, 34, 35, 37, 38, 39, 40, 41, 42.

Most gains after the cyclone:
  Mean income-equivalents 1977: Assets 4.4; Claims 1.4; Stocks 0.4: Total 6.2.
  Mean income-equivalents 1988: Assets 5.4; Claims 3.2; Stocks 0.5: Total 9.1.
Increase in investments 1983–88:
  Mean income-equivalents 1977: Assets 11.0; Claims 5.0; Stocks 1.7: Total 17.7.
  Mean income-equivalents 1988: Assets 13.5; Claims 7.1; Stocks 2.8: Total 23.4.
Decrease in investments 1983–88:
  Mean income-equivalents 1977: Assets 5.4; Claims 1.9; Stocks 0.5: Total 7.8.
  Mean income-equivalents 1988: Assets 5.9; Claims 3.4; Stocks 0.7: Total 10.0.

until sometime after 1983 when they declined to more or less their pre-cyclone positions. More than half the households who failed to make gains after 1983 were the same as those who had gained after 1977 (Figure 6.4). While the income-equivalent of their assets more or less remained the same over the period they too became increasingly dependent on income from claims (Appendix 4). In both these groups the income-equivalents from assets and stocks in 1988 does not lift them above the cut-off level we have referred to. Their increasing dependence on loans suggests that they were probably more vulnerable to outside shocks in 1988 than they were in 1977 since most of their income-equivalent in 1988 was from loans and outside intervention, and as we have seen the extent of loans had decreased by 1988 (Appendix 6). There is a wide gap between households whose income-equivalent from all their investments increased from 1983 until 1988 and those whose income-equivalent from all their investments did not. Apart from NGO intervention there may be some clues as to the reasons for this gap when we look to the characteristics of these households.

Change based on household characteristics

The gap between those households whose income-equivalents from investments had increased substantially or not increased between 1983 and 1988 can be partly explained by the noticeable difference in the numbers of workers in the respective households. Another significant factor appears to have been the substantial difference in the number of illnesses between the two groups. When we were discussing recovery (Table 6.1) we noted that the number of deaths did not appear to have had a significant effect on the increase or decrease in income-equivalents from investments; here we see the same pattern again. At this stage this suggests that casualties in cyclones may not have such serious economic effects as might have been thought. The ratio between workers and non workers again does not appear to have had any effect on increasing or decreasing income-equivalents from investments.

TABLE 6.2: *Change: means of measures of household characteristics in households classified by most gains after the cyclone, increase or decrease of investments, 1983–88*

Household type	Number of households N	Total workers[a] x	Worker: non-worker[b] x	Total deaths[c] x	Total illnesses[d] x
Most gains after cyclone	21	10.0	0.52	1.3	2.7
Increase 1983–88	8	12.0	0.43	2.4	2.0
Decrease 1983–88	28	9.4	0.54	1.7	3.2

Source: Fieldwork.

[a] Total number of workers pre-cyclone to 1988.
[b] Worker-dependent ratio pre-cyclone to 1988.
[c] Total deaths 1977–88 including deaths in cyclone.
[d] Total illnesses post-cyclone to 1988.

In the matrix below we see that 15 of the 21 households whose income-equivalents increased within a year of the cyclone failed to continue to do so between 1983 and 1988, suggesting that without the intervention of the NGOs their plight in 1988 might have been far worse than it was, and, sadly, that the NGO intervention did not seem to have had any lasting effects.

FIGURE 6.4: *Change: matrix showing relationship between households classified by gains after the cyclone, and the increase or decrease in investments, 1983–88*

Household type	(N)	1	2	3	4	5	6	7	8	9	10	11	12	13	14	15	16
Main gains after cyclone	(21)			★		★			★				★	★	★	★	
Increase: 1983–88	(8)	★			★			★									★
Decrease: 1983–88	(28)			★		★		★	★	★	★	★	★	★	★		

17	18	19	20	21	22	23	24	25	26	27	28	29	30	31	32	33	34	35	36	37	38	39	40	41	42
	★			★		★		★	★	★	★		★	★			★	★	★	★					
★	★			★				★																	
			★			★	★					★	★	★	★	★	★	★	★		★	★		★	★

Source: Appendix 4.

6.1.3   Characteristics

Characteristics of vulnerability based on income-equivalents from assets, claims and stores

In Figure 6.6 we compare two pairs of household types. In each case, one of them could be said to have the most patent characteristics of vulnerability; the first pair consists of those households with the highest and lowest income-equivalents from assets from before the cyclone to 1988 (**highest assets** and **lowest assets** in Figures 6.5 and 6.6; and Table 6.3); the second pair consists of those with the highest income-equivalents from investments and the highest relative differences in income-equivalents from 1977 to 1988 and those households with the lowest totals and relative differences (**highest** and **lowest totals/differences**in Figures 6.5 and 6.6; and Table 6.3).

The gap between the top and bottom ends of both groupings is fairly dramatic. The total income-equivalents from all investments of households with the highest totals and differences steadily increased from suffering relatively substantial losses in the cyclone to 1988, whilst once again the less well off households declined after 1983. The less well-off households, especially the households with the lowest totals and least differences, are relying on income-equivalents from claims to take them to barely above the cut off level of an income-equivalent of Rs 5,500. The least well-off group – those households with the lowest relative differences and the lowest totals – were still pretty much in the same boat as they were in 1977 (i.e., barely able to make ends meet). The two groups at the top end of the scale seem to have maintained their 1983 position.

Characteristics of vulnerability based on household characteristics

There is a positive correlation between the numbers of workers and high and low income-equivalents from assets. We see a 25 per cent overall difference in the numbers of workers between households with the highest income-equivalents from assets and the highest differences and totals, and their opposite numbers. The difference in the numbers of workers is also reflected in the incidence of illnesses, so clearly there is a link between health and worker availability and economic improvement. The pattern for the number of deaths that we saw before seems to be confirmed – i.e., that the number of deaths does not appear to have significantly influenced the progress or consolidation of the better-off households.

In Figure 6.6 we see that five households out of 12 with the lowest income-equivalents from assets also have the least relative differences and the least total of income-equivalents, whilst two out of five households with the highest

FIGURE 6.5: *Characteristics: mean income-equivalents from total investments of households with the highest (– – –) and lowest (– · –) numbers of assets, from before the cyclone to 1988; and households with highest and lowest totals (———) and highest and lowest differences (· · · · ·), 1977–88 as for Figure 6.1. The two points marked for 1977 are pre-cyclone (left) and post-cyclone (right)*

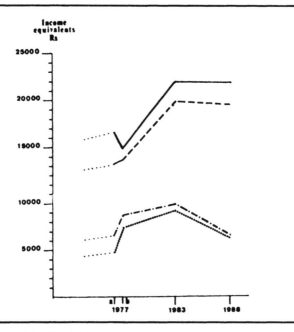

Source: Appendix 3 (Table A 3.4).

Income-equivalents from assets 1977–88 more than Rs 43,000 in households: 1, 3, 4, 6, 7, 15, 16, 18, 20, 25, 26, 31.

Mean of 42 households: 25.0; median: 21.1; standard deviation: 13.9; range: 5.1–71.21.

Income-equivalents from assets 1977–88 less than Rs 33,000 in households: 3, 8, 9, 10, 22, 29, 30, 32, 33, 34, 36, 37.

Income-equivalent from investments with more than 50 per cent differences 1977–88 and total investments 1977–88 exceeding Rs 43,000 in households: 1, 2, 14, 15, 16.

Income-equivalent from investments with less than 10 per cent increase and total investments 1977–88 less than Rs 33,000 in households: 3, 8, 9, 10, 22, 29, 30, 32, 33, 34, 36, 37.

Highest assets:
  Mean income-equivalents 1977: Assets 10.8; Claims 4.7; Stocks 1.6: Total 17.2.
  Mean income-equivalents 1988: Assets 11.8; Claims 6.7; Stocks 2.4: Total 20.9.
Lowest assets:
  Mean income-equivalents 1977: Assets 3.5; Claims 1.1; Stocks 0.2: Total 4.7.
  Mean income-equivalents 1988: Assets 3.7; Claims 2.5; Stocks 0.2: Total 6.4.
Highest totals/differences:
  Mean income-equivalents 1977: Assets 8.3; Claims 3.6; Stocks 1.2: Total 13.1.
  Mean income-equivalents 1988: Assets 11.5; Claims 5.7; Stocks 2.2: Total 19.4.
Lowest totals/differences:
  Mean income-equivalents 1977: Assets 4.8; Claims 1.2; Stocks 0.3: Total 6.3.
  Mean income-equivalents 1988: Assets 4.3; Claims 2.1; Stocks 0.3: Total 5.7.

TABLE 6.3: *Characteristics: means of household characteristics in households classified by highest and lowest number of assets from before the cyclone to 1988; and highest and lowest total income-equivalents from investments, and highest and lowest differences in income-equivalents, 1977–88*

Household type	Number of households N	Total workers[a] x	Worker: non-worker[b] x	Total deaths[c] x	Total illnesses[d] x
Highest assets	13	11.0	0.45	1.8	2.7
Lowest assets	12	8.0	0.56	1.6	3.7
Highest totals/differences	5	10.0	0.45	1.6	2.2
Lowest totals/differences	10	8.6	0.51	2.2	4.4

Source: Fieldwork.
[a] Total number of workers pre-cyclone to 1988. [b] Worker-dependent ratio pre-cyclone to 1988. [c] Total deaths 1977–88 including deaths in cyclone. [d] Total illnesses post-cyclone to 1988.

income-equivalents from assets also have the largest relative differences and total income-equivalents.

In the matrix below we see that 5 households out of 12 with the lowest income equivalents from assets also have the least relative differences and the least total of income equivalents whilst 2 out of 5 households with the highest income equivalents from assets also have the largest relative differences and total income equivalents.

6.2 THE MOST VULNERABLE HOUSEHOLDS

When looking at households grouped to ascertain recovery we noted that while claims were on the increase in all households, claims in those households with the lowest assets in 1977 were a higher proportion of total income-equivalents in 1988 than they were in 1977 and that these households were more or less still at subsistence level in 1988 – in other words the effects of development and the combined interventions of the government and NGOs had barely raised them beyond their pre-cyclone levels. When looking for the character-istics of these households we noted that the number of workers was the only significant characteristic that separated households with the lowest assets from the others. The matrix showed us that exposure was correlated with the number of deaths although there was some evidence that there were more households with the highest income-equivalent from assets (i.e., the highest losses) living in the exposed areas than households with the lowest income-equivalents from assets.

When we looked at change we saw again that the proportion of income-equivalents from claims was on the increase and that income-equivalents from

FIGURE 6.6: *Characteristics: matrix showing relationship between households with highest and lowest assets from before the cyclone to 1988; and households with highest and lowest totals and lowest differences, 1977–88*

		Households															
Household type	(N)	1	2	3	4	5	6	7	8	9	10	11	12	13	14	15	16
Highest assets	(9)	★		★	★		★	★							★	★	
Lowest assets	(12)		★						★	★	★						
Highest totals/differences	(5)	★	★												★	★	★
Lowest totals/differences	(10)		★						★	★	★						

Households																										
17	18	19	20	21	22	23	24	25	26	27	28	29	30	31	32	33	34	35	36	37	38	39	40	41	42
★		★					★	★						★								★			
				★								★	★			★	★	★		★	★				
				★								★	★			★	★	★		★	★				

Source: Appendix 4.

claims in the households that had gained after the cyclone, notably as a result of government and NGO intervention, were higher in 1988 than in 1977. The distinguishing feature of households whose total income-equivalents increased after 1977 and then declined sometime after 1983 and households whose total income-equivalents continued to increase after 1983 was the difference in the numbers of workers in those households and the number of illnesses. The matrix showed us that NGO intervention, however shortlived, was crucial in helping many households to recover to some extent.

We then looked for the characteristics of the households with the highest and lowest income-equivalents from assets and those with the greatest and least totals and differences. We found the pattern of income-equivalent from claims being a relatively larger proportion of income-equivalent from assets repeated again in the households with the lowest income-equivalents from assets and least differences and totals. The number of workers and the number of illnesses were again significant features of the differences between the well-off and less well-off households. The matrix showed us clearly that the households with the lowest income-equivalent from assets had the least differences in total income-equivalents from 1977 to 1988, telling us that the income-equivalent of assets in the less well off households were diminishing at an alarming rate. From all this we deduced that certain households had particular characteristics that prevented them from improving or getting to a point of relative invulnerability.

6.2.1 Seven types of household

From the 17 groupings of households which we have examined in this and the preceding chapter we have taken seven groupings with the lowest total income-equivalents from all their investments as being the most demonstrative of vulnerability, from which we will select *the most vulnerable households in 1988*. They are households which had:

- the least total income-equivalents from all their investments from 1977–88;

- the lowest total income-equivalents in 1988 and the least differences in income-equivalents from 1977–88;

- the least income-equivalents from assets in 1977;

- the lowest income-equivalents from assets 1977–88;

- registered increased income-equivalents from all their investments within a year of the cyclone;

- failed to increase income-equivalents from all their investments after 1983; and

- the most illnesses after the cyclone to 1988.

We have excluded households who lived in the most exposed areas and the ones who suffered the most casualties after the cyclone because they were not among households with the least income-equivalents from investments.

From the above categories we have selected 14 households who belong to at least four of them (these households are effectively those in the lowest quartile of the distribution) and have compared their characteristics and the components of their income-equivalents with the mean figures for the sample distribution in Table 6.4. This comparison should help others to spot the most vulnerable households when they carry out socio-economic surveys. With the range and mean of a distribution one can quickly target certain households that do not fall comfortably into the usual socio-economic classifications of caste, occupation, house-type and so on.

A sample of 14 households is a very small sample from which to extricate the most vulnerable people. However, the 42-household sample derived from a carefully stratified random sample of 202 households which was in turn representative of some 3,142 households within the DSSSS socio-economic survey (Chapter Three; section 3.4), which in turn was representative of the larger population on Divi Seema of 120,000. The 42 case-study households all, more or less, gained benefits (partial or otherwise) from the government *and* NGO interventions in their villages. The point we would like to make here is that if we find that one third of the sample population has a mean total income-equivalent of Rs 6,600 from its investments in 1988 while the mean income-equivalent for the total sample is Rs 12,400 then how many people were economically vulnerable in Divi Seema in 1988?

Before we briefly discuss the findings in these last tables we should elaborate more on the value of knowing the total number of workers in a household over a period *as well as*, of course, the number of people at any one time. To this end, the following example is offered. Over the last 10 years in household X there has been a total of, say, 12 workers but at the time of the decision as to who to help with what, there are only two workers; in household Y there have been eight workers over the same period but at the moment there are three. Which is the more vulnerable household? The household with the lower number of workers (household X) would appear to be less well-off than and more vulnerable than household Y – so should we help X rather than Y?

Throughout this analysis we have seen a positive and recurring correlation between the numbers of workers in a household and the value of its assets – households with a higher total number of workers have consistently had higher income-equivalents from assets than those with low assets and low total numbers of workers. So we would say that household Y is more vulnerable because it has not been able to build up the same extent of assets as household X, although things look rosier now. That is not to say that household X might not become vulnerable and could now decline, but, assuming that we have to make a choice, then household Y is the one to help.

In Table 6.4 we see that the number of workers in the vulnerable households was virtually the same as the sample in 1977 but that the numbers

TABLE 6.4: *Means of household characteristics of the 14 most vulnerable households, and the mean of household characteristics of the 42-household sample*

Household type	Household	Workers 1977	Workers 1988	Total	Worker-dependent ratio	Total deaths	Total illnesses
	(N)	(x)	(x)	(x)	(x)	(x)	(x)
Most vulnerable[a]	14	2.7	2.1	8.8	0.55	1.9	4.0
Mean of sample	42	2.9	2.6	10.2	0.50	1.7	2.8

Source: Fieldwork.
[a] **Households**: 3, 8, 9, 10, 22, 30, 33, 34, 35, 36, 37, 38, 40, 41.
  Family type: eight were extended families and six were joint Hindu families; **Caste**: Kapu 1, Gouda 3, Golla 1, Pallecarlu 3, Harijan 6, Others 0; **Occupation**: 10 marginal farmers; 4 landless.

TABLE 6.5: *Mean income-equivalents from all investments of the most vulnerable households in the 42-household sample*

Household type	Household (N)	Total income-equivalents							
		Assets		Claims		Stocks		Totals	
		1977	1988	1977	1988	1977	1988	1977	1988
Most vulnerable[a][1]	14	4.3	3.8	1.1	2.6	0.3	0.2	5.7	6.6
42-household sample[2]	42	6.2	7.2	2.4	4.2	0.7	1.0	9.3	12.4

Source: Fieldwork.
[a] As for Table 6.4.
[1] **Most vulnerable households**:
  Range of Assets: 1977: 1.5–7.4; 1988: 1.0–5.7.
  Range of Claims: 1977: 0.5–1.9; 1988: 0.5–4.5.
  Range of Stocks: 1977: 0.0–1.0; 1988: 0.0–0.8.
[2] **42-household sample**:
  Range of Assets: 1977: 1.5–16.8; 1988: 1.0–21.5.
  Range of Claims: 1977: 0.5–10.5; 1988: 0.5–15.0.
  Range of Stocks: 1977: 0.0–4.0; 1988: 0.0–6.0.

had fallen by 20 per cent by 1988, reflected in the total number of workers over the period. The very slight difference in the worker-dependent ratio tells us little more than that there tend to be fewer workers in the less vulnerable households and that the less vulnerable households can afford to "carry" a few non-workers at less risk to its survival than a poorer one. There is no significant difference in the number of deaths over the period (including the cyclone) but there is a marked difference in the number of illnesses between the most vulnerable households and the mean of the sample.

The income-equivalent from assets (Table 6.5) declined in the most vulnerable households from 1977 to 1988 while that of the 42-household sample had risen slightly in the same period. Income-equivalents from claims rose in both cases by similar proportions which indicates that both moneylenders' credit was on the increase and bank loans were still trickling through despite the assertions made by the people who had said that bank loans had dried up once the DSSSS had left. Income-equivalents for stocks remained the same for both the most vulnerable households and those in the overall sample. Returning to our earlier assertion that a minimum total income-equivalent of Rs 5,500–6,500 per year only guaranteed a meagre existence, then we can see that the most vulnerable were still hovering on the cut-off point in 1988 despite the massive development that had taken place in Divi Seema since the cyclone.

TABLE 6.6: *The most vulnerable people*

Location	Case-study number	Description	Occupation and assets	Way of life	Nature of household
Most exposed Coastal *Nali Pallecarlu*	22	Two old adults (M, F) who missed out on free *pucca* concrete house; living in one-pole house in the centre of village.	Agricultural labour; some fishing; shares 0.5 acre with son.	Dependent only on moneylender's credit; two families living off 0.5 acre.	Small household; old age and declining health; no assets.
Coastal *Nali Pallecarlu*	41	Two adults (M, F); son marries and leaves village; living in *pucca* house on edge of village.	Agricultural labour; 0.5 acre of unfertile land.	Dependent on NGO and moneylender's credit; both migrate.	Small household; poor health; no assets.
Tidal flat *Ramanthapuram Pallecarlu*	9	Old man who lost his family in cyclone; died in 1983; nephew and wife take over *pucca* house, situated on edge of village next to irrigation drain.	All agricultural labour; old man used to fish; 0.5 acre unfertile encroachment land.	Dependent on government and NGO interventions; no access to formal credit; both migrate.	Small household; old age and death, then poor health; animal asset.
Exposed Tidal flat *Mandapakala Harijan*	37	Single man, lost wife and two children in cyclone, new wife left him in 1983; living in *pucca* house on low-lying land on edge of village.	Agricultural labour; some ditch fishing but penalised by higher castes.	Dependent only on moneylender's credit; migrates.	Small household; poor health and insanity; no assets.

Tidal flat *Mandapakala Harijan*	38	Two adults (M, F) and one child, lost brother and children in cyclone; living in *pucca* house on low-lying land on edge of village.	Agricultural labour; no land.	Dependent only on moneylender's credit; both migrate.	Small household; long spells of poor health for both; animal asset.
Tidal flat *Mandapakala Kapu*	40	Two adults (M, F), lost wife and son in cyclone; living in one-pole house on low-lying land near centre of village.	Agricultural labour; some ditch fishing; 0.5 acre of poor encroachment land.	Dependent on NGO, and moneylender's credit; both migrate.	Small household; some sickness; animal asset only.
Inland Inland plain *Bellamkomdadibba Gouda*	3	Two adults (M, F), old man and young wife; lost previous wife in cyclone; living in hut on low-lying ground on edge of village.	Agricultural labour; shares 0.5 acre of fertile land with two brothers next door.	Dependent only on moneylender's credit; both migrate.	Small household; no sickness; no assets.
Inland plain *Goudapalem Gouda*	8	Widow living with youngest son (14) and dependent on other sons nearby; living in one-pole house on high ground in poorer part of village.	Intermittent agricultural labour; no land having given it to sons.	Formal credit after cyclone; no help from NGOs, otherwise moneylender's credit.	Very small household; old age and declining health curtails earnings; no assets.
Inland plain *Goudapalem Christian*	10	Two adults (M, F) and two young children, lost wife and two children in cyclone; living in one-pole house on low-lying land in richer part of village next to irrigation drain.	Agricultural labour; 0.8 acre unfertile encroachment land.	Dependent on NGO and moneylender's credit; only one migrates.	Below average size household; poor health dominates life; two animal assets.

TABLE 6.6: *The most vulnerable people*

Location	Case-study number	Description	Occupation and assets	Way of life	Nature of household
Inland plain *Lingareddipalem Kapu*	30	Two adults and two young children, crippled husband; living in hut until 1986, then one-pole house, on edge of village.	Intermittent agricultural labour; 0.5 acre fertile land, dependent on wife's parents next door.	Dependent only on moneylender's credit; health problems curtail migration; missed out initially on NGOs (higher caste).	Small household; poor health and disability, operations; sold animal asset.
Inland plain *Lingareddipalem Harijan*	33	Old couple (M, F); living in *pucca* house on edge of village near irrigation drain.	Intermittent agricultural labour, 0.5 acre unfertile land.[b]	Dependent only on moneylender's credit; one migrates.	Small household; old age and declining health; son has animal asset.
Inland plain *Lingareddipalem Harijan*	34	Two adults (M, F) son marries and leaves village; living in *pucca* house on low-lying land on edge of village near irrigation drain.	Messenger for *muncif*; wife does some agricultural labour.	Dependent only on moneylender's credit.	Small household; no assets.
Inland plain *Lingareddipalem Harijan*	35	Old man and his granddaughter (11); living in *pucca* house on low-lying land on edge of village near irrigation drain.	Too old for labouring; some ditch fishing.	Dependent only on moneylender's credit; migrates.	Small household; old age and declining labour power; no assets.
Inland plain *Lingareddipalem Harijan*	38	Two adults (M, F) and child (7), lost brother and his own children in cyclone; living in *pucca* house on low-lying land on edge of village near irrigation drain.	Agricultural labour; no land.	Dependent only on moneylender's credit; migrates.	Small household; intermittent sickness; no assets.

Source: Fieldwork 1981, 1982, 1983, 1988.

6.2.2 The most vulnerable people

We come now to who are are the most vulnerable people, and in what households they live, and what questions one should ask if one is to help them with aid and development programmes. Let us start with the 14 households we have decided are the most vulnerable.

Summary

The most vulnerable households all share common characteristics; they are characterised by their small size and their dependence on single workers. Just under half the households suffered casualties in the 1977 cyclone which throws the previous findings about the significance od cyclone deaths into some question. This finding goes some way to substantiate the government's efforts to reduce casualties. However, just over half the households lived in the most sheltered areas, signifying that vulnerability is not determined by location and partly substantiating the alternative hypothesis that we put forward previously (Chapter Two, section 2.2). All households had to depend on moneylenders' credit and most had to migrate for work to earn enough money to keep alive, and most households suffered from prolonged ill-health or other incapacities that had serious effects on their earning potential. The summary table (Table 6.7) illustrates these characteristics.

From these findings we could suggest that the following could be classified as **target households**:

- Small households especially those with old people and single workers;
- Households with a record of illness, disability and infirmities;
- Households who depend entirely on labouring;
- Households with access only to the informal market for loans;
- Households who depend only on their families for financial support.

6.3 SUMMARY:
HOW TO FIND THE MOST VULNERABLE PEOPLE

We can now ask if and how the conceptual model of vulnerability (Chapter Two, section 2.6, Figure 2.6) has helped us find the most vulnerable households. Its most useful feature has been its facility to have a common measure (income-equivalents) applied to a whole range of resources (investments) held by households. In this instance this has enabled us to estimate the value of Government and NGO interventions and loans which taken *together* with assets revealed the chronic dependence of the most vulnerable households on claims and the relatively high proportion of the income-equivalents of

TABLE 6.7: *Characteristics of vulnerability of the most vulnerable households*

Location	Number of households	Small households[a]	Deaths in cyclone	Prolonged bad health	Old age	Ag. lab. as main occupation	Migrate for work	Informal credit only	Without assets
Coastal	6	6	4	4	2	6	5	4	4
Inland	8	7	3	4	3	3	5	7	6
Total	14	13	7	8	5	9	10	11	10

Source: Fieldwork.
[a] Two or less people.

174

claims of the poorest and most vulnerable households. The correlation between low income-equivalents of all investments with household characteristics enabled us to suggest which characteristics to look for in seeking out the most vulnerable people. However, to answer the question rigorously we have to relate household characteristics back to the larger conceptual model and apply its components in sequence, so that future users might benefit from its use.

First of all we should start with **physiography** and *where* people live. We found that nearly all the most vulnerable households lived in the worst areas – i.e., on low-lying land prone to all types of flooding and usually on the edges of the villages (Table 6.6, description) because the higher ground was always occupied by the richer households in the most favourable areas of the villages; in other words the poorest were more or less physically marginalised at the local level. Even in the most exposed areas we found that the richer households lived on the higher ground and even though there was often less than 1 m difference between sites occupied by the poorest and the richest, the difference was significant when it came to sea or ground flooding. We found a colony of *Harijans* (Table 6.6, column 1) living on the edge of the village on land that was prone to flooding even after moderate rainfalls in Lingareddipalem, the most protected village in the inland plain. Therefore, in any search for the most vulnerable people in cyclone-prone areas we should focus not only on those living in the most exposed areas but also on those living on the edges of villages or close to the worst type of land – i.e., with poor drainage and susceptibility to flooding.

Next we should look at the **social relations of production** and find out *what* people do for a living. We found that the most poorest and vulnerable households had the least remunerative employment and the least assets. Occupations can be a useful guide but within the same occupational groupings we found quite wide differences in conditions of vulnerability and potential to recover (Table 6.5, note [a]). The best guide we have to assessing households' potential vulnerability and recoverability therefore is to look at their position at any given moment and relate it to the wider context of the social relations of production. In the search for the most vulnerable households, questions should include the following:

- How large is the household?
- How many people can work?
- How many people actually work and for how long?
- How many non-working members does the household have to support?
- How many people have worked over the past five years?
- What is the age composition of the household?
- What is the predominant occupation of the household?
- Is labouring the predominant occupation?
- How many people migrate for (extra) work?

Next we should look at the historic and current **development policies** which will tell us *why* certain groups live where they do and also what work they do. We found, again, that the most vulnerable households had been spatially marginalised but it does not follow that spatially marginalised people are necessarily economically marginalised (the most exposed: Figure 6.1). There was evidence that the most vulnerable households were economically marginalised by the fact that they had the fewest employment opportunities and the least assets (Figures 6.1 and 6.5) and this resulted directly from development policies over the years (Chapter Three, section 3.2.3, and Chapter Four, section 4.5).

These three variables – physiography, the social relations of production, and development policies – provide us with the essential context in which households should be evaluated.

Next we should look at the households' **production, exchange and consumption relationships** – i.e., their specific relationship to the market. We found that the poorest and most vulnerable had the least resources to sell (i.e., their labour power), the least assets to realise (see Tables 6.6 and 6.7) and consequently a significantly marginal relationship with the market. We also found that their consumption was predominantly of staple foods and they consumed almost as much rice as the richer households, but little else. They had less to spend on clothes, medical services and transport, and so not only looked poor but were not seen far from their own villages. Amongst the questions we should ask in seeking out the most vulnerable households there is one crucial one:

- What are the households' sources of credit?

The others should include:

- What has the household to sell?
- What stocks has the household to withstand any contingencies?
- Apart from staples, what else forms the basic diet of the household?
- How many assets have been sold or exchanged recently, and why?

Next we come to **household characteristics** and we have seen what the characteristics of the most vulnerable households are (Tables 6.3 and 6.4, Figures 6.5 and 6.6). In any search for the most vulnerable people the following questions should be included:

- What has been the health of household members over the last five years?
- What illnesses have they suffered from?
- Have these illnesses been treated?
- To what extent does the household depend on its other family members outside the household?
- What other claims can the household make on people outside the family members?

Finally, we should look at the *whole* range of **shocks** that people are likely to be exposed to and their **risk-reduction strategies** to cope with them. It is important to open the "Pandora's box" of climatic *and non-climatic* shocks that can befall people in any given place and recognise their full potential along the lines we discussed (Chapter Two, section 2.4). Among the questions we should ask households, are the following:

- What are the level of assets and resources at their disposal?
- What losses are they likely to sustain in a variety of conditions?
- What will be the likely effects of those losses?
- What are their likely chances of recovering or improving on them?
- What sort of assistance do they require to recover those lost assets?
- What are the future levels and values of their assets likely to be?

This concludes our search for the most vulnerable households. Whether these searches are incorporated into rapid appraisals or longer term studies will depend on a number of factors we discuss in our final chapter when we will be drawing all the strands together and suggesting some golden rules for disaster managers, the voluntary agencies and governments.

7

Some Golden Rules for Disaster Management

7.1 REVIEW OF THE PRECEDING CHAPTERS

In Chapter One we became aware of the awesome and destructive nature of cyclones and how the "savagery of nature" was held to blame for the widespread devastation after cyclone strikes, and the perpetuation of poverty that was characteristic of many coastal areas (section 1.2.1.). We saw how policies evolved over 20 years, with the work of the Cyclone Distress Mitigation Committee in 1971 and the 1977 cyclone acting as the catalysts for change, and how cyclone mitigation policy had progressed from trying to cure the effects of cyclones after they had happened to trying to prevent the loss of life and assets before they happened (section 1.2.2).

The critique raised some doubts about the reliance on the mass evacuation of coastal areas (section 1.4.2) and the over-emphasis on some of the protection programmes, because they might become the substitute for improving other aspects of life in the coastal areas (section 1.4.3). Another criticism was that cyclone mitigation programmes ignored the significance of power relations and were proscribed by the lack of integration with the anti-poverty programmes. The government's perception of cyclone vulnerability was illustrated in diagrammatic form by the Conventional View taking the details from the 1977 cyclone (Figure 1.1) followed by a diagram showing government's perception of cyclone vulnerability and poverty (Figure 1.2).

In Chapter Two we traced the development of disasters research from the 1950s to the end of the 1970s which resulted in perceptions of natural disasters progressing faster and on a wider front than governments' perceptions over the same period. We described how Gilbert White's work laid the foundations of a political economy model of disasters (section 2.1) which was developed by other social scientists, which set out the processes and interrelationships affecting vulnerability at the household scale, gathered into a representative Alternative View (section 2.2, and Figure 2.2), again taking the details from the 1977 cyclone.

The comparison between the Alternative View and the Conventional View had by now alerted us that cyclone vulnerability was more complex than might have been first imagined. We turned our attention to unpacking the concept of vulnerability, starting with a definition that linked vulnerability to a wider range of external events than cyclones (section 2.3.1), followed by an examination of some of the components of vulnerability – i.e., the characteristics of shock events and the impact of losses, and ended with a discussion of the traditional methods of coping with shocks and losses in the form of risk-reduction and risk-diffusion strategies (sectiion 2.4). Into the analysis we introduced a model which identified the relationship between the household and the external world through its production, consumption and exchange relations which incorporated tangible and intangible assets and integrated it with the larger-scale political economy model (section 2.5.1). This fed into a conceptual model of vulnerability (section 2.6) which became the basis for our subsequent analysis.

In Chapter Three we introduced the study area and its underlying power relations, and the fieldwork and methodology. We started with the agricultural calendar and the incidence of cyclones to illustrate how precarious was the balance between the climate and agriculture (section 3.2.1). We described the social features of the island of Divi Seema in the same order as we had described the components of vulnerability in Chapter Two, and showed how the development of Divi Seema and the introduction of irrigation, had produced social relations of production that had transformed the area to the detriment of many and reinforced the power relations existing on the mainland (sections 3.2.3–3.2.5). After this we analysed risk-reduction strategies and ranges of choice which households could use to cope with the exigencies of the climate and socio-economic relations within the society (section 3.2.7), but concluded that choices for the minority were severely limited.

From this descriptive analysis of the social and economic structure of Divi Seema, two possible causes of cyclone vulnerability emerged; first, the climate and secondly and more important, the underlying man made forces that shaped the society. On the one hand we saw cyclones recurring at the same time as the harvest, tipping the balance between survival and destitution; and on the other we saw how the distorted power relations exacerbated the climatic risks.

We then described our fieldwork programme and how the methodology had to respond to the underlying hypotheses of the Conventional and Alternative Views (section 3.4) and why the sampling frame changed in 1983 from 202 households to 42 households as we became more aware of the complexities of vulnerability and the nature of choice and power relations.

In Chapter Four we returned to the terrible cyclone of 1977 and described the aftermath and appalling devastation and trauma which followed, illustrated by losses (section 4.1). We analysed development in Divi Seema since the cyclone to 1988 through the changes in the numbers of households' assets (sections 4.2 and 4.3) and found that, generally, the people with the least assets had not made relatively as many gains as those with the most assets. From this panoramic analysis we discerned, first, the relative importance of government and NGO interventions in changing economic conditions and attitudes and the positive and negative implications of their interventions, and, secondly, a conflicting picture of much change and little change. The conclusion we drew was that the least well-off households, whilst not becoming destitute, appeared to be as vulnerable as they were in 1977 and the best-off households were far less vulnerable in 1988. We concluded by posing questions about the efficacy of government programmes, first raised in Chapter one, and the extent to which NGOs should intervene. The questions in effect set the scene for the second half of the book, moving from description and generalised critique to analysis.

In Chapter Five we presented the first stage of the detailed analysis of differential vulnerability in terms of the effects of losses and the nature of recovery. We measured the vulnerability of households with the least and greatest differences in their investment values over the period, and, those households with the lowest and highest totals in 1988, by explanatory and response variables which we described in detail (section 5.3). We found that while the total investments had increased relatively equally in all four household types there had also been a significant increase in claims as a percentage of total values in all cases and especially in the poorest households, i.e. those with the least assets before the cyclone (section 5.4). This is alarming because the claims figures were not the result of increasing government or NGO intervention, in fact the opposite, but an increasing reliance on the informal market for loans. We concluded that location was not as important a causal factor of vulnerability as the numbers of workers in a household and their health. Land, of course, was the major asset.

In Chapter Six we chose three more groupings of households according to what had now emerged as the most potent measures of vulnerability: the capacity for recovery, the capacity for positive change, and particular household characteristics of vulnerability. Examining vulnerability measured by recovery (section 6.1.1) we found a link only between exposure and casualties. We also found that while claims had increased in all households, those with the least assets in 1988 were depending more on claims than they had been in 1977 and and as a result were possibly worse off in 1988 than they had been in 1977. These households were characterised by low numbers of workers and high levels of illness. Examining vulnerability measured by change (section 6.1.2) we found that the pattern of low numbers of workers and high incidence of illness characterised the households who had failed to consolidate their gains whereas we found the opposite for those who had improved. In examining the perceived characteristics of vulnerability (section 6.1.3) we found again that low numbers of workers and a high incidence of illness characterised the households with the lowest totals. In the final section we saw that prevalence of illness, deficiency in worker availability and small size characterised the most vulnerable households (section 6.2) and to conclude we suggested how to identify the most vulnerable people in a larger distribution (section 6.3) and how the overall conceptual model of vulnerability could be applicable to other situations.

7.2 SUMMARY:
THREE THEMES: POWER, CHOICE AND VULNERABILITY

What has become apparent from the preceding chapters is that vulnerability is a very complex condition heightened not only by cyclones and other natural calamities but by complex processes within societies and their inability to deal with them. To respond to cyclone vulnerability or other forms of vulnerability, disaster management has to become an all-embracing activity not confined to producing preparedness plans and training programmes, however necessary they may be, but one which has within its curtilage *all aspects of social and economic development*. In the course of this book we have discussed many interlinked activities connected with development but there are many that we have barely touched on (Drabek 1987). However, we hope that we have explained *differential vulnerability* well enough for the reader to comprehend its variable and diffuse nature and we hope also to have brought out three major themes concerning vulnerability.

The first theme is **power**. In many if not all countries, governments tend to represent the rich and the powerful sections in their societies more than the poorer sections and in many countries the politicians who are democratically elected to power through the ballot box find themselves in governments presiding over civil-service apparatuses that are compelled by law to serve them. Many politicians abuse these systems and encourage bureaucracy, nepotism and corruption as a means of gaining and retaining personal wealth and power. These activities are by-and-large supported by the affluent middle classes who exist in both rural and urban areas and who work closely together creating a powerful alliance.

> The characteristic of this alliance, where it occurs, is that both groups refuse to redistribute assets and incomes, and even less so in a general context of crisis and decline; they refuse to eliminate corruption in the private and public spheres; they refuse to reorganize the State in order to make it capable of implementing selective policies and effective redistribution and they refuse to contribute, through just taxation, to the well being of the poor. (World Development 1987: Appendix III: 257.)

The refusal to act is often called, mistakenly, lack of political will. It is, in fact, self-interest. Susan George advises those who want to help the poor to **"study the rich and powerful, not the poor and powerless"** (George 1986: 296).

In a critique of IRDP programmes an Indian economist has this to say about the rich and powerful:

> A good part of what is given to the poor through IRDP will be taken away through the social process and market operations by the rich and powerful. (Kurian 1987.)

We have seen how the most powerful people in our sample – i.e., those with the largest landholdings and the most assets before the cyclone – recovered well and increased the size of both landholdings and assets, and we noted the opposite trend with those with the least landholdings and assets (Figure 6.1). This was no accident. As they said during our conversations, they had contacts with other powerful people on whom they could make claims, on the island and on the mainland and with people in government, all of whom belonged to a sort of rural élite, which although widespread *excluded* the majority of farmers and artisans, thus giving the small minority an inbuilt advantage in having access to resources.

The second theme is **choice** and the importance of expanding it. People with few choices have the least effective strategies, and their strategy is often to put themselves "into the hands of God". Choice relates to the assets base of people, in the widest sense, and therefore it was of vital importance for the NGOs *and* the government to concentrate on "building up the asset base" of the poorest people (Chapter Four, section 4.2). Choice at its simplest is "money in the bank". In the case of cyclones, people with no assets have nothing to lose except their lives, but people with even the smallest (immovable) assets will often take the gravest risks and stay in their huts even when they know that they are in the path of the cyclone, because they cannot afford to lose even the smallest asset if it may help them raise a loan to safeguard survival and reduce future vulnerability.

Expanding choice is the key to successful disaster management and government policies have in some degree focused on expanding choice (Chapter One, sections 1.2.2 and 1.2.3) but they have not developed sufficiently. Durable houses give people some choice, in that having been warned about a cyclone strike the people can calculate whether it is worth staying in their house with their belongings or going elsewhere; the construction of cyclone shelters in the villages has given the people more choice – i.e., whether to stay in the village or leave and go to higher ground. Choices can be widened by having durable shelters to protect people's assets but having assets elsewhere – i.e., outside the low-lying areas – widens that choice, and having assets elsewhere *and* influential contacts expands that choice still further. People with assets elsewhere have been able to diversify spatially as well as economically and in so doing have been able to spread their risks (Chapter Four, sections 4.2 and 4.3). If we wish to reduce the risks that the poorest have to take and widen their choices then we should concentrate on building up their economic base.

Most poor people do not choose to put all their eggs in one basket. Rather they seek to reduce risk, increase adaptability and seek a degree of autonomy by developing and maintaining wider options, through the ability and willingness of different household members to do different things in different places. (Heyer 1989: 3.)

But choices are determined by priorities and these are governed not only by the climate but by the power relations inherent in societies.

The fact that the majority of people do not construct elaborate or even simple defences against the exigencies of the environment is not at all surprising, nor is it necessarily a special case due to extreme poverty, but rather a matter of priorities and choice . . . . The message is simple – disaster preparedness whether it be adopting earthquake resistant building techniques or constructing [individual] flood defences will be undertaken when development [of a household and area] has reached a level sufficient for the majority to choose to allocate a portion of their income to protect themselves from what they consider to be a likely catastrophe. (D'Souza 1984: 306.)

The third theme which combines the other two is the **nature of vulnerability**. Vulnerability is a dynamic condition which alters, often from day to day, and certainly from season to season. The condition is influenced by exposure to risk events but is governed by the ability of a person or a household or a community to recover from risk events; this recovery is dependent basically on assets and resources and not on the degree of exposure. Anyone looking at Divi Seema from late 1983 to early 1985, unless they understood the nature of vulnerability, could have been excused for thinking that the people had recovered well enough to withstand the vicissitude of further cyclones. A research snapshot taken at the time would have shown that five years after the cyclone some 80 per cent of the storm-surge affected population had recovered to and beyond their pre cyclone levels and those that had not were well on their way, thanks to the combined efforts of Government and NGO long-term rehabilitation and development programmes (Winchester 1986). The snapshot would not have shown the fragile nature of the recovery or the time dimension of vulnerability and the significance of particular indicators **over time** – i.e., worker availability and health.

We can ask what lessons we can draw from this experience and how might our findings help those who are actively engaged in disaster management? It would be as foolish as Icarus to soar from one case-study to an overview of the whole of disaster management but it might help if we use our experience and the findings from the fieldwork to conclude with some **Golden rules** for those involved in disaster management, the NGOs and the Government.

7.3 GOLDEN RULES

We presented a conceptual model of vulnerability early on in this book and applied it to cyclone vulnerability. It has served its purpose. It became the vehicle for an examination that widened our approach and in doing so widened our understanding of vulnerability. We have not ended up with a model of vulnerability because, in our view, such models are too simplistic and static. Life is not static; it changes from day to day and hour to hour so that this year's model could become next year's doorstop. Nor have we ended up with guidelines. Although guidelines can be as wide or as narrow as one chooses they too can be restrictive and can be swept away by a new administrative broom as easily as yesterday's model.

We have decided instead to finish up with golden rules which concentrate our minds and are proscriptive for those working in disaster management. Each golden rule is not an end in itself but is more of a starting point since each rule should provoke a number of questions. Only by asking questions may we perhaps come to some broad answers that recognise the multifarious nature of reality and not cosy compartmentalised versions of it. By asking questions we will find that we invariably end up with people, not models or ideas or policies, but people and responsibilities. That should give us a good start for looking at vulnerability. For confirmation of the veracity of the rules we will refer the reader to preceding sections in the text.

The first two rules are directed towards disaster managers and administrators, the next two are directed towards the voluntary agencies, and the last rule is directed towards government. Each rule, of course, is applicable to any of the other groups and hopefully to a wider range of people but we have separated them here for clarity.

7.3.1 Rule One: Focus on the people whose daily lives are a disaster

This rule recognises that disasters are incipient and endemic within societies and stem from everyday conditions of life. It focuses our attention on the fact that for many people living in cyclone-prone coastal areas (and for millions of people in disaster-prone areas of the world) *everyday conditions* are as much a catastrophe as the occurrence of natural and man-made disasters. For them life is a daily disaster. They barely earn enough to keep alive; they are subject to the vagaries of government officials and powerful people; they have few if any medical facilities and no economic safety net, beyond their family and caste allegiances, to prevent them from falling into destitution and misery. A cyclone will accelerate this process, not cause it. The essence of this rule is that it uncouples disaster specifically from cyclones and its focus is on time, people and place.

We have shown that everyday occurrences such as illness, inadequate worker availability, inadequate resources, the absence of economic safety nets (Chambers 1989) are more closely connected with vulnerability than are cyclones. The traditional safety nets of caste and faction may still be there in Divi Seema, but they may have been eroded beyond repair for the weakest sections by the use of technology replacing people and new men coming in taking up common lands. (Chapter Four, section 4.5). In terms of *power* we have seen that uneven power relations resulted in inequal distribution of resources – i.e., water for tail-end lands, roads, electrification and the expanded irrigation network which in effect severely limited the extent of *choice* in the area (Chapter Four, section 4.5).

Choice is governed not only by access to resources, but by restrictions and penalties. For instance, choosing whether to stay in the area or leave, whether to stay in the village or leave when a cyclone strikes, whether to put spare resources into building a stronger house, building a stronger animal shelter, educating a son, putting the money aside for a dowry for a daughter, paying off private debts, paying bribes, spending money on ceremonies, or whatever, depends largely on what assets people have *and their priorities*. But the priorities are to a large extent governed by the power relations which determine which choices carry benefits and which carry penalties.

Visiting an irrigation project in a drought-prone area of North India, I noticed that the aqueduct of simple pipes and troughs bringing water from miles away to the parched and bare lands in the project, was broken in one place. One pipe lay on the ground and there was no water either. I asked the Project Officer how long it had been like that. "Oh, about a year now." – "But it's quite simple to mend, why has it taken so long?" – "Because every time we repair it they (the powerful landlords) come back and break it." (Winchester 1981: 159–162.)

7.3.2 Rule Two: Welcome complexity; don't simplify issues

If this book had done nothing else it has, we hope, shown the reader the complexity of vulnerability. The reader knows from his or her own experience that life is full of complex relationships which constrain or propel them in their daily actions. The key point about complexity is not to confuse the process with the product; having to go through a complex process of analysis does not necessarily mean a complex solution although some of the solutions may be complicated. But if that is reality, then our task is not to simplify but to deal with it.

As everyone knows, many social and political issues are very complicated, and one way for those who have power in societies to retain it is to simplify issues so that a semblance of power "sharing" is given. Many of these issues are reduced into unquantifiable aims whose moral tones are appealing and which appear to enable the weakest sections of societies to have more choice over their own lives. Sometimes this can work (Fernandez 1987) but mostly the chanting of the slogans that are associated with power-sharing is a cruel deception. Many programmes have noble aims such as to respect "human dignity", create "self-reliance", encourage "participation", lead to "self-sufficiency", and focus on "community development" amongst many others.

Each one of these aims should be questioned as to whom the beneficiaries are; for instance, self-reliance *from whom?*, participation *by whom?*, self sufficiency *from whom?* and so on.

Few of these abstract ideas exist in the slums and gutters of Third-World cities, and even less so in the villages; their use as slogans in briefs and reports puts many outsiders working at a disadvantage, compounded by the fact that most outsiders are commissioned to tackle *problems already defined by the governments*. These problems are normally set out for professional experts to solve in the form of briefs, but, briefs prepared by governments are usually simplifications of problems that lead invariably to *producing* something – a sea wall, a training programme, an irrigation system, a plan, or a housing layout all of which are visible manifestations of effort, within parameters already defined by the government, according to their perception of the problem. They very rarely lead to structural changes within the societies. On the subject of briefs and the relationship between professionals and governments, what Baker (1981: 4) has to say is relevant:

> . . . most aid is requested rather than offered . . . consequently aid responds to problems already defined by the authorities in the recipient countries so that . . . the social and economic *status quo* becomes implicit.

Technology is assumed to be scale neutral – i.e., it affects everybody equally – and it is inherently excluded from the context of the political economy as defined here. The conventional attitude of the technocrat and often the scientist can be summed up in a concluding passage of Baker's paper:

> Frequently those in the technical fields actually resent or resist more profound explanations of the causation of physical phenomena with derisory accusations of 'politics' or simply that they cannot be held responsible for what non scientists do to abuse their skills and advice. Worst of all is the statement that they are 'simply doing a job and doing it well'. Indeed the technocratic approach, rather like neo-classical economics, is often seen by its practitioners as being apolitical. In fact, it operates on the premise that the political economy as a variable is held constant. (Baker 1981: 28.)

If there are doubts about the validity of a project then a simple criterion used by Mahatma Gandhi can be applied:

> Recall the face of the poorest and most helpless person whom you may have seen and ask yourself if the step you contemplate is going to be of any use to him. Will he be able to gain anything by it? Will it restore him to control over his own life and destiny? In other words, will it lead to *swaraj*, self-rule, for the hungry and also spiritually starved millions of our countrymen?

In terms of choice, the process of simplification of issues usually means reducing the variety of choices because not everybody wants the *same* thing – i.e., not everybody wants a pump set, or another irrigation canal or a community shelter – mainly because to the majority with onerous debts and insecure livelihoods these things probably do not bring them any advantages or alleviate their everyday disastrous conditions (Chapter Three, section 3.2.7, Table 3.6). The simplification of issues such as the perception that cyclones cause poverty may actually increase vulnerability by diverting resources from a social security system to a physical-security system in which mainly the better off benefit.

Disaster management or disaster prevention is an integral part of human affairs and should not be activated only when a disaster occurs. It is easier to deal with one thing at a time and to compartmentalise issues, events and crises. These invariably become simplified for communication purposes and in the simplification process much is excluded, including millions of people. Recognising complexity entails laborious and time consuming work and more people to share the analytical and decision-making processess which would not only be a drain on resources, it would also undermine the "power" of those with access to the information, something at which Hewitt was hinting (1983).

Risk-aversion strategies are constrained by choice and are usually the result of weighing up a complex range of opportunities and penalties. Blanket solutions such as mass evacuation, community protection, even improved physical infrastructure, may not be the appropriate risk-aversion strategies for people who only work for four months a year and who have to spend half their annual income on medical treatment.

7.3.3   Rule Three: "Leave the money at the airport"

This applies specifically to foreigners and is a caricature of saying "let the choice be theirs". "Theirs" in this case are national governments to whom one is sending aid, or local people. The remark may raise some hackles but hopefully it will also raise some questions; such as, who do you leave it with? Who can you trust with it? But this is a risk that outsiders have to take, otherwise most aid projects become mere palliatives and fail to address the underlying cause of the distress they want so much to alleviate. There are bound to be leakages (a euphemism for theft) in whatever system of distribution is taken up. If the reduction of vulnerability can be measured by "money in the bank" then the question is "whose bank?".

In terms of power relations, whoever the money is left with at the airport is unlikely to channel it in the way the donor would wish, and, anyway, outsiders are *bound to get it mostly wrong*. We cannot pretend there are no mistakes; the world is strewn with development failures on a gigantic scale and the errors of commission far outweigh the errors of omission (Bernstein 1973; Seers 1979; Wijkman and Timberlake 1984) and most of these failures have stemmed from the desire of the most powerful sections of the world's community for prestige projects for their own, and, possibly, their country's, international image.

In terms of vulnerability "leaving the money at the airport" may be the best thing to do given the twist to the phenomenon of "cargo cults", where the over-response by government and the NGOs to the 1977 cyclone, and others since, has resulted in people in the coastal areas lobbying the politicians at the *first* cyclone warning to bargain for relief, whether the cyclone hits their area or not. This activity has now become part of the risk-reduction strategies of the people in the coastal areas and has produced mixed results, one being a wariness of NGOs to become involved in post-disaster work for fear of being duped by clamorous victims, and another is increasing scepticism by the government about the validity of the villagers' claims.

NGOs are unlikely to consider this rule as one of any value because it undermines their reasons for existence and their credibility in the eyes of their donors. They also feel that there is little or no guarantee that the aid they might bring and "leave at the airport" would not fall into the hands of the powerful sections in the society, but the evidence of the failure of "trickle down" and "trickle up" development should have convinced them by now. Underlying their resistance to heed this advice is the gnawing suspicion that whatever they do the NGOs are having little effect within the political realities in which they work. As long as their work is tied to projects and programmes of one sort or another they are likely to have doubts similar to those expressed by Susan George:

> . . . very little can be done to help the rural [and urban] poor without overwhelming social changes in their own countries. Most projects can therefore be little more than palliative measures serving the élites, in the final analysis, as alibis for maintaining the *status quo*. Thus I would urge people to give support to national liberation and minority political groups whose goal is to change the whole society, but there are probably few charitable organisations willing to go that far. (George 1986: 296.)

7.3.4 Rule Four: If you have to come then be prepared to stay forever

The essence of this rule is that **TIME** is needed in one place to understand the complexities within any society. There are two important aspects to note: first, it takes time to understand what is going on underneath the surface; and, secondly, it takes more time to implement programmes. For anyone working in a foreign culture perhaps the most important thing they can do is to become more aware as why things *don't* change rather than why they do change, and of course this takes time. Every generation attempts to change something it inherits and the reasons why things do not change reveal the underlying forces that operate within societies (Moore 1969: 313). Only long-run studies will reveal what forces operate within societies and how vulnerability alters over time and perhaps even 10 years in one area is not enough. (Even the presence of two highly creditable NGOs in Divi Seema for four and seven years was not enough to have any lasting effects except on a handful of people.)

Staying "forever" requires a long-term commitment of its resources by an NGO and this is difficult for many of them, given the voluntary nature of their funding and their desire to assist as many disadvantaged people as they can. However, many indigenous NGOs in India, with limited resources, are turning to "social activities" (Sheth 1983; 1985; Nandy 1987; World Development 1987) as disappointments with NGO development projects increase.

One reason for stressing the need for a long-term commitment by NGOs is their need to achieve an effective relationship with government (Chatturvedi 1987; Garilao 1987; Clark 1991) so that they achieve more than just "bandaging" operations; another reason is that, too often, NGOs fail to create indigenous leadership structures capable of safeguarding a community's new-found strengths, *after their departure* (Chapter Four, sections 4.2 and 4.4). However, NGOs have difficulties that are not unique to them. For instance, NGOs compete for resources amongst themselves and in many cases depend for their success on the charismatic qualities of one person. When this person leaves, either by choice or as a result of "internal politics", the resources tend to dry up and a potentially self-reliant community is put at risk. This applies equally to NGOs who focus on social activism as it does to NGOs who go in for long-term projects.

A cruel choice for many NGOs with limited time and money is where to put their resources. By staying in one place "forever" they may put another group at a disadvantage; a miserable double bind. But staying must have its rewards, otherwise many agencies and individuals would not do it. Occasionally, when the television cameras focus on an event that makes its way into the headlines, it is discovered that priests or voluntary workers have been in some slum or other or in some remote place for 20-odd years. Staying is certainly less glamorous than "academic tourism" and yet the most cost effective agencies and people, not just Jesuit priests but many others, are those that **stay** in one place for years. The main difficulty with staying is NOT for the agency or individuals to identify with the people, but the other way round – the people have to identify with the outsider, and this can take years and years. The "outsider" has to be seen as part of the **same** society, suffering the same sorrows and enjoying the same pleasures and successes as the people.

An educated man (M) and his wife, a nursing sister (T) lived in a community of 5,000 *Harijans*. The land was owned by large farmers who leased it to the community. For seven years M and T practised what they preached, drawing funds from many sources. They set up a school, to which their son went, opened a clinic and an animal husbandry unit and raised loans for the villagers through the banks. Through the continuous presence of M and T, life for the villagers improved way beyond what they had experienced before. One year, after a poor harvest, the tenant villagers were unable to pay what they owed the landlords so the landlords came with their *goondals* (hooligans) and burned the crops, poisoned the water in the tanks, burned down the school and clinic and beat up several villagers. M and T complained to the police and spent time and money to get the case into the courts where it was thrown out. Next year the harvest failed again and the landlords repeated what they had done the year before but this time their hooligans beat up M and T so severely that M had to spend a month in hospital. When the family returned to continue their work, the headman of the village said to them: "They treat you like one of us, so now you are one of us".

Probably the most useful and ultimately rewarding activity an outsider can undertake, before starting to propose projects is to observe and record, in other words "look before you leap". Rapid appraisals can be useful, providing they are carried out by people who have sufficient experience to understand the underlying processes within the society, but in many cases they are used by professionals as substitutes for spending time in a place and getting to know it. We saw how accurate the surveys carried out by the DSSSS and the Salvation Army were in terms of the relevance of their diagnosis, and their example should be followed by all concerned with the alleviation of suffering and misery. Time is not of the essence here, but accuracy is.

7.3.5 Rule Five: Government: you have the power; you are in charge

Governments have the power and the resources to mitigate the worst effects of cyclones and other catastrophic natural events, alongside which, in most countries, the resources of the NGOs are negligible. We touched on the conflicting political pressures governing the allocation of resources in cyclone prone areas in India (Chapter One, section 1.3.1). One of the tasks facing disaster managers, in India and elsewhere, is to lessen these pressures and to convince governments that disaster mitigation is development in another form. Any field of activity or area of expertise should be included in disaster management and the concept underlying disaster management should be enlarged beyond the narrow confines of physical phenomena.

Viewed from the perspective of this book, there are two possible ways for disaster management to develop. One way is to continue focusing on preparedness to deal with the physical and economic aspects of the impact of physical phenomena – i.e., improving administrative procedures and logistics, perfecting technical evaluations, improving building standards, stockpiling and improving forecasting, warning and evacuation systems and procedures, building better sea walls, more cyclone shelters and more and better "durable" housing, producing better training programmes for officials and potential victims, publishing more manuals and plans to alert all concerned, training more disaster managers in administration, and so on, and so on, and so on. But will all this effort change the fundamental causes of disasters?

"More of the same" disaster management may also increasingly become its own victim of political and commercial competition. Those working in disaster management will inevitably be drawn into auctions between themselves and forced to provide increasingly generous promises of aid, or durable houses, or training programmes and so on, and the disaster industry will acquire the nature of the motor car industry, each consultant or organisation promising a better model this year, with more extras and so on.

Although current disaster mitigation programmes are geared towards prevention, they are still "waiting for something to happen". In the meantime, the everyday disasters continue:

> . . . past crisis interventions have often come too late, after poor people have become poorer by disposing of productive assets, or after they have taken debts or obligations which prejudice their livelihoods, and their future interventions should come earlier. (Chambers 1989: 4.)

The other approach for disaster management is for it to become a development process which includes all forms of development activity, from providing permanent health services and creating employment before disasters to reconstruction afterwards. The current disaster mitigation programmes could then be reduced to a minimum, concentrating on relief only. Instead of building up the *physical infrastructure* of disaster-prone areas, mitigation programmes would put resources into building up the long-term *economic infrastructure* of the poorest **people** so that their everyday disastrous conditions are reduced. Many would argue that building up the physical infrastructures of disaster-prone areas is the same as building up the economic infrastructure of the poorest people, but, we have shown that the post-disaster development in one disaster-prone area, Divi Seema, had, by and large, only benefited those with the capital and resources to take advantage of it (Chapter Four, section 4.4).

Chambers proposes that governments should "provide floors underneath the vulnerable" and he cites the Maharashtra Employment Guarantee Scheme which:

> . . . provides a model of how, given the administrative capability to respond, poor people can be empowered to demand and receive work and renumeration when they need it. Food for work schemes require less sustained administration and can have the same effect – putting a floor under the poor to enable them to survive a bad time without having to become poorer. It seems more cost-effective as well as being more humane to use such means to reduce vulnerability and prevent impoverishment than, once people are poorer or destitute, to try and enable them to recover (Chambers 1989: 5),

and he goes on to suggest (p. 6) that:

> Guaranteed markets at good prices for whatever poor people sell at bad times are another form of floor . . . . Cheap and accessible food is another form of floor. Whatever their defects, programmes such as the Andhra Pradesh's cheap rice help the poorest, providing they have access to buying it. Assuring basic food at low prices is one of the safest ways of mitigating poverty and reducing vulnerability.

In the second approach, the bulk of the resources normally devoted to disaster prevention, on the lines we have discussed above, would be diverted to building up a type of welfare-state system, with people qualifying for resources and/or assistance **before** disasters. Disaster-prone areas might become mini welfare states on the same lines, in principle – along the lines that exist in the drought-prone areas of the state of Maharashtra.

One drawback with this idea is that the people in non-disaster-prone areas would demand equivalent favours and concessions and the designation of such areas would become tangled up in the myriad complexities of politics. If qualifications for benefits were to be regulated by "ceilings" and "floors" then they too could be the subject of abuse such as happened with the Land Ceiling Acts in the 1960s. But the idea has some merit in so far as it pinpoints the dichotomy between prevention and cure. A concept of a welfare **system** instead of a concept of welfare *projects* may restrict the huge amounts of money that go into prestige projects which either collapse, are never finished, are never used or occasionally never start.

Perhaps as important as a food security system is the need to provide low-cost or free health services, which our own fieldwork has substantiated.

Health services which are cheap or free and are accessible and effective are more important than ever. These services have a greater role in reducing vulnerability and limiting impoverishment than has previously been recognised. Adult health, especially the health of breadwinners, is more important than many supposed for the nutrition and health of children. (Chambers 1989: 6.)

Improved health services gives more choice to the most vulnerable and should form an integral part of any disaster mitigation programmes. Only governments have the power and resources to tackle this problem effectively.

What are the implications for disaster management? We have brought forward evidence to show that the concept of differential vulnerability differs from the conventional concept of vulnerability that pervades disaster management, with its focus on the physical aspects of disasters, and that programmes which ignore the varied differentiations between groups of people within the same disaster prone areas condemn millions to misery and perpetual insecurity. The focus of disaster management on prevention is correct. By focusing on the prevention of losses and suffering from physical causes, disaster management begs the question for whom is the natural disaster a disaster?

We hope we have convinced the reader that a disaster is as much the loss of a wage earner which plunges a family into debt, an illness that drains a family's resources and forces it to sell everything, a disabling accident that prevents taking on work or finishing a training programme, a corrupt official who cancels a loan, a venal politician who requires a bribe that takes five years to pay back, as a cyclone strike. Our evidence suggests that any one of these disasters could set a family back 10 years (Chapters 5 and 6).

Even a cyclone strike will not set everyone back to an irretrievable economic level since we have seen quite clearly that even the poorest people recover relatively quickly from a cyclone (Figure 6.3), *provided they are helped*, and the most practical method of help for them and best use of resources is within a welfare security system (Ahmed *et al.* 1991).

> Equity-oriented policies and programmes pursued within the cast iron iniquitous economic structure of ownership of assets [that prevails today in India] will not only be self-defeating, but may prove counterproductive, through a "trickle up" [process]. More simply a direct attack on poverty without an equally direct attack on the structure which has bred poverty and continues to do so is an illusion at best, fraud at worst. (Dantwala 1985.)

7.4 CONCLUDING REMARKS

The evidence we have presented in this book has unearthed some major defficiencies in government policy in the study area, such as the provision of health services that do not financially cripple those that want to use them, a lack of medical programmes to decrease the incidence of illness, the lack of opportunities for obtaining crisis credit, the widely prevalent lack of formal credit among the poorest groups and lack of alternative employment. We would argue that programmes to counter these omissions should be regarded as part of cyclone mitigation policy and therefore policy should change.

However, there would be considerable opposition to large-scale change. Since policies are normally advocated, and their implementation supervised, by people who are in some way committed to them, changes in policies of a certain magnitude must therefore involve changes of personnel in the policy-making structures. The dominant individuals and groups in the policy-making structure and the Indian political economy are intricately but firmly linked at many different levels, and, in the villages the powerful people are those with links outside the villages. These people are concerned mainly with preserving the *status quo* and maintaining their vested interests in the agricultural economy. Policies of least change are generally the same ones that maximise safety and do least to upset the powerful sections of the community and so are most likely to be accepted.

Maximising safety instead of security, as a basis for a policy in cyclone-prone areas, not only directs attention away from the real causes of social weakness and disadvantage, but also gives a plausibility and credibility on the emotional level which leads to the confused debate about the "value of a human life". To "minimise unhappiness" (suffering) is not just the negative formulation of the notion "maximise happiness". It is not possible to know exactly how to make people happy, but it is known how to reduce their suffering. This important precept is made explicit by Karl Popper:

. . . from the ethical point of view [there is] no symmetry between suffering and happiness or between pain and pleasure . . . human suffering makes a direct moral appeal, namely the appeal for help while there is no similar call to increase the happiness of a man who is doing well anyway. A further criticism of the utilitarian formula 'maximize pleasure' is that it assumes, in principle, a continuous pleasure pain scale which allows us to treat degrees of pain as negative degrees of pleasure . . . . Instead of the greatest happiness for the greatest number one should demand, more modestly, the least amount of avoidable suffering for all. (Popper 1966, Volume I: 284–285.)

This precept reinforces our scepticism about the philosophy of maximising safety as an exclusive basis for cyclone policies, by raising the question: "At what stage are people safe and is the top priority to make them safe against cyclones?" The notion of safety has been thought of purely in technical terms but it has far deeper political implications. The strongest instinct we have is the instinct for survival and so the strongest need is probably the need for security. People are therefore prepared to shift the responsibility for their security only to someone or something else in whom they have greater confidence than in themselves. People want a release from fear and most fears – i.e., death, the consequences of their actions, the future, and so on – are basically forms of fear of the unknown. People need assurances that the unknown is known, but if the focus of their fear is on something that is beyond their control – i.e., natural phenomena – then the random devastations of such phenomena can only be explained by metaphysics, cosmic determination (Hewitt 1983), and the savagery of nature.

If the source of the problem of safety is claimed to be outside society and the solution is large-scale protection, then the onus of responsibility, and subsequent dependence, falls increasingly on governments who are the only agency with sufficient resources. If the source of the problem was seen to be equally, or to some extent, due to the actions of powerful sections in society then the focus on fear of something beyond anyone's control would be replaced by greater criticism of policy and might lead to changes in policy.

It is in the interests of certain powerful sections in society to increase the dependency of subject groups and in this they can be greatly assisted by ill informed technical experts. As long as technical experts perceive the solutions to vulnerability in terms of technical adjustments **in isolation from political realities,** then solutions will only treat symptoms and not causes, and spirals of dependency and expectation will inevitably be created which in time may create their own political cyclones.

Bibliography

Ahmad, A. (ed.). 1981. *Workshop Proceedings: Disaster Management Preparedness and Response*. Administrative Staff College of India (ASCI) and Appropriate Reconstruction Training Information Centre (ARTIC): Hyderabad, 16–18 February 1980.

Ahmad, E., Dreze, J., Hills, J. and Sen Amartya (eds). 1991. *Social Security in Developing Countries*. Oxford: Clarendon Press.

Amin, S. 1974. "Accumulation and Development: A Theoretical Model". *Review of African Political Economy* (cited by Baird *et al.* 1975: 29).

Andhra Pradesh, Government of. 1971. *Final Report of the Cyclone Distress Mitigation Committee*. Hyderabad: Office of the Chief Engineer, Major Irrigation.

Andhra Pradesh, Government of. 1973. *District Census Handbook, Andhra Pradesh, Krishna District*. Village and Town Directory; Village and Town Primary Census Abstract. Series 2. Parts X. A & B.

Andhra Pradesh, Government of. 1977a. *Statement on Cyclone and Tidal Wave on 19th November 1977 by Sri Vengala Rao, Chief Minister of Andhra Pradesh*. Hyderabad: Government Secretariat Press.

Andhra Pradesh, Government of. 1977b. *Andhra Pradesh District Gazetteers, Krishna*. Hyderabad: Government Secretariat Press.

Andhra Pradesh, Government of. 1978. *Fifth Five Year Plan (1978–1983)*. Finance and Planning Department. (Housing Policy 77–83). Hyderabad.

Andhra Pradesh, Government of. 1979a. *Note on the Recent Cyclone by Dr. M. Channa Reddy, Chief Minister of Andhra Pradesh*. Hyderabad: Government Secretariat Press.

Andhra Pradesh, Government of. 1979b. *Statement showing proposed expenditures on Shelter Belt Planting and protection in Tidal Wave affected areas*. Hyderabad: Revenue Department.

Andhra Pradesh, Government of. 1980a. *Community Cyclone Shelter Construction Programme for Cyclone-Prone Areas of Andhra Pradesh*. Hyderabad: Revenue Department.

Andhra Pradesh, Government of. 1980b. *Sixth Five Year Plan (Draft) (1980–1985). Vol.I; Vol. II; Vol. III*. Finance and Planning Department. Hyderabad: Government Secretariat Press (Housing Policy for Cyclone Prone Areas 392–393).

Andhra Pradesh, Government of. 1980c. "Rehabilitation and Construction of Permanent Houses in Cyclone-Affected Areas in Krishna District". Masulipatnam: Office of the Collector of Krishna district.

Andhra Pradesh, Government of. 1981a. "Note on Cyclone Damages Relief and Rehabilitation regarding the Cyclones of November 1977 and May 1979 in Guntur District". Annexure I: Cyclone 1977. Sectorwise damages and its value. Annexure II: Details of Cyclone Relief Measures and Relief Works Undertaken. Annexure III: Progress of Construction of Cyclone Housing Colonies in Guntur District up to the End of February 1981. Annexure IV: Statement showing progress in the construction of Cyclone Shelters in Guntur District up to the end of

BIBLIOGRAPHY

February 1981. Annexure V: Cyclone in May 1979. Annexure VI: Relief Measures undertaken – May 1979 Cyclone. Hyderabad: Revenue Department.

Andhra Pradesh, Government of. 1981b. *The Andhra Pradesh Natural Calamities (Relief and Rehabilitation) Act 1981.* Legislative Assembly Bill 38. 1981. Andhra Pradesh Gazette. Part IV A – Extraordinary. Hyderabad: Government Central Press.

Andhra Pradesh, Government of. 1981c. "Statement showing losses of crops, cattle, human lives and other wealth, devastated by the cyclones in November 1977 and May 1979". Hyderabad: Revenue Department.

Andhra Pradesh, Government of. 1981d. *Cyclone Contingency Plan of Action.* Hyderabad: Revenue Department.

Andhra Pradesh, Government of. 1981e. "Statement showing the expenditure incurred on construction of housing colonies and provision of infrastructure in the tidal-wave-affected area of the Krishna district". (December). Masulipatnam: Office of the Collector of Krishna district.

Andhra Pradesh, Government of. 1982a. *Rice in Andhra Pradesh. A Study in Intra State Variations, Kharif 1978. Part I, Report.* Waltair: Agro-Economic Research Centre, University of Andhra Pradesh.

Andhra Pradesh, Government of. 1982b. "Statement showing the progress of the construction of the houses by various voluntary organisations, Krishna and Guntur districts". Masulipatnam and Guntur: Offices of the Collectors of Krishna and Guntur districts to Director of Andhra Pradesh Housing Corporation.

Andhra Pradesh, Government of. 1982c. *Map showing distribution of Housing colonies, cyclone shelters, in Divi taluk, projected and built.* Hyderabad: Office of the Assistant Director, District Survey and Land Records.

Andhra Pradesh, Government of. 1982d. "Cyclone housing in Divi *taluk.* 31.8.82". Masulipatnam: Office of the Collector of Krishna district. Internal paper. CR 14721/78.

Andhra Pradesh, Government of. 1982e. *Report on Housing and Land Colonisation Programmes for the Rural Poor,* prepared by the Centre for Planning and Development Studies: Technical Cell. Andhra University, Waltair. Hyderabad. Government Press.

Andhra Pradesh, Government of. 1982f *Manual for E.W.S Housing Programmes.* Vols 1 and II; Hyderabad: Directorate of Weaker Sections Housing.

Andhra Pradesh, Government of. 1983a. "*Rehabilitation and Construction of Permanent Houses in Cyclone-Affected Areas in Krishna District*". Office of the Collector of Krishna district: Internal paper CR 132111/78.

Andhra Pradesh, Government of. 1983b. *Budget Estimates (Non-Plan) for the year 1983–84, Volume III. Part I. Details of demands for Grants.* Minister for Finance. Hyderabad: Government Central Press.

Andhra Pradesh, Government of. 1983c. *Budget Estimates (Non Plan) for the year 1983–84. Volume III. Part I.* Details of demands for Grants. Minister for Finance. Hyderabad: Government Central Press.

Andhra Pradesh, Government of. 1983d. *Budget Estima⁝s (Plan) for the year 1983–84. Schemes in the Plan, Volume III. Part II. Details of demands for Grants.* Minister for Finance. Hyderabad: Government Central Press.

van Apeldoorn, G. 1981. *Perspectives on Drought and Famine in Nigeria.* London: George, Allen and Unwin.

Arrow, K. J. and Hahn, F. H. 1971. *General Competitive Analysis.* San Francisco: Holden Day Inc., and Edinburgh: Oliver Boyd.

Ayyar, R. V. V. 1980. *Problems of housing in cyclone-prone areas.* Administrative Staff College of India, Hyderabad, Internal Paper and annexures. [Also published in A. Ahmad (ed.) 1981, *op. cit.*, pp. 51–62].

Baird, S., O'Keefe, P., Westgate, K. N. and Wisner, B. 1975. *Towards an Explanation and Reduction of Disaster-Proneness.* Disaster Research Unit Occasional Paper No. 11, University of Bradford.

196

BIBLIOGRAPHY

Baker, P. R. 1981. *Land Degradation in Kenya: Economic or Social Crisis.* School of Development Studies Discussion Paper No. 82, School of Development Studies, University of East Anglia, Norwich.

Balasubramaniam, K., *et al.* 1982. "Interaction of the two cyclones of November 1977 over Indian seas". *Mausam*, 2: 207–210.

Barkun, N. 1974. *Disaster and the Millenium.* New Haven: Yale University Press.

Barry, R. G. and Chorley, R. J. 1976. *Atmosphere, Weather and Climate.* (Third Edition). London: Methuen.

Beck, Tony. 1989. "Survival Strategies and Power amongst the Poorest in a West Bengal Village". *IDS Bulletin*, 20: 23–31.

Beckinsale, R. P. 1969. "The Nature of Tropical Rainfall". *Tropical Agriculture*, 34: 76–98.

Bernstein, H. (ed.). 1973. *Underdevelopment and Development: The Third World Today.* Harmondsworth: Penguin.

Bernstein, H. 1979a. "Sociology of Underdevelopment versus the Sociology of Development?" in D. Lehmann (ed.). *Development Theory: Four Critical Essays*, pp. 77–106. London: Frank Cass.

Bernstein, H. 1979b. "African Peasantries: Theoritical framework". *Journal of Peasant Studies*, 6: 420–444.

Beteille, A. 1965. *Caste, Class and Power.* Berkeley: University of California Press.

Bhaskara Rao, N. S., and Mazumdar, S. 1966. "A Technique for Forecasting Storm Waves". *Indian Journal of Meteorology and Geophysics*, 17: 333–346.

Binswanger, H. P. and Sillers, D. A. 1983. "Risk Aversion and Credit Constraints in Farmers' Decision Making: A Reinterpretation". *Journal of Development Studies*, 20(1): 5–21.

Blaikie, P. M. 1981. "Class, Land Use and Soil Erosion". Paper presented at Development Studies Association Annual Conference, Oxford, September 1981. [Reprinted in *ODI Review*, 1981(2): 57–66).

Blaikie, P. M. 1985. *The Political Economy of Soil Erosion.* London: Longmans.

Bremen, J. 1974. *Patronage and Exploitation: Changing Agrarian Relations in South Gujarat.* Berkeley: University of California Press.

Britton, N. 1987. "Towards a Reconceptualisation of Disaster for the Enhancement of Social Preparedness" in Dynes *et al.* (eds) 1987, *op. cit.*, 31–55.

Brodhead, T. 1987. "NGOs: In One Year, Out the Other?" *World Development*, 15: 1–6.

Burton, I., and Kates, R. W. 1964. "The Perception of Natural Hazards in Resource Management". *Natural Resources Journal*, 3: 412–441.

Burton, I., Kates, R. W. and White, G. F. 1968. *The Human Ecology of Extreme Geophysical Events.* Department of Geography, Natural Hazard Research Working Paper No. 1, Department of Geography, University of Toronto.

Burton, I., Kates, R. W. and White, G. F. 1978. *The Environment as Hazard.* New York: Oxford University Press.

Chambers, R. 1982. "Health, Agriculture and Rural Poverty: Why Seasons Matter". *Journal of Development Studies*, 18(2): 218–238.

Ch mbers, R. 1983. *Rural Development: Putting the Last First.* Harlow: Longmans.

Chambers, R. 1988. *Poverty in India: Concepts, Research and Reality.* Discussion Paper No. 241, Institu e of Development Studies, University of Sussex.

Chambers, R. 1989. "Vulnerability, Coping and Policy" *IDS Bulletin*, 20: 1–7.

Chambers, R., Longhurst, R. and Pacey A. 1981. *Seasonal Dimensions to Rural Poverty.* London: Frances Pinter.

Chatturvedi, T. N. (ed.) 1987. *Voluntary Organisations and Development: Their Role and Functions.* [Special Number, *Indian Journal of Public Administration*, Vol XXXIII, No. 3 (Delhi).]

Chen, L. C. (ed.) 1973. *Disaster in Bangladesh.* New York: Oxford University Press.

Clark, J. 1991. *Democratizing Development. The Role of Voluntary Organisations.* London: Earthscan

Connell, J., Dasgupta, L. and Lipton, M. 1976. *Migration from Rural Areas*. Delhi: Oxford University Press.

Cook, S. 1975. "Production, Ecology and Economic Anthropology". *Social Scientific Information*, 12: 25–52 (cited by M. Watts in K. Hewitt 1983).

Corbett, J. 1989. "Poverty and Sickness: The High Costs of Ill-Health". *IDS Bulletin*, 20: 58–67.

Cuny, F. C. 1984. *Disasters and Development*. New York: Oxford University Press.

Dantwala, M. L. 1985. "Garibi hatao: strategy options". *Economic and Political Weekly*, Vol. 20, No. 11. March 16.

Das, P. K., Sinha, M. C. and Balasubramanyan, V. 1974. "Storm Surges in the Bay of Bengal". *Quarterly Journal, Royal Meteorological Society*, 100: 437–449.

Davis, I. R. 1981a. *Shelter after Disaster*. Oxford: Oxford Polytechnic Press.

Davis, I. R. 1981b. *Disasters and the Small Dwelling*. Oxford: Pergamon.

Desai, B. N., *et al.* 1979. "Role of Mountains in the Development of the Indian Summer Monsoon Circulation and the Associated Weather". *Mausam*, 80(4): 463–468.

Divi Seema Social Service Society (D.S.S.S.S.). 1978. *Socio-Economic Survey Conducted during May 1978: Six Months after the Tidal Wave Tragedy of November 1977*. (Nagayalanka), mimeo.

Drabek, A. G. 1987. "Development Alternatives: The Challenge for NGOs – An overview of the Issues". *World Development*: ix–xv.

D'Souza, F. 1984. "The Socio-Economic Cost of Planning for Hazards: An Analysis of Barkulti Village, Yasin, N. Pakistan" in J. Miller (ed.) *International Karakoram Project, Vol. 2*, pp. 303–321. Cambridge: Cambridge University Press.

Dube, S. K., Sinha, P. C. and Rao, A. D. 1981. "The Response of Different Wind-Stress Forcings on the Surges along the East Coast of India". *Mausam*, 32: 315–320.

Dynes, R. R., Haas, J. E. and Quarantelli, E. L. 1967. "Administrative, Methodological and Theoretical Problems of disaster Research". *Indian Sociological Bulletin*, 4: 215–217.

Dynes, R. R., de Marchi, B. and Pelanda, C., 1987. *Sociology of Disasters: Contribution of Sociology to Disaster Research*. Milan: Franco Angeli.

Dynes, R. R. and Quarantelli, E. L. 1977. *Organisational Communications and Decision-making in Crises*. Report, Series 17. Columbus, Ohio. Disaster Research Centre, The Ohio State University.

Dynes, R. R., Quarantelli, E. L. and Kreps, G. A. 1972. *A Perspective on Disaster Planning*. Columbus, Ohio. Disaster Research Centre, The Ohio State University.

Elliott, C. M. 1970. "Caste and Faction among the Dominant Caste: The Reddis and Kammas of Andhra", in R. Kothari (ed.) *Caste in Indian Politics*, pp. 129–171.

Evans, T. 1989. "The Impact of Permanent Disability on Rural Households: River Blindness in Guinea". *IDS Bulletin*, 20: 41–48.

Fernandez, A. P. 1987. "NGOs in South Asia: People's Participation and Partnership". *World Development*, 15: 39–49.

Frank, A. G. 1966. "The Development of Underdevelopment". *Monthly Review*, September.

Frank, A. G. 1973. *Dependent Accumulation and Underdevelopment*. London: Macmillan.

Frank, N. L. and Husain, S. A. 1971. "The Deadliest Tropical Cyclone in History". *Bulletin, American Meteorological Society*, 52(6): 438–444.

Garilao, E. D. 1987. "Indigenous NGOs as Strategic Insitutions: Managing the Relationship with Government and Resource Agencies". *World Development*, 15: 113–120.

George, S. 1986. How the Other Half Dies: The Real Reasons for World Hunger. (Reprint.) Pelican.

Gosh, S. K. 1977. "Prediction of Storm Surges on the East Coast of India". *Indian Journal Meteorology, Hydrology and Geophysics*, 28: 157–168.

Government of India. 1932. *Map of the Krishna Delta: Irrigation and Land Use*. Office of the Surveyor-General, Madras: Government press. (Amendments 1938.)

Government of India. 1973. *District Census Handbook, Andhra Pradesh, Krishna District. Village and Town Directory; Village and Town Primary Census Abstract*. Series 2. Parts X. A & B.

Government of Andhra Pradesh, Government Secretariat Press, Hyderabad.

Government of India. 1977. *Sarvekshana. Housing condition NSS 28th Round (1973–74)*. Department of Statistics and Planning. New Delhi.

Government of India. 1978. *Report of the Finance Commission*. Delhi. Government Press.

Government of India. 1981. *Report of the Group on Disaster Preparedness and Management*. New Delhi. Government Central Press.

Government of India. 1983. *District Census Handbook, Andhra Pradesh, Krishna District. Village and Town Directory; Village and Town Primary Census Abstract*. Series 2. Parts X. A & B. Government of Andhra Pradesh, Government Secretariat Press, Hyderabad.

Government of Madras. 1859. *Administration Report of the Madras Public Works for the Official Year 1957–58*. Madras: Fort Saint George Gazette Press.

Government of Madras. 1878. *Annual Progress Reports of the Irrigation Branch of the Public Works Department in the Madras Presidency*. Madras: Government Gazette Press.

Government of Madras. 1883. *A Manual of the Kistna District in the Presidency of Madras*. G. Mackenzie. Madras: Lawrence Asylum Press.

Government of Madras. 1902. *Administration Report for the Year 1901–02, Part II*. Irrigation Public Works Department, Madras Presidency. Madras: Government Press.

Government of Madras. 1908. *Administrative Report of the Irrigation Branch of the Public Works Department in the Madras Presidency for the Year 1907–08*. Madras. Government Press.

Government of Madras. 1915. *Gazetteer of the Kistna District*, Vol. 2. Madras: Government Press.

Government of Madras. 1934. *Gazetteer of the Kistna District*, Vol. 2. Madras: Government Press.

Government of Madras. 1938. *Administrative Report of the Irrigation Branch of the Public Works Department in the Madras Presidency for the Year 1937–38*. Madras. Government Press.

Government of Maharashtra. 1981. *Report of the Group on Disaster Preparedness and Management*. New Delhi: Office of the State Planning Board.

Government of Tamil Nadu. 1979. *Socio-Economic Impact of Disasters: Nilgiris District*. Madras: Directorate of Town and Country Planning.

Gray, W. M. 1968. "Global View of the Origin of Tropical Disturbances and Hurricanes". *Monthly Weather Review*, 96: 669–700.

Griffin, K. 1974. *The Political Economy of Agrarian Change*. London: Macmillan.

Guhan, S. 1980. "Rural Poverty: Policy or Play Acting?" *Economic and Political Weekly*, Vol 15, No. 47, November 22.

Guhan, S. 1986. "Reaching out to the Poor". *Economic Times*, December 19.

Handmer, J. and Penning-Rowsell, E. (eds). 1990. *Hazards and the Communication of Risk*. London: Gower.

Hartmann, B. and Boyce, J. K. 1983. *A Quiet Violence: A View from a Bangladesh Village*. London: Zed Press.

Hewitt, K. 1976. "Earthquake Hazards in Mountains". *Natural History*. May: 30–37.

Hewitt, K. 1983. "Calamity in a Technocratic Age" in K. Hewitt (ed.) *Interpretations of Calamity*, 3–30. New York: Allen and Unwin.

Hewitt, K. and Burton, I. 1971. *The Hazardousness of a Place: A Regional Ecology of Damaging Events*. Department of Geography Research Publication No. 6, Department of Geography, University of Toronto.

Heyer J. 1989. "Landless Agricultural Labourers' Asset Strategies". *IDS Bulletin*, 20: 33–39.

Hoover, R. A. 1957. "Empirical Relationships of Central Pressures in Hurricanes to the Maximum Surge and Storm Tide". *Monthly Weather Review*, 85: 167–174.

Indian Meteorological Department (I.M.D.) 1960. *Monsoons of the World*. Delhi: I.M.D.

Institute of Development Studies. 1986. "Seasonality and Poverty". *IDS Bulletin* 17(3):.

Institute of Development Studies. 1989. "Vulnerability: How the Poor cope". *IDS Bulletin*, 20(2).

Islam, M. A. 1971. *Human Adjustment to Cyclone Hazards: A Case Study of Char Jabbar*. Natural Hazard Research Working Paper No. 18, Institute of Behavioral Science, University of Colorado. Colorado.

BIBLIOGRAPHY

Islam, M. A. 1974. "Tropical Cyclones: Coastal Bangladesh" in G. White (ed.) *Natural Hazards*: 19–25.

Islam, M. A. 1981. "Human Adjustment to Cyclone Hazards in Coastal Bangladesh" in K. M. Elahi (ed.) *Perspectives on Bangladesh Geography*. Bangladesh National Geographical Association.

Jeffrey, S. E. 1980. *Our Usual Landslide: Ubiquitous Hazard and Socio-Economic Causes of Natural Disaster in Indonesia*. Natural Hazards Research Working Paper No. 40, University of Colorado, Boulder.

Jeffrey, S. E. 1982. "The Creation of Vulnerability to Natural Disaster: Case Studies from the Dominican Republic". *Disasters*, 6(1): 36–43.

Jodha, N. S. 1976. "Famine and Famine Policies: Some Empirical Evidence". *Economic and Political Weekly*, Vol. 10, No. 41, October 11.

Jodha, N. S. 1978. "Effectiveness of Farmers' Adjustments to Risk". *Economic and Political Weekly*, Vol. 13, No. 25, June 24.

Jodha, N. S. 1981. "Role of Credit in Farmers' Adjustments against Risk in Arid and Semi-Arid Tropical Agricultural Areas of India". *Economic and Political Weekly*, Vol. 31, No. 14, October 16.

Jodha, N. S. 1983. "Market Forces and Erosion of Common Property Resources". Paper presented to the International Workshop on Agricultural Markets in the Semi-Arid Tropics, ICRISAT, Hyderabad, India.

Joseph, P. V. 1980. "Ocean Atmosphere Interaction on a Seasonal Scale over North Indian Ocean and Indian Monsoon Rainfall and Cyclone Tracks". *Mausam*, 32: 237–46.

Kates, R. W. 1962. *Hazard and Choice Perception in Flood Plain Management*. Research Paper No. 78, Department of Geography, University of Chicago.

Khan, W. 1982. *Financial Resources for the Plan* [Sixth Five Year Plan: 1980–85]. Centre for Economics and Social Studies, Discussion Paper No. 1, CESS, Hyderabad.

Koteswaram, P. N. 1958. "The Easterly Jet Stream in the Tropics". *Tellus*, 10: 43–57.

Koteswaram, P. N. 1981. "Cyclone Warning Systems: Dissemination to the Grass-Roots Level". Paper presented to Conference on Disaster Management, in A. Ahmad (ed.) *Workshop Proceedings*, 86–96.

Kothari, R. 1981. "On Eco-Imperialism". *Alternatives* (Delhi) 7: 385–394.

Kothari, R. 1983. "The Party and State in our times; the Rise of Non-Party-Political Formations". *Alternatives* 9: 595–618.

Kothari, R. 1986. "Masses, Classes and the State". *Alternatives*: 167–183.

Kumar, P. V. S. 1982. "The Awakening: The Story of Divi Seema Social Service Society". Indo-German Social Service Society, Vol. 9, No. 4, New Delhi.

Kurian, N. J. 1987. "IRDP: How relevant is it?" *Economic and Political Weekly*, Vol. 22, No. 52, November 30.

Lehmann, D. 1979. *Development Theory: Four Critical Studis*. London: Frank Cass.

Lockwood, J. G. 1965. "The Indian Monsoon". *Weather*, 20: 2–8.

Mitchell, J. K. 1974. *Community Response to Coastal Erosion*. Research Paper No. 156, Department of Geography, University of Chicago.

Mitra, A. 1977. *Terms of Trade and Class Relations: An Assay in Political Economy*. London: Frank Cass.

Moore, J. B. Jnr. 1969. *The Social Origins of Dictatorship and Democracy*. Harmondsworth: Penguin.

Mukherjee, A. K., Gupta, H. V. and Guranadham, G. 1979. "On Interaction between Tropical Cyclones over Indian Seas and Neighbourhood". *Mausam*, 30(4): 457–462.

Nageswara Rao, K. 1980. *Landforms and Land Uses in the Krishna Delta, India*. Unpublished Ph.D. thesis, Department of Geography, University of Andhra Pradesh, Waltair.

Nageswara Rao, K. and Prasad, T. 1979. "Effect of Landforms on the Pattern, Size and Spacing of Rural Settlements in the Krishna Delta". *Indian Geographical Journal*, 54(1): 31–39.

Nageswara Rao, K. and Vaidyanaham, R. 1978. "Geomorphic Features in the Krishna Delta and its Evolution". *Proceedings Symposium of Morphological Evolution of Land Forms*: 120–130, University of Delhi (cited by K. Nageswara Rao *et al.* in K. Nageswara Rao 1979, 1981).

Nandy, A. 1987. "Development and Authoritarianism: An Epithaph on Social Engineering", *Lokayan Bulletin*, 5(1): 39–50.

National Academy of Sciences. 1978a. *The Role of Technology in International Disaster Assistance: Proceedings of the Committee on International Disaster Assistance Workshop, March 1977.* Washington: National Academy of Sciences.

National Academy of Sciences. 1978b. *The U.S. Government Foreign Disaster Assistance Program.* Washington: National Academy of Sciences.

National Institute for Rural Development (NIRD). 1985. *Administrative Arrangements for Rural Development: Proceedings of the National Workshop held at the National Institute for Rural Development (Hyderabad).* Government of India Publications.

Natural Hazards World Map. 1980. "Risiko und politische Verantworteng". Aus Politik und Zeitgeshichte, Beilage Das Parlement, 7 (16.2), Bonn. (In German.)

O'Keefe, P., Westgate, K. N. and Wisner, B. 1976. "Taking the Naturalness out of Natural Disaster". *Nature*, **260**, April 15: 566.

Oxall, I., Barnett, A. and Booth, D. (eds) 1975. *Beyond the Sociology of Development.* London: Routledge and Kegan Paul.

Palmen, E. H. 1948. "On the Formation and Structure of Tropical Hurricanes". *Geophysica*, **3**: 26–38 (cited by I. Subbaramayya *et al.* 1981).

Parthasarathy, G. N. 1971. *Agricultural Development and Small Farmers: A Study of Andhra Pradesh.* Delhi: Vikan.

Parthasarathy, G. N. 1985. "Re-orientation of Rural Development Programmes: A Note on some Basic Issues". *Economic and Political Weekly*, Vol. 20, No. 48, November 30.

Pelanda, C. 1982. "Disaster and Sociosystemic Vulnerability" in B. Jones and M. Thozevic (eds) *Social and Economic Aspects of Earthquakes*, pp. 67–91. Skopje: Institute of Earthquake Engineering and Engineering Seismology, University of Kiril and Metodij.

Popper, K. R. 1966. *The Open Society and Its Enemies, Vol. I, Plato*, London: Routledge & Kegan Paul.

Popper, K. R. 1966. *The Open Society and Its Enemies, Vol. 2, Hegel and Marx*. London: Routledge & Kegan Paul.

Pryer, J. 1989. "When Breadwinners fall ill: Preliminary Findings from a Case Study in Bangladesh". *IDS Bulletin*, 20: 49–57.

Ragharan, K. R. 1967. "Influence of Tropical Storms on Monsoon Rainfall in India". *Weather*, 22: 250–255.

Raghavulu, C. V. and Cohen, S. 1979. *The Andhra Cyclone: A Study in Mass Death.* Bombay: Vikas.

Raghavulu, C. V. 1981. *Disaster Preparedness: A Study in Community Perspectives.* Hyderabad: ARTIC.

Riehl, H. and Simpson, R. H. 1981. *The Hurricane and its Impact.* Oxford: Blackwell.

van Schendel, W. 1981. *Peasant Mobility: The Odds of Life in Rural Bangladesh.* Assen: Van Gorcum.

Scott, J. C. 1976. *The Moral Economy of the Peasant: Rebellion and Subsistence in S.E. Asia.* Yale: The University Press.

Seaman, J. 1980. "The Effects of Disaster on Health". IDI Working Paper No. 4, International Disaster Institute, London.

Seers, D. 1979. "The New Meaning of Development" in D. Lehmann (ed.) *Development Theory*, pp. 9–30.

Sen, A. K. 1975. *Employment, Technology and Development.* Oxford: Clarendon Press.

Sen, A. K. 1981. *Poverty and Famines: An Essay on Entitlement and Deprivation.* Oxford: Clarendon Press.

201

BIBLIOGRAPHY

Sheth, D. L. 1983. "Grass-roots Stirrings and the Future of Politics". *Alternatives*, 9: 1–24.

Sheth, D. L. 1987. "Alternative Developments as Political Practice". *Alternatives*, 12: 155–171.

Simpson, R. H. 1971. "The Decision Process in Hurricane Forecasting", NOAA Technical Memorandum NWS SR-53, Fort Worth, Texas (cited by G. White (ed.): 74).

Slovic, P., Kunrenther, H. and White, G. F. 1974. "Decision Processes, Rationality and Adjustment to Natural Hazards" in G. F. White (ed.) *Natural Hazards*, pp. 187–205. Oxford: Oxford University Press.

Srinivas, M. N. (ed.) 1960. *India's Villages*. New York: Asia Publishing House.

Srinivas, M. N. 1962. *Caste in Modern India and other Essays*. Bombay: Asia Publishing House.

Srinivas, M. N. 1976. *The Remembered Village*. Berkeley: The University of California Press.

Subbaramayya, I. and Fujiwhara, S. 1981. "On the Maximum Wind in Tropical Cyclones". *Meteorological Magazine*, 110: 87–91.

Subbaramayya, I., Ramanadham, R. and Subba Rao, M. 1979. "The November 1977 Andhra Pradesh Cyclone and the Associated Storm Surge". *Indian National Science Academy*, 45, Part A. 4: 293–304.

Subbaramayya, I. and Subba Rao, M. 1981. "Cyclone Climatology of North Indian Ocean". *Indian Journal of Marine Sciences*, 10: 366–368.

Subrahmanyam, V. P. and Hema Malini, B. 1978. "Drought-Prone Areas of Andhra Pradesh". *Deccan Geographer*, 17: 441–49.

Swift, J. 1989. "Why are Rural People Vulnerable to Famine?" *IDS Bulletin*, 20: 9–14.

Torry, W. I. 1979. "Hazards, Hazes and Holes: A Critique of 'The Environment as Hazard' and General Reflections on Disaster Research". *Canadian Geographer*, 23: 517–540.

United Nations Disaster Relief Organisation. 1979a. *Disaster Prevention and Mitigation: A Compendium of Current Knowledge, Volume XI. Preparedness Aspects, Volume 7, Economic Aspects*. New York, UNDRO.

United National Disaster Relief Organisation. 1979b "Natural Disasters and Vulnerability Analysis". Report of Expert Working Group Meeting, 9–12 July. Geneva: UNDRO.

United Nations Disaster Relief Organisation. 1981. "National, Regional and International Aspects of Disaster Management". Paper presented to *Conference on Disaster Management Preparedness and Response*. Hyderabad: ASCI/ARTIC *Proceedings*: pp. 57–63.

United Nations Disaster Relief Organisation. 1982. *Shelter after Disaster: Guidelines for Assistance*. New York: United Nations.

Wade, R. 1982. "The System of Administrative and Political Corruption: Canal Irrigation in S. India". *Journal of Development Studies*, 18(3): 287–328.

Wade, R. 1984. "The Market for Public Office: Why the Indian State is not better at Development". Discussion Paper No. 194, Institute of Development Studies, the University of Sussex.

Washbrook, D. A. 1976. *The Emergence of Provincial Politics: The Madras Presidency 1880–1920*. Cambridge: The University Press

Watts, M. 1983. "On the Poverty of Theory: Natural Hazards Research in Context" in K. Hewitt (ed.) *Interpretations of Calamity*. New York: Allen and Unwin.

Westgate, K. N. and O'Keefe, P. 1976. *Some Definitions of Disaster*. Disaster Research Unit Occasional Paper No. 4, Department of Geography, University of Bradford.

White, A. 1974. "Adjustments to the Hazard of Tropical Cyclones". in G. F. White (ed.) pp. 255–265.

White, G. F. (ed.) 1961. *Papers on Flood Problems*. Research Paper No. 70, Department of Geography, University of Chicago.

White, G. F. 1964. *Choice of Adjustments to Floods*. Research Paper No. 93, Chicago: Department of Geography, University of Chicago.

White, G. F. (ed.). 1974. *Natural Hazards: Local, National, Global*. Oxford: Oxford University Press.

White, G. F. and Haas, J. E. 1975. *Assessment of Research on Natural Hazards*. Cambridge. M.I.T.

202

BIBLIOGRAPHY

Wijkman. A. and Timberlake. L. 1984. *Natural Disasters: Acts of God or acts of Man?* London: International Institute for the Environment and Development.

Winchester, P. J. 1979. "Report on a Conference about Relief Operations after 1977 Cyclone". *Disasters*, 3(2): 173–177.

Winchester, P. J. 1981. "From Disaster to Development: Notes from India". *Disasters*, 5(2): 154–163.

Winchester, P. J. 1986. *Cyclone Vulnerability and Housing Policy in the Krishna delta, South India, 1977–83.* Unpublished Ph.D. thesis. School of Development Studies, University of East Anglia, Norwich.

Winchester, P. J. 1990. "Economic Power and Response to Risk: A Case Study from India" in Handmer and Penning-Rowsell (eds), pp. 95–109.

Wisner. B. 1976. "Man-made Famine in Eastern Kenya: The Interrelation of Environment and Development". Discussion Paper No. 96, Institute of Development Studies, University of Sussex.

Woodcock, A. and Davis, M. 1978. *Catastrophe Theory.* Harmondsworth: Penguin Books.

World Development. 1987. *Development Alternatives: The Challenge for NGOs.* Vol. 15 (Supplement). Autumn. Oxford: Pergamon.

World Development. 1987. *Appendix III: Final Statement of the UN/NGO Workshop on Debt, Adjustment and the Needs of the Poor.* Oxford, UK, 19–22 September 1987.

Zeeman, E. C. 1978. *Catastrophe Theory: Selected Papers (1972–77).* Reading, Mass: Addison-Wesley.

Appendix 1: Housing

To be read with Chapter One, section 1.4.4.

1.1 SPACE STANDARDS IN HOUSING COLONIES AND TRADITIONAL VILLAGES

TABLE A 1.1: *Comparison of use of space in housing colonies and traditional villages/hamlets as percentage of totals*

Village/hamlet	Total number of households	Roads %	Irrigation %	Public buildings %	Unusable space %	House sites[a] %
Housing colonies						
Nali	245	19	6	3	8	63
Kammanamolu	226	21	7	4	7	61
Chodavarem	130	19	3	7	5	66
Mean percentage		19.6				63
Standard deviation		1.4				2.7
Traditional villages						
Lingareddypalem	209	11	5	6	3	76
Goudapalem	146	17	4	1	1	77
Bellamkondadibba	109	12	3	1	7	77
Mean percentage		13.3				76.8
Standard deviation		3.2				0.2

Source: Fieldwork 1983.
[a] Includes storage.

Land in traditional villages is sparingly used; public open space is limited to roads for bullock carts. There are narrow alleyways between houses and larger spaces around temples, tanks, wells and where richer households share land for haystacks. The use of land for housing is restricted by its value for agricultural purposes, although there are wide variations in the sizes of house sites, depending on economic status; for instance, the richer households in an inland village live on quarter-acre sites in the middle of the village while the poorest live in huts by the side of the road. Except for the landless and other poor people, each house is surrounded by its own paddy store, haystack, animal shelter and other additions such as a separate kitchen and/or "bathroom". Housing density is higher in traditional villages than in the housing colonies; the average number of people per household living in two- and four-truss houses and two- and one-pole houses, ranges from 6.9 to 3.7, compared to a range of the average number of 4.7 to 3.4 in the concrete houses.

TABLE A 1.1.2: *Comparison of spaces in traditional villages and housing colonies as a percentage of total area*

Village type	Number of villages	Number of households	Roads as % of total area		House sites as % of total area[a]	
Housing colonies[b]	14	1,165	Mean	18.5	Mean	62.4
			s.d.	5.4	s.d.	7.4
Traditional[c]	10	1,021	Mean	13.3	Mean	73.7
			s.d.	3.2	s.d.	2.3

Source: Fieldwork 1983.

[a] Total area includes land for irrigation, public buildings and unusable space. In the traditional villages the mean total is 13.0%; in the housing colonies the mean total is 19%.

[b] This includes many traditional houses in the housing colonies.

[c] Not all these households were within the sample interview area.

Extensions

One of the ways envisaged to make the concrete housing programme cost-effective was to put the houses on sites that were sufficiently large for the families to build-on extensions; but this happened rarely. In 50 per cent of the colonies surveyed the houses were built so close together that it was impossible to build extensions or leave enough room between the houses for foodgrain or fodder storage. Where extensions for kitchens or verandahs for sleeping had been built then the cores were used as lock-up storage as intended. In a separate survey of 877 *katcha* houses and 604 concrete houses in 1981 we noted that 50 per cent of the households in the concrete houses had built separate or attached kitchens compared to 11 per cent in the *katcha* houses and 33 per cent of the households in the concrete houses had built animal shelters compared to 37 per cent in the *katcha* households. Less than half the concrete houses had been extended to be the same size as *katcha* houses which might signify restricted house sites and/or lack of money. This is not surprising since most of the housing colonies were built in the coastal areas where poorer people predominated and for the poorest groups inland.

1.2 DURABILITY AND PERCEPTIONS OF SAFETY

Durability

The case for durable housing is evident from Table A 1.2.1. All the mud-and-thatch one-pole houses and most of the mud-and-thatch two-pole houses were destroyed in the 1977 cyclone – irrespective of location. Only just over half the traditional *pucca* old-style brick-and-tile houses were destroyed, due partly to the better quality of the materials, but mainly to the structure and plan shape of the buildings (Winchester 1986: 267).

TABLE A 1.2.1: *Numbers of traditional houses destroyed and people killed in 1977*

House type	Number of houses in 1977	Number of houses destroyed	Number of houses damaged	Number of houses standing	Number of households with >1 killed	Number of people killed
2t/4t (*pucca*)[a]	38	20	4	14	12	16
Two-pole (*katcha*)	80	62	16	2	20	44
One-pole/hut	72	72	–	–	28	73
Totals	190	154	20	16	60	133

Source: Fieldwork 1981–82.
[a] 2t/4t are two- and four-truss houses

By 1983 28 housing colonies had been built in the storm-surge-affected areas for approximately 25,000 people (30 per cent of the population). A special study of the durability of concrete houses was incorporated into the survey of 1,165 concrete houses carried out by two Cambridge architectural graduates during the second stage of fieldwork in 1983. The survey was carried out in 14 housing colonies built between 1978 and 1980 with a population of 6,000.

Except in one colony (Chodavarem) the concrete houses were not built to the government's technical criteria, mainly due to the use of sub-standard materials enabling huge cost savings to be channelled elsewhere by the contractors. Added to the leakages was a catalogue of incompetence and technical failures; first there seemed to have been a complete misunderstanding of the nature of the soil and ground conditions as shown by widespread subsidence of houses and severe scale erosion of the materials; the chronic workmanship was shown by widespread cracking and peeling in many houses and the use of construction specifications to urban standards proved to be quite unrealistic in such a remote area. Government's claim that the provision of durable concrete houses would enhance protection and reduce vulnerability appears to be unfounded, judging by the evidence of the survey (Table A 1.2.2) which suggests that by 1990 at least half the houses would be uninhabitable.

TABLE A 1.2.2: *Distribution of failures by type in 1,165 houses*

	Eaves cracks	Structural failure in walls	Erosion at ground level	Poor condition of adjacent ground
N	234	296	402	308
N as percentage of total	20	25	35	27

Source: Structure and condition survey September–October 1983.

In 1988 we observed that over 50 per cent of the houses had been abandoned as living places and were being used for storage while the families lived in cramped extensions beside them. Approximately 25 per cent of the concrete houses in the same colonies as surveyed in 1983 had been abandoned altogether.

Perceptions of safety

Of the 102 households living in concrete houses in 1981–82, 28 thought that they were safe, the remaining 75 per cent thought they were quite unsafe. However, from the same sample it was found that 63 households would have preferred to live in concrete houses, if they had been built to higher standards as per the two-room brick house of 500 sq ft with a concrete roof built by EFICOR for Rs 10,000.

1.3 EMPLOYMENT POTENTIAL

A housing colony of 150 houses took about three months to build; the approximate breakdown of mandays *per house* was: skilled men – nine days;

unskilled attached labour – nine days; unskilled local labour – five days. At that rate 60 villagers, or say about a third of the working population of a village, had the opportunity of building work for three months. But many of the colonies were started in the first months of 1978 during which time the villagers were working on clearing the irrigation network, rebuilding the tidal bund or the all-weather link roads, or were fully engaged in clearing their own fields and planting a second crop. In nearly all cases the colonies were totally built by outside labour. (Personal communication with a building contractor who supplied labour for building work and roads, case 31.) A major drawback to the concrete houses was their running costs. Repairs and replacement were virtually impossible due to the high cost of cement and lack of local skills so that free provision of concrete houses on their own, in housing colonies, had not been significantly advantageous, except for one aspect in saving people money.

1.4 SAVINGS POTENTIAL

Reducing recurrent repair and replacement costs of traditional houses

The concrete houses may not have achieved many of their technical criteria but their free provision led to savings in replacement costs according to many respondents who claimed that as a result they had not had to divert scarce resources into housing. For instance in the case of fishermen and marginal farmers the one-off saving could have amounted to 25 per cent of one year's income; for landless labourers it would probably have been more.

The figures in Table A 1.4.1 are based on the assumption that NO repairs were necessary to the concrete houses for at least 12 years (the only cost their

TABLE A 1.4.1: *Comparison of rebuilding and repair costs between "katcha" and "pucca" concrete houses, and potential savings in Rupees at 1981 prices*

House type	Rebuilding costs	Replacement costs[a] (12 years)	Savings (12 years)	Annual savings	Savings as % of household income[b]
Hut	850	2,260	1,440	120	5
One-pole	1,150	3,900	4,680	390	16
Two-pole	1,950	4,580	6,000	500	20
Concrete	400[c]	1,560			

[a] Takes into account the likely occurrence of two cyclones over the period.

[b] The average income for a male and female whose principal income is agricultural labouring of Rs 2,470 p.a. at 1981 rates.

[c] The costs for an extension.

recipients would have to bear would be costs of extensions).

The savings in replacement and repair costs are significant if they are compared to agricultural wages. For instance, by living in a concrete house instead of in a two-pole house the annual savings to a household could have been the equivalent of an additional 55 per cent of the annual wages of a female agricultural worker (Rs 890 p.a.) or 30 per cent of the annual wages of a male agricultural worker (Rs 1,580 p.a.). For those living in huts (20 per cent of the population) the annual savings would have been less valuable (less than five per cent of an average household's income). However, savings could have been of greater value if they could have been diverted into asset accumulation, increased credit availability (a savings account) or in other directions (medical or crop insurance – if they existed), but these possibilities and choices depend more on government policies and power relations than just having the spare "savings".

Comparison between two groups of households

As the last measure of the value of savings, we took two groups of households – those that had been given free concrete houses and those that had not – to see if the potential savings from the provision of concrete houses had had any effect on their levels of asset accumulation over a short period.

The two groups were as comparable as possible in every other way bar the provision of houses, in so far as they had lived in similar houses before the cyclone and had similar asset types and similar sized landholdings – for

TABLE A 1.4.2: *Asset accumulation in two groups of households of similar economic status: (1) those living in traditional houses; (2) those provided with free concrete houses, taken from 202-household sample*

Classification of house type	Number of households	Plough teams	Carts	Milch animals
Concrete houses				
Before cyclone	–	11	17	81
By 1983	80	18	23	85
Increase/decrease		+ 7	+ 6	+ 4
Traditional houses				
Before cyclone	160[a]	16	39	106
By 1983	84	27	44	119
Increase/decrease		+ 9	+ 5	+ 13

Source: Fieldwork 1981–83.

[a] Since the cyclone, 12 households had set up on their own. Previously these household members were living in their parental houses.

instance, a household that lived in a two-truss house before the cyclone and was living in a concrete house in 1981 would be compared to a household that was living in a two-truss house in 1981, and so on.

We found less differences in the asset levels between the two groups than might have been expected, or according to the claims made by the donors of the concrete houses. The difference in the numbers of plough teams and carts between the two groups was not significant enough to indicate that savings (?) had been channeled into them, but there was a marked difference in the ownership of milch animals. However, the difference in the numbers of milch animals owned by the two groups can be partly explained by the fact that generally the occupants of the concrete houses came from the poorest and most marginalised groups, i.e. the Harijans, the Girijans (tribals), the Fishermen and the Small and Marginal Farmers living in the coastal areas and that some of these (the Landless and possibly the Fishermen) would not have had the resources to raise the loans in the first place. Another explanation could be that the poorest groups buy and sell milch animals far more often than the less poor groups, for reasons we discussed before (Chapter 4: Section 4.3.2).

Our findings did not indicate that the provision of concrete houses had had any economic effect for their occupants. Any savings they might have made would in any event have gone straight into paying off old debts, redeeming pawned goods (jewellery), paying bribes, buying necessary utensils and perhaps improving their diet.

APPENDIX 2 *Mean distribution and numbers of assets and resources of 202 households, in 1977, 1981 and losses in 1977, classified by occupation and topography*

Topography 1: Coastal flat (30 households)

Occupation^a	Castes^b	Dates	Household size	Labour power^c	House types^d	Land holding^e	Land type^f	Land quality^g	Plough teams	Carts	Milch animals
1 (n=1)		1977	6 (6)	3.0	(1×1)	3.0			1 (1)	1 (1)	4 (4)
		Lost	2 (2)	1.5	(lost)				1 (1)	1 (1)	4 (4)
	(1×1)	1981	4 (4)	2.5	(1×1)	3.5	Pa=3.5 Le=0 Enc=0	Fe=2.5 Me=1.5 Po=0	1 (1)	1 (1)	2 (2)
2 (n=3)		1977	2.0 (6)	1.2	(3×3)	1.8			0.3	0.3 (1)	1.0 (3)
		Lost	1.0 (3)	0.6	(lost all)				0.3	0.3 (1)	1.0 (3)
	(3×3)	1981	3.0 (9)	1.6	(3×2)	1.8	Pa=1.2 Le=0.6 Enc=0	Fe=0.5 Me=0.8 Po=0.5	0.3	0.3 (1)	2.5 (7)
3 (n=17)		1977	4.8 (81)	2.1	(8×3; 5×4)	1.3			0.1	0.4 (13)	1.1 (18)
		Lost	1.4 (19)	0.6	(lost all)				0.1	0.4 (13)	1.1 (18)
		1981	5.3 (90)	2.3	(17×2)	1.6	Pa=0.9 Le=0.3 Enc=0.4	Fe=0.3 Me=0.8 Po=0.5	0.1	0.3 (9)	1.2 (21)
4 (n=2)		1977	4 (8)	1.4	(2×3)	2.0			–	– (–)	1.0 (2)
		Lost	1 (2)	0.3	(lost all)				–	– (–)	1.0 (2)
	(1×1; 1×3)	1981	6 (12)	2.2	(2×4)	2.3	Pa=1.6 Le=0.7 Enc=0	Fe=0.2 Me=1.2 Po=0.9	–	0.5 (1)	2.0 (4)
5 (n=6)		1977	4.5 (27)	2.3	(2×3; 4×4)	1.6			0.2	0.3 (2)	1.5 (9)
		Lost	1.2 (6)	0.6	(lost all)				0.2	0.3 (2)	1.5 (9)
	(2×1; 4×3)	1981	3.5 (21)	1.8	(6×2)	1.7	Pa=1.0 Le=0.5 Enc=0.2	Fe=0.2 Me=0.7 Po=0.8	0.2	0.3 (2)	1.5 (9)
6 (n=1)		1977	3 (3)	0.8	(1×4)	0			–	– (–)	– (–)
		Lost	1 (1)	0.5	(lost)	0			–	– (–)	– (–)
		1981	2 (2)	0.5	(1×2)				–	– (–)	– (–)
Totals		1977	131				Pa =25.6 Le =14.8 Enc =12.0 — 51.4		4	17	36
		Lost	33						4	17	36
		1981	138						4	14	43

211

APPENDIX 2 *continued*

Topography 2: Tidal flat (63 households)

Occupation[a]	Castes[b]	Dates	Household size x̄ (N)	Labour power[c]	House types[d] (N)	Land holding[e] x̄	Land type[f]	Land quality[g]	Plough teams x̄ (N)	Carts x̄ (N)	Milch animals x̄ (N)
1 (n=5)		1977	5.0 (25)	2.6	(3×1; 2×3)	4.8			1.6 (8)	2.2 (11)	3.8 (19)
		Lost	0.2 (1)	0.1	(lost all)				1.0 (5)	1.6 (8)	3.0 (15)
	(1×1; 2×2; 2×4)	1981	5.6 (28)	3.0	(2×1; 3×2)	5.6	Pa=5.6 Le=0 Enc=0	Fe=4.0 Me=1.6 Po=0	2.0 (10)	2.4 (12)	4.4 (22)
2 (n=22)		1977	5.5 (121)	2.9	(10×1; 4×3; 8×4)	2.6			0.6 (14)	0.9 (21)	3.0 (66)
		Lost	1.4 (29)	0.7	(9×1; 4×3; 8×4)				0.6 (14)	0.9 (21)	3.0 (66)
	(3×1; 12×2; 2×3; 4×4; 1×5)	1981	4.9 (108)	2.6	(1×1; 5×2; 5×3; 8×4)	2.5	Pa=1.5 Le=0.4 Enc=0.6	Fe=0.7 Me=1.1 Po=0.7	0.4 (9)	0.8 (18)	2.3 (49)
3 (n=7)		1977	5.3 (37)	2.4	(1×1; 2×3; 3×4)	1.2			0.1 (1)	0.6 (4)	0.9 (6)
		Lost	2.0 (14)	0.9	(lost all)				0.1 (1)	0.6 (4)	0.9 (6)
	(7×3)	1981	3.9 (27)	1.8	(6×2; 1×3)	1.76	Pa=1.0 Le=0.2 Enc=0.4	Fe=0.3 Me=1.0 Po=0.4	0.1 (1)	0.3 (9)	1.3 (9)
5 (n=16)		1977	4.2 (66)	1.7	(3×3; 11×4)	1.2			0.1 (1)	0.4 (6)	1.5 (20)
		Lost	1.1 (17)	0.4	(lost all)				0.1 (1)	0.4 (6)	1.5 (19)
	(3×1; 6×2; 6×5; 1×4)	1981	4.2 (67)	1.7	(9×2; 3×4; 4×5)	1.4	Pa=0.8 Le=0 Enc=0.6	Fe=0.3 Me=0.5 Po=0.6	– (–)	– (–)	1.1 (17)
6 (n=13)		1977	3.2 (245)	1.5	(1×1; 10×4)	0.8			– (–)	– (–)	0.6 (5)
		Lost	1.3 (16)	0.7	(lost all)				– (–)	– (–)	0.6 (5)
	(4×2; 4×4; 5×5)	1981	3.2 (44)	1.5	(8×2; 2×4; 3×5)	0.3	Pa=0 Le=0.1 Enc=0.2	Fe=0 Me=0.1 Po=0.3	– (–)	– (–)	0.2 (3)
Totals		1977	293				Pa =78.6 Le =15.0 Enc=30.2 ‾‾‾‾ 123.8		24	42	116
		Lost	77						21	39	111
		1981	274						20	38	100

APPENDIX 2 *continued*

Topography 3: Levees (18 households)

Occupation[a]	Castes[b]	Dates	Household size x̄ (N)	Labour power[c]	House types[d] (N)	Land holding[e] x̄	Land type[f]	Land quality[g]	Plough teams x̄ (N)	Carts x̄ (N)	Milch animals x̄ (N)
2 (n=8)	(4×1; 4×3)	1977	3.8 (31)	1.8	(2×1; 4×3; 2×4)	1.3			– (–)	0.4 (3)	1.8 (14)
		Lost	–	–	(lost all)				– (–)	0.3 (2)	1.2 (9)
		1981	4.3 (35)	1.9	(8×2)	1.5	Pa=1.2 Le=0.3 Enc=0	Fe=0.5 Me=0.8 Po=0.2	– (–)	0.4 (3)	1.2 (9)
3 (n=1)	(1×3)	1977	3 (3)	1.5	(1×2)	1.0			– (–)	– (–)	– (–)
		Lost	1 (1)	0.5					– (–)	– (–)	– (–)
		1981	3 (3)	1.5		1.0	Pa=0.5 Le=0 Enc=0.5	Fe=0.1 Me=0.4 Po=0.5	– (–)	– (–)	1 (1)
5 (n=4)	(3×1; 1×3)	1977	4.3 (17)	1.8	(1×3; 3×4)	1.1			0.3 (1)	0.3 (1)	0.8 (3)
		Lost	0.3 (1)	0.1	(lost all)				0.3 (1)	0.3 (1)	0.6 (2)
		1981	4.3 (17)	1.8	(4×2)	1.0	Pa=0.6 Le=0 Enc=0.4	Fe=0.2 Me=0.4 Po=0.4	– (–)	– (–)	0.8 (3)
6 (n=5)	(1×1; 1×4; 3×5)	1977	4.6 (23)	2.2	(1×3; 2×4; 2×5)	0			– (–)	– (–)	0.6 (3)
		Lost	0.6 (3)	0.3	(lost all)				– (–)	– (–)	0.6 (3)
		1981	4.4 (22)	2.1	(5×2)	0.7	Pa=0.2 Le=0 Enc=0.5	Fe=0 Me=0.2 Po=0.5	– (–)	– (–)	0.6 (3)
Totals		1977	74				Pa =13.5 Le =2.4 Enc=4.6		1	4	20
		Lost	77						1	3	14
		1981	274				20.5		0	4	16

Notes:

Landholdings in areas (1–3):	Total acreage as *patta*	117.7	(60%)
	Total acreage as lease	32.2	(16%)
	Total acreage as encroachment	46.8	(24%)
	Total	196.7	

APPENDIX 2 *continued*

Topography 4: Inland flat (29 households)

Occupation[a]	Castes[b]	Dates	Household size x̄	Household size (N)	Labour power[c]	House types[d] (N)	Land holding[e] x̄	Land type[f]	Land quality[g]	Plough teams x̄	Plough teams (N)	Carts x̄	Carts (N)	Milch animals x̄	Milch animals (N)
1 (n=3)		1977	4.3	(14)	1.7	(2×1; 1×3)	5.6			1.6	(5)	2.0	(6)	2.6	(8)
		Lost	–	–	–	(1×3)				0.3	(1)	0.3	(1)	0.6	(2)
2 (n=16)	(3×1)	1981	5.0	(15)	2.0	(2×1; 1×3)	5.6	Pa=5.6 Le=0 Enc=0	Fe=4.8 Me=0.8 Po=0	2.3	(7)	2.7	(8)	4.6	(14)
		1977	4.8	(77)	2.1	(8×1; 7×3; 1×4)	1.5			0.1	(1)	0.9	(14)	2.3	(37)
		Lost	0.1	(2)	0.1	(8×1; 5×3; 1×4)				0.1	(1)	0.8	(13)	1.9	(30)
	(11×1; 3×2; 2×5)	1981	5.0	(80)	2.2	(5×2; 8×3; 3×4)	1.9	Pa=0.9 Le=0.7 Enc=0.3	Fe=1.0 Me=0.4 Po=0.5	0.2	(2)	0.9	(14)	2.4	(39)
5 (n=4)		1977	3.9	(16)	1.8	(1×3; 3×4)	0.5			–	(–)	0.5	(2)	0.8	(3)
		Lost	0.8	(3)	0.4	(lost all)		Pa=0.3 Le=0.8 Enc=0	Fe=0.1 Me=0.5 Po=0.5	–	(–)	0.5	(2)	0.8	(3)
	(2×1; 2×2)	1981	3.5	(14)	1.6	(2×2; 1×3; 1×4)	1.1			–	(–)	0.3	(1)	1.0	(4)
6 (n=5)		1977	3.0	(19)	1.5	(4×3; 2×4)	0			–	(–)	–	(–)	0.5	(3)
		Lost	–	(1)	0.1	(lost all)				–	(–)	–	(–)	0.5	(3)
	(5×5)	1981	3.5	(22)	1.6	(5×2; 1×5)	0			–	(–)	–	(–)	0.5	(3)
Totals		1977		126				Pa = 32.4 Le = 14.4 Enc = 4.8			6		22		51
		Lost		6							2		16		38
		1981		131				51.6			9		23		60

APPENDIX 2 *continued*

Topography 5: High ground (62 households)

Occupation[a]	Castes[b]	Dates	Household size x̄ (N)	Labour power[c]	House types[d] (N)	Land holding[e] x̄	Land type[f]	Land quality[g]	Plough teams x̄ (N)	Carts x̄ (N)	Milch animals x̄ (N)
1 (n=9)	(8×1; 1×4)	1977	7.4 (67)	3.2	(7×1; 2×3)	5.0			1.4 (13)	1.7 (15)	3.7 (34)
		Lost	- (-)	-	(1×1; 2×3)				0.3 (3)	0.3 (3)	1.2 (11)
		1981	7.7 (70)	3.2	(6×1; 3×3)	4.8	Pa=4.8; Le=0; Enc=0	Fe=4.8; Me=0; Po=0	1.8 (16)	2.3 (21)	4.0 (36)
2 (n=23)	(3×1; 10×4; 10×5)	1977	4.7 (108)	2.5	(2×1; 12×3; 6×4; 1×5)	1.4			0.2 (4)	0.5 (11)	1.0 (23)
		Lost	0.1 (1)	0.1	(1×1; 9×3; 5×4; 1×5)				0.2 (4)	0.4 (9)	0.7 (15)
		1981	5.1 (117)	2.7	(2×1; 3×2; 7×3; 7×4; 5×5)	1.3	Pa=1.2; Le=0.1; Enc=0	Fe=0.5; Me=0.8; Po=0	0.2 (5)	0.6 (13)	1.6 (32)
3 (n=2)	(2×4)	1977	4.5 (9)	1.4	(1×1; 1×4)	0.5			0.5 (1)	0.5 (1)	2.0 (4)
		Lost	- (-)	-	(1×4)				- (-)	- (-)	2.0 (4)
		1981	5.5 (11)	1.8	(1×1; 1×5)	0.7	Pa=0.7; Le=0; Enc=0	Fe=0; Me=0.5; Po=0.2	0.5 (1)	0.5 (1)	1.0 (2)
4 (n=9)	(2×1; 5×4; 2×5)	1977	5.4 (49)	2.8	(3×1; 4×3; 2×4)	1.0			- (-)	- (-)	0.7 (6)
		Lost	0.1 (2)	0.1	(2×1; 3×3; 2×4)				- (-)	- (-)	0.4 (4)
		1981	5.7 (51)	3.0	(2×1; 2×2; 2×3; 2×4; 1×5)	0.9	Pa=0.5; Le=0.4; Enc=0	Fe=0.4; Me=0.3; Po=0.2	- (-)	0.5 (4)	1.2 (11)

APPENDIX 2 *continued*

Topography 5: High ground (62 households)

Occupation^a	Castes^b	Dates	Household size x̄	(N)	Labour power^c	House types^d (N)	Land holding^e x̄	Land type^f	Land quality^g	Plough teams x̄	(N)	Carts x̄	(N)	Milch animals x̄	(N)
5 (n=6)	(3×1; 1×4 2×5)	1977	5.8	(35)	2.2	(3×3; 3×4)	0.8			0.3	(2)	0.3	(2)	1.0	(6)
		Lost	0.3	(5)	0.1	(2×3; 3×4)			Fe=0.1 Me=0.6 Po=0	0.3	(2)	0.3	(2)	0.5	(3)
		1981	6.2	(37)	2.3	(3×2; 2×3; 1×5)	0.7	Pa=0.2 Le=0.5 Enc=0		0.2	(1)	0.2	(1)	0.8	(5)
6 (n=13)	(2×1; 2×4; 9×5)	1977	3.8	(45)	1.6	(3×3; 8.4; 1×5)	0			–	(–)	–	(–)	–	(–)
		Lost	0.2	(4)	0.1	(lost all)			Fe=0 Me=0 Po=0.3	–	(–)	–	(–)	–	(–)
		1981	4.2	(51)	1.8	(6×2; 1×4; 6×5)	0.3	Pa=0 Le=0 Enc=0.3		–	(–)	–	(–)	0.5	(3)
Totals		1977	313							20		29		74	
		Lost	12							9		14		38	
		1981	337					Pa =78.0 Le =8.9 Enc=2.1 — 89.0		23		40		93	

Source: Fieldwork 1981–2.

a Occupations 1–6 are as follows:

1 Own cultivation, employing others but not working for others, combined with business interests inside and outside the villages.

2 Own cultivation and agricultural labour for others and one other occupation, i.e., caste occupation (toddy tapping, herding), animal husbandry; three occupations.

3 Own cultivation and agricultural labour and sea-fishing (mainly). (N.B. Two of this group are canal fishermen); three occupations.

4 Own cultivation and agricultural labour plus job as minor government official, or, petty shop or tradesman occupations; three occupations.

5 Own cultivation and agricultural labour; two occupations.

6 Little or no cultivation of own land (i.e., almost landless) and agricultural labour; minor caste occupations; 1–5 occupations.

b Castes 1–5 are as follows:

1 *Kapu* (cultivator);

2 *Gouda* (toddy-tapper);

3 *Pallecarlu* (fisherman);

4 Others (*Gollalu* – herders, Muslims);

5 *Harijan* (scheduled caste).

c Labour power is calculated at the rate of 1.0 units per adult male; 0.5 per adult female and adolescent male; 0.3 per adolescent female. The unit calculation is related to wage rates applying in 1981–82. The calculation of labour power in 1977 (and lost) is based on the same proportion of labour power 1981 to household size 1981.

d House types 1–5 are as follows:

1 2-truss and 4-truss brick-and-tile houses;

2 New concrete houses provided after the cyclone;

3 2-pole mud-and-thatch or leaf house;

4 1-pole mud-and-leaf house;

5 Mud-and-leaf hut.

The number of houses in 1977 corresponds to the numbers of households in 1981 who were not living in their parental homes in 1977 (i.e., there are twelve new households). The number of houses in 1981 is for the full 202-sample survey.

e The size of landholdings in 1977 does not take account of households in 1981 living in parental homes in 1977 and accounts to some extent for the difference in the size of landholdings 1977–81.

f Pa *Patta* land;

Le Leasehold land;

Enc Encroachment land (i.e., with no title).

g Fe Fertile, with an average yield of 20 bags/acre;

Me Medium, with an average yield of 15 bags/acre;

Po Poor, with an average yield of 10 bags/acre.

Categories derived from farmers' own estimates and subsequently cross-checked.

APPENDIX 3 *Income-equivalents*

TABLE A 3.1: *Mean income-equivalents from total investments of households with least and most differences in 1977–88; and lowest and highest totals in 1988*
to be read with Figure 5.3.

Household type	Assets				Claims				Stores			
	'77i	'77ii	'83	'88	'77i	'77ii	'83	'88	'77i	'77ii	'83	'88
Least differences	5.7	3.6	5.9	4.9	2.0	5.3	5.4	2.8	0.6	0.1	0.6	0.6
Most differences	5.3	3.6	7.1	7.3	2.0	5.6	5.8	4.4	0.5	0.2	0.9	1.0
Lowest totals	3.8	2.8	4.5	3.9	1.1	4.5	4.6	2.5	0.2	0.1	0.2	0.2
Highest totals	11.8	7.4	13.5	13.4	5.9	7.8	8.8	7.9	2.2	0.5	2.6	3.2

TABLE A 3.2: *Recovery: Mean income-equivalents from total investments of the most vulnerable households, classified by lowest assets, and highest exposure before the cyclone; and the highest losses of assets, and the highest casualties after the cyclone*
to be read with Figure 6.1.

Household type	Assets				Claims				Stores			
	'77i	'77ii	'83	'88	'77i	'77ii	'83	'88	'77i	'77ii	'83	'88
Most losses in 1977	11.4	6.6	12.9	13.1	5.3	7.5	8.2	7.5	2.0	0.5	2.4	3.1
Most deaths in 1977	6.5	2.9	7.7	7.8	1.9	6.0	5.8	3.7	0.4	0.2	0.7	0.7
Least assets in 1977	3.5	3.2	4.8	4.2	1.2	4.9	4.9	3.0	0.3	0.1	0.4	0.4
Most exposed in 1977	6.9	3.8	8.3	7.8	2.6	6.8	6.9	4.9	0.7	0.2	0.8	1.0

TABLE A 3.3: *Change: Mean income-equivalents from total investments in households classified by gains after the cyclone, increase or decrease in investments 1983–8*

to be read with Figure 6.3.

Household type	Assets				Claims				Stores			
	'77i	'77ii	'83	'88	'77i	'77ii	'83	'88	'77i	'77ii	'83	'88
Gains after cyclone	4.5	3.4	5.9	5.4	1.4	5.4	5.4	3.2	0.4	0.1	0.5	0.5
Increase 1983–8	11.0	6.5	12.5	13.4	5.0	6.9	7.3	7.1	1.7	0.5	2.0	2.9
Decrease 1983–8	5.5	3.4	6.7	5.9	2.0	5.9	6.0	3.5	0.5	0.2	0.7	0.7

TABLE A 3.4: *Characteristics: Mean numbers of measures of household characteristics of households with the highest and lowest assets from before the cyclone to 1988; and households with highest and lowest totals and highest and lowest differences 1977–88.*

to be read with Figure 6.5.

Household type	Assets				Claims				Stores			
	'77i	'77ii	'83	'88	'77i	'77ii	'83	'88	'77i	'77ii	'83	'88
Highest assets 1977–88	10.1	6.3	11.8	11.8	4.7	7.6	8.14	6.7	1.6	0.5	2.0	2.4
Lowest assets 1977–88	3.5	2.8	4.4	3.7	1.1	4.3	4.5	2.5	0.3	0.1	0.2	0.2
Highest values 1977–88	8.3	6.3	10.5	11.5	3.6	7.5	7.5	5.7	1.2	0.4	1.9	2.2
Lowest values 1977–88	4.8	3.1	4.8	4.3	1.2	4.8	4.8	2.1	0.3	0.1	0.3	0.3

Source: Fieldwork 1981, 1982, 1983 and 1988.

APPENDIX 4: Matrix of 42 households to be read with Chapters 5, section 5.4, and Chapter 6, sections 6.1–6.3.

Households

Household type	(n)	1	2	3	4	5	6	7	8	9	10	11	12	13	14	15	16	17	18	19	20	21	22	23	24	25	26	27	28	29	30	31	32	33	34	35	36	37	38	39	40	41	42
Most losses: 1977	(10)	*	*									*	*				*	*	*																		*	*	*	*		*	
Most deaths: 1977	(14)	*												*	*							*	*	*	*									*			*	*		*	*	*	*
Lowest assets pre-1977	(11)		*			*	*	*						*						*			*			*								*			*				*		
Most exposed pre-1977	(17)					*	*						*	*	*				*	*	*	*	*	*	*												*	*		*	*	*	
Most gains after cyclone	(22)			*		*		*					*	*	*			*	*	*	*	*	*	*	*	*	*	*	*	*					*		*	*	*				*
Improve: 1983–8	(6)			*	*					*						*	*	*																									
Decline: 1983–8	(22)		*		*	*	*	*	*	*	*	*	*	*	*				*					*			*	*					*		*			*		*	*		*
Highest assets overall	(9)						*	*	*																	*						*	*				*						
Lowest assets overall	(11)				*	*				*										*	*	*				*	*		*	*					*	*							
Highest values overall	(3)							*																							*												
Lowest values overall	(11)			*	*				*	*	*	*																							*	*	*						
Most illnesses overall	(13)			*	*				*	*				*								*	*						*		*			*	*		*	*					
Least illnesses overall	(10)																							*	*	*			*				*	*		*							
Concrete-house owners	(22)	*				*	*			*			*				*	*	*	*	*	*	*	*	*						*		*	*	*	*	*	*	*				*
Traditional-house owners	(20)	*	*	*		*		*			*	*	*			*	*	*	*	*	*	*		*		*	*	*	*	*				*	*	*	*	*					*

Index